FAMILY MATTERS

The Importance of Mattering to Family in Adolescence

GREGORY C. ELLIOTT

WILEY-BLACKWELL
A John Wiley & Sons, Ltd., Publication

This edition first published 2009

Blackwell Publishing was acquired by John Wiley & Sons in February 2007. Blackwell's publishing program has been merged with Wiley's global Scientific, Technical, and Medical business to form Wiley-Blackwell.

Registered Office
John Wiley & Sons Ltd, The Atrium, Southern Gate, Chichester, West Sussex, PO19 8SQ, United Kingdom

Editorial Offices
350 Main Street, Malden, MA 02148-5020, USA
9600 Garsington Road, Oxford, OX4 2DQ, UK
The Atrium, Southern Gate, Chichester, West Sussex, PO19 8SQ, UK

For details of our global editorial offices, for customer services, and for information about how to apply for permission to reuse the copyright material in this book please see our website at www.wiley.com/wiley-blackwell.

Library of Congress Cataloging-in-Publication Data

Elliott, Gregory.
Family matters : the importance of mattering to family in adolescence / Gregory C. Elliott.
p. cm.
Includes bibliographical references and index.
ISBN 978-1-4051-6242-5 (hardcover : alk. paper) — ISBN 978-1-4051-6243-2 (pbk. : alk. paper) 1. Adolescent psychology. 2. Teenagers—Family relationships. 3. Teenagers—Conduct of life. 4. Parent and teenager. I. Title.
BF724.E49 2009
155.5′18—dc22

2008028045

A catalogue record for this book is available from the British Library.

Set in 10.5/13pt Galliard by Graphicraft Limited, Hong Kong
Printed and bound in Malaysia by Vivar Printing Sdn Bhd

1 2009

Family Matters

To Nan:
Congratulations! You
matter to your children

[signature]

I dedicate this book with great love, admiration, and respect to Morris Rosenberg. Manny, as his friends and colleagues knew him, was the pre-eminent scholar of the self. His works, including *Conceiving the self* (which earned him the Distinguished Contribution for Scholarship Award from the American Sociological Association) and *Society and the adolescent self-image*, became the foundation for much of the sociological and psychological studies of the self that followed. His methodological expertise, exemplified in *The logic of survey analysis* and *The language of social research* (with Paul Lazarsfeld), assured a precise and rigorous empirical analysis to substantiate the theories he developed.

When I arrived at the University of Maryland, College Park, for my first academic appointment in Sociology, I was very fortunate that Manny soon took me under his wing. As a superb mentor and colleague, he provided advice, support, and guidance that made everything I did better. Our collaborative research taught me so much about the lore of research and data analysis; he helped me choose appropriate outlets for my manuscripts; and, perhaps most important, his professional and personal encouragement helped me find my own niche in the discipline. Manny was very generous with his assistance, while allowing me autonomy. He was the ideal mentor. More than that, he was a true friend.

Thank you, Manny. In your own words, you matter.

Contents

Preface

Ever since I began studying social psychology, my primary interest has been the self. Inspired by Erving Goffman, my dissertation research focused on the processes by which we present ourselves to others. When I accepted my first position as an assistant professor at the University of Maryland, College Park, I was fortunate to have Morris Rosenberg as my mentor. He trained me, both conceptually and methodology, in the social psychology of the self-concept, and it was from him that I learned the concept of mattering: the extent to which people believe they make a difference in the lives of others.

This book represents the culmination of my efforts. I believe that mattering is the fundamental human motivation; to be a social nonentity is intolerable, and people will do anything to escape this plight. When Prof. Richard Gelles generously invited me to include the mattering index I had developed (as well as Rosenberg's self-esteem index) in his study of dysfunctional behavior among adolescents, I had the opportunity to relate mattering (in this case, mattering to one's family) to behavior. The results give powerful evidence that mattering is indeed an essential part of the self-concept, in that failing to matter precipitously increases the likelihood of anti-social and self-destructive activity.

The intended audience for this book includes social psychologists, psychologists, sociologists, and social workers. It is pitched at the level of professional practitioners in each of these disciplines. In the university curriculum, the book is appropriate for an upper level undergraduate or graduate course in social psychology, the self-concept, adolescence, deviant behavior, and risky behavior. It could be a required book in any of the courses mentioned above. In a general social psychology course, it would be appropriate for a unit on the self-concept. The empirical analyses of the data are presented in an accessible fashion for students at any level of study.

I endeavored to make the book accessible to non-professionals, as well. I intend the chapter on research method to be detailed enough to convey an adequate sense of how research is done, without dwelling on complex issues. For those interested in more detail and discussion, I describe the intricacies of the research process in the Appendix. In addition, the final chapter includes a guide for parents and other authority figures (teachers, counselors, coaches) to inducing mattering in young people.

Because mattering is a relatively new concept in social psychology, there has been little published in this area. Research on the concept to date has appeared only in articles from peer-reviewed journals and a single piece in an edited book of readings. Further, the research has mainly focused on the antecedents to mattering (death of a loved one, social status and role) or the intrapersonal consequences of mattering (depression, self-esteem). This book is the first large-scale analysis of the powerful impact of mattering on behavior. It will open the gates for a new direction in the study of the self and will bring an understanding of a fundamental motivation that has been only implicitly recognized in social psychology to this time.

Acknowledgments

My deep thanks go to Morris Rosenberg, for his support over the years. Until his death, Manny was a source of great wisdom to me, both in learning how to think like a sociological social psychologist and in how to shape my career from these interests. His constructive suggestions, gently and eagerly communicated, gave me confidence that I was on the right track, and his generosity as a colleague helped me recognize that mentoring is about encouraging others to develop their own insights and skills.

Equally important, Richard Gelles has long been a significant part of my intellectual growth. His beneficence in inviting me to include my Mattering Index in the Youth at Risk survey is an outstanding act of collegiality. And his understanding of the process of book publishing proved invaluable to this novice.

All of the results, as powerful as they are, would mean nothing if they were not presented in a coherent, organized manner. Christine Cardone, my extraordinary editor at Wiley-Blackwell, has been constructive, supportive, and, most importantly, patient. She has steered me away from the common pitfalls of a first book and helped me present my theoretical arguments, and the empirical results that support them, in accessible and persuasive prose. When we disagreed, she carefully explained her perspective on publishing, and, invariably, I ended up concluding that she was correct. Thank you, Chris, for all that you have done for me.

Kudos to Kelly Basner of Wiley-Blackwell for her meticulous attention to detail and her occasionally necessary reminders that things were due to her. Thanks also to the production and copyediting staff (Hannah Rolls, Janey Fisher and Eldo Barkhuizen) who took the manuscript through its final stages.

My peers who volunteered to review the manuscript deserve a special commendation. Their constructive contributions and pertinent insights have made the book so much stronger. Their enthusiasm for the project strengthened my confidence, and their suggestions for connections to other theories in social psychology widened my understanding of the place of mattering in the discipline. Their altruism in what some have characterized as a thankless task makes them truly valuable colleagues. In that spirit, I thank Michael Hogg and James Cote. Any remaining errors in the book are solely my responsibility.

My colleagues at Brown University have been marvelous in their support and assistance. I especially thank my departmental confreres, Calvin Goldscheider and John Modell, for reading my proposal and offering their astute suggestions for its improvement. I greatly appreciate the assistance of fellow sociologists Phil Brown, Dennis Hogan, and David Meyer for their advice regarding the intricacies of book publishing. My erstwhile fellow graduate student and continuing close friend John Fleishman, of the Agency for Healthcare Research and Quality, was particularly helpful in providing suggestions for additional quantitative analyses.

Hongwei Xu, a graduate student in the Department of Sociology, has been a godsend in carrying out the final computer analyses using the software package SAS. His sharp eye for detail and spotting possible mistakes added much to the efficiency of these efforts. I am also very grateful to the undergraduate students who participated in the Group Research Project that I sponsored to engage in the preliminary data management and initial quantitative analyses. Their enthusiasm and willingness to learn how to manipulate the data made these early stages enjoyable and productive. So, thanks to Michelle Katzow and Serin Marshall for their work on mattering and violence; Jon Glasser and Kate Mason for mattering and binge drinking; Frances Cowhig and Drew Horton for mattering and substance abuse; Christopher Chin and Evin Isaacson for religiosity and mattering; and Sara Bloch and Audrey McIntyre for the structural antecedents to mattering. Thanks to my son, Brendan; you were a living example of the importance of mattering, and you matter so much to me.

Finally, a special thanks to my wife and colleague Susan Cunningham, of the College of the Holy Cross. She encouraged me throughout the long haul, from the initial germ of an idea to the final drafts of the manuscript. More importantly, she read every page of every draft and contributed valuable and productive insights that made the prose more accessible and persuasive. She provided me with several points of sociological theory that gave greater depth to my reasoning. I am blessed that Susan is both a superb colleague and supportive spouse. Thank you, Susan, with all my heart.

1

What Does It Mean to Matter?

Introduction: A Thought Experiment

Imagine for a moment that you are in a world in which you pass by others unnoticed. You cannot capture anyone's attention and are ignored by all around you. No one takes an interest in your activities, shares your joys, or comforts you in your sorrows. People in a quandary do not seek advice or emotional support from you, nor does anyone care about your opinions. In short, you are virtually invisible. You make a difference in no one's life. You feel alone in the company of your family, in your workplace, and in your community.

Now, shrug off this dreadful image. Return to your world and recognize with great relief that you are indeed connected to people in a meaningful way. Others are usually aware of your presence and notice when you come or go. They recognize you in social gatherings. Your successes are a source of pride to many of them. They are willing to listen to your problems. They may even feel close enough to you to criticize you for your own good. You recall that others have turned to you when they were in need and trusted you with things that are important to them. You *do* make a difference in the world around you. Put succinctly, you *matter*.

Defining Mattering: What It Is

Cellophane,
Mister Cellophane
Shoulda been my name.
Mister Cellophane.
'Cause you can look right through me,
Walk right by me,
And never know I'm there . . .

Chicago: The Musical

Because the notion of "mattering" can have a wide range of connotations, it is important to define the term carefully. In an earlier work I define "mattering" as "the perception that, to some degree and in any of a variety of ways, we are a significant part of the world around us" (Elliott, Kao, & Grant, 2004: 339). One can matter to specific others (a friend, a lover, a teacher), social institutions (such as the family or a business firm), one's community as a whole, or even society at large. This web of meaningful associations plays a vital role in our understanding of who we are.

First conceptualized by the sociologist Morris Rosenberg (Rosenberg & McCullough, 1981), mattering is an important aspect of the protective power of social connection. To matter to others enables a person to avoid behavior that would threaten the negotiation of a personally and socially rewarding path through the life course. When we matter, we know that any anti-social or self-destructive behavior would be a disappointment to the people or institutions to which we are connected; there is a bond of nurturance and approval that would be jeopardized by such acts.

On the other hand, those who believe that they do not matter recognize that they are isolated from the people and institutions who help give their lives meaning in a complex and often confusing society. Failing to matter, especially to the significant others and organizations in a person's life, is experienced as a profound rejection of the self in its entirety. Such a terrifying realization can hardly be borne. It feels shameful, for if one has nothing to capture another's attention, nothing worth investing in, or nothing to offer, it is prima facie evidence that one is a socially worthless person. To be wholly without merit is perhaps the most painful social image in a society that rewards the ability to distinguish oneself from the ordinary on the basis of personal development.

In this dire strait, people will do almost anything to rid themselves of the status of a "non-person." In some cases, the usual inhibitions against anti-social behavior are overcome by the need to matter at any cost. It is better to matter negatively, to be the focus of anger and opprobrium, than not to matter at all. Alternatively, self-destructive behaviors are not so threatening for a person who does not matter. What is the loss to the world or to the individual if a nonentity disappears forever?

An example from a popular film may make the point. George Bailey (James Stewart), the lead character in Frank Capra's *It's a Wonderful Life*, actually had the opportunity to discover how much he mattered to his family, friends, and the whole town of Bedford Falls, because he managed the town's Savings and Loan Institution. Discouraged by his failure to live out his dreams, George attempts suicide but is saved by an angel named Clarence. Unable to convince George that he has played a significant part in the world around him, Clarence arranges for George to experience Bedford Falls (now called Potterstown, after the mean, avaricious banker who wanted to take over the town) as it would have been if he had never been born. The stark contrast between the productive, happy Bedford Falls and the miserable, dark Potterstown soon makes clear to George how much he has mattered to everyone.

Occasional doubts about mattering are common in everyday personal experience. Many people experience dark times in which they wonder whether others know or care that they exist. After serious introspection or a check of their relationships to the people and institutions in their lives, they find that they are, indeed, significant, even if only in some small way, to the world around them. The anxiety passes.

I focus, in contrast, on the possibility that some people may *chronically* question their social significance, whereas others may be relatively free of such distressing suspicions. In constructing the theory of mattering, I begin with an axiom common to the two paradigms I use to elaborate the theory: One must learn how to be a human being.

In this view, very little of human nature is innate. To be sure, all human beings are born with impulses, embedded in our genetic and biological make-up. These impulses supply the energy for human activity, and they can be quite powerful. But the energy from such impulses is diffuse and undirected. If that were all there was to human beings, life would be chaotic, indeed.

Building a self is a social process that begins at birth and continues throughout the life course. It is predicated upon the development of cognitive capacities, a development that is determined both by genetic make-up and the socialization provided to us by those around us. The kind of self that one constructs is a product of everyday experiences as a person matures.

Sociologists call the process of learning how to be human "socialization." The teachers in the socialization process are the significant others in a person's life, beginning with parents and other family members, continuing with friends, other peers, and teachers, and extending throughout the life course to include lovers, neighbors, employers, and even one's own children. We never stop learning more about who we are.

As cognitive capacities develop, the structure of the self becomes an increasingly complex and sophisticated construct, arranged in a way that is significant and meaningful to a person. There are individual differences in the complexity and sophistication of the self-concept, based on cognitive development and socialization experiences, but each of us has developed a unique and reasonably coherent understanding of who we are.

One of the most important things we learn is the extent to which we matter to other people, social institutions (such as the family), our community, and even society as a whole. People come to differ in the extent to which they believe they matter because of their different experiences of the socialization process that prepares them to be functioning members of society. How people are treated by another, especially someone who looms large in their lives, will teach them whether or not they matter in this world. Most will learn that they are significant to their significant others, at least to some degree. A notable minority will not. In short, I am interested in mattering as a continuum of the self along which people vary. It is our placement on this dimension that will strongly influence how we orient to ourselves and others and how we engage with the world around us.

Further, it is the *subjective* sense of mattering that is critical in my account. As the sociologist W. I. Thomas (Thomas & Thomas, 1928, p. 572) asserted long ago: "If [people] define situations as real, they are real in their consequences." There may be many objective indicators that a person is significant to others, but if that person does not understand this to be so, it is effectively not so. For example, parents may point to all the material goods they have lavished on their children as evidence that their children really matter to them. The children, in turn, may sense that these things are a poor substitute for the lost time that their parents could have spent with them. Those who intend to communicate mattering and those on the receiving end of the communication may have different notions of what truly signals mattering to another. But the impact on a person's behavior will come from mattering as it is *perceived* by the person and not by some "objective" criteria.

Forms of Mattering

Awareness

> *Dear Abby:*
>
> *I have a problem that may not seem like a big deal to most people, but it really bothers me.*
>
> *I meet people, and the next time I see them, they do not remember having met me. While I can't always remember the name of a new acquaintance, I can at least remember having met the person.*
>
> *Abby, it's a blow to my ego when someone has no recollection of having met me. I admit that I am on the shy and quiet side; perhaps that is why I am not remembered.*
>
> *Is there anything I can do to make a lasting impression?*
>
> Abigail Van Buren, Mr. Forgettable

Mattering can take several forms. The first involves being the focus of others' attention. Such awareness is purely cognitive: We matter in the merest sense if others realize that we exist. Recognizable to others as an individual, a person who matters is distinguishable from the masses that populate the surroundings. If others greet us whenever we walk into a crowded room, we know that others are mindful of us, and we have reaffirmed the fact that we matter. In contrast, if we fail to attract the attention of others when we are in their presence, we may literally feel like a nonentity. Unacknowledged by anyone around us, we may feel that people are looking right through us, which strongly suggests that we do not matter.

Importance

> *I'll find somebody new,*
> *And, baby, we'll say we're through,*
> *And you won't matter anymore.*
>
> Paul Anka, (I guess) it doesn't matter anymore

Two other forms of mattering are more complex, in that they imply a relationship between the person and the others to whom one matters. With importance, we feel that we matter to others if we are the object of their concern. They may provide us with emotional support, inconvenience themselves to see that our needs are met, or take pride in our achievements. The fact that people invest time and energy in us in order to promote our welfare suggests that we are a significant part of their world. For example, the teacher who tutors a student after classes are done for the day is communicating that the student is important to the teacher. Instead of going home to throw off the demands of the job, the teacher is spending precious time on the student. It is unlikely that the message will be lost on the youth, even if it is not articulated explicitly. In contrast, if people continually do not care what happens to us or will not bother to help us, we realize how unimportant we are to others.

Reliance

> *"That job did wonders for her. I think about that every time I hear somebody say there's such a thing as 'natural adjusted rate inflation-unemployment,' or 'structural unemployment.' That there's always gonna be five or six percent of the work force with no jobs. Nothin' the government can do about it. It's something that can't be helped. Well* bullshit; *that's what I say.* 'Find *something the poor bastards can do.' Government has* got *to deal with it. That's what the government's* for. *It's a moral obligation, and I mean that. It's not just havin' no money that drags people down; it's feelin' like they don't* matter, *don't count any more. They lost the parts they had to play."*
>
> George V. Higgins, *A change of gravity*

Finally, mattering to other people can take the form of their reliance on us. We matter to others if they look to us for the satisfaction of their needs or desires. The joy that engulfs us upon being told that our lover needs us is due to the realization that we matter to him or her. Another poignant example of reliant mattering is the link between parent and child. The knowledge that the child will not survive without the care of the parents is a clear signal to the parents that they matter.

Reliance can be onerous. To have another depend on us in critical ways may become a burden, in that the other's needs may too often have to take precedence over our own. An emotional attachment to the other may help compensate for the efforts expended as a consequence of reliance, but even so, this form of mattering may prove exhausting. The ambivalence sometimes found in this form of mattering can be difficult for a person to resolve. The father who works two jobs so that his children can attend college may resent the need to do so, but perhaps the resentment is mitigated by the knowledge that his children need him.

Once again, popular culture can make the point very effectively. In the film *About Schmidt*, Warren Schmidt (Jack Nicholson), learns to his dismay how little he meant to his firm once he retired – and even before. As he prepares for his retirement, Schmidt meticulously catalogues and boxes all his files, along with helpful hints for his successor. A few days later, he impulsively revisits the firm, only to find his presence most unwelcome. Upon leaving, he happens to pass by the disposal center for the business. There, stacked and never opened, he sees the boxes of his files. (When I first presented a paper on mattering at a colloquium sponsored by my own Department of Sociology, a colleague who had recently ended his tenure came to me after the talk and said to me, "Do you want to know what it means not to matter? Just retire.")

In both relationship forms of mattering, it is the element of choice that is crucial. To realize that one has been singled out from all the people who might have benefited from others' investment or who could provide what the others seek is to know that one matters. Indeed, although being uniquely qualified to receive or give resources is prima facie evidence that one matters, the fact that one has been chosen from a pool of people may indicate an even stronger degree of mattering. If no one else is around, so that another's attention must be focused on me or nothing at all; if there are no others in whom a benefactor can invest time and resources; if I am the only person who could provide for another's need, then I cannot be confident that

I matter as deeply as I might like. It is possible that someone is turning to me simply because there is no one else. But when there are many who could fill the bill and the person notices *me*, is concerned for *me*, or asks *me* for help, I can be more certain that there is something about me that sets me apart from all the others. I can be more confident that I really do matter.

Distinguishing Mattering: What It Is Not

Social psychologists have posited many elements of the self-concept, and to introduce mattering as a new dimension requires that it be conceptually distinguished from those already recognized. Mattering may have a superficial similarity to other dimensions, and because elements of the self-concept can have a wide range of connotations in the public parlance, it is especially important to define mattering, in part, by pointing out its differences from other notions. I focus on four existing constructs, each well established in social-psychological theory and empirical research: perceived social support, self-esteem, self-monitoring, and self-consciousness. All of these constructs are associated with mattering, but I will argue (and point to evidence) that they are conceptually distinct from mattering. The following explication is taken from my initial analysis of mattering (Elliott, Kao, & Grant, 2004).

Perceived Social Support

Perceived social support is the sense that others provide the resources (material, psychological, and emotional) that help one carry on. Although perceived social support should be positively associated with mattering (especially importance), the two are distinguishable concepts. Perceived social support is generally defined as the extent to which one expects that others will provide for a person's specific needs (such as emotional support during a trying time or financial assistance when things are bad economically). In contrast, importance is considered to be a more general awareness, involving a continual interest in one's welfare by others, beyond the provision of specific forms of support. We can be aware that others invest in us even when specific needs are not at issue: The friendly card that arrives in the mail for no specific reason reminds us that we matter.

In addition, importance implies that others are investing in us because they are sincerely interested in furthering our welfare. However, not all social support arises from altruism; occasionally, there is an ulterior motive that is hidden during the interaction. Suspicion of bad faith is not likely to lead to an attribution that one matters to another. If we are merely useful to another person, a means to an end, we are more likely to resent the other as a manipulator than value him or her as a source of mattering.

Self-Esteem

Self-esteem is the global evaluation of one's own personal characteristics; it is the extent to which a person considers him- or herself a worthwhile person (Rosenberg, 1979). Those with low self-esteem believe that they are seriously deficient in important ways. They find little in themselves to be proud of and lack self-respect. They have difficulty acknowledging any positive understandings of themselves, because of the need to maintain a consistent understanding of who they are; the few positive aspects are overwhelmed by the many negative aspects. As a consequence, the person experiences continual self-rejection.

The social psychologist Roy Baumeister (1993) has more to say about the nature of low self-esteem. As he eloquently argues:

> People with low self-esteem lack a clear, consistent, unified understanding of who they are, which leaves them at the mercy of events and changing situations and which makes it difficult for them to manage their affairs optimally. They favor self-protection over self-enhancement . . . even if this strategy means giving up some opportunities for success and prestige (Baumeister, 1993, p. 217).

People with low self-esteem would like to think better of themselves. However, they are inhibited in doing so by an anxiety arising from their recognition that they lack the personal resources to back up their behaviors. The risk of discovering that they are as worthless as they fear they might be prevents them from taking the risks necessary to establish a self-concept that deserves approbation.

In contrast, high self-esteem people consider themselves persons of value. They respect themselves because they find that, overall, their good points outweigh their bad points. It is important to note that high self-esteem does not imply a feeling of superiority or arrogance. The person enjoying high self-esteem realizes that there is always room for improvement in the self-concept. It is more that the central elements of the self are valued positively enough that they can feel good about themselves. A person with realistic high self-esteem feels "good enough."

There are important distinctions between mattering and self-esteem. In its essence, mattering is a purely cognitive process, an attribution of one's connection to the social order. To be sure, the inference about whether one matters does not occur in a vacuum. The social and structural contexts of people's existence will play a large role in their understanding of their social significance. To know that I matter means that others take note of me and relate to me in ways that evince my connection to them, but there is no immediate evaluation of the self involved in this awareness.

In contrast, assessing one's self-esteem entails both cognitive and affective processes. In our society, we are taught to evaluate what we know about ourselves, to be satisfied with physical, social, and moral aspects of the self that are deemed positive and to react with regret, guilt, or shame when undesirable aspects of the self come to light. However, self-esteem can entail a focus on the self independent of one's relations with others. There are many contributors to a person's self-evaluation, and mattering is one of them.

Indeed, I will argue below that attributions about mattering comprise a fundamentally important foundation for inferences about self-worth. But mattering is not, in itself, a judgment about one's worthiness as a human being. Once the cognitive appraisal of the extent to which one matters is finished, the emotional appraisal of one's self-worth will soon follow. Self-evaluation is a consequence of mattering, not a part of it. Conceptually, they are distinguishable.

Self-Monitoring

According to the social psychologist Mark Snyder (1974, 1987), self-monitoring refers to the extent to which people observe and regulate the self-presentations that they proffer in everyday social interactions. The sociologist Erving Goffman (1959) argues that everyone engages in impression management, orchestrating their behavior in major or minor ways to achieve the goals they seek in a given encounter with others. The concept of self-monitoring carries this understanding further and asserts that people differ in the ways that they present themselves. For example, high self-monitors look to their immediate environment (including the behavior of others) for cues that will signal conduct appropriate to goal attainment; in contrast, low self-monitors prefer to look within themselves for guidelines of appropriateness (Elliott, 1979).

The strategies and tactics of self-presentation are different from the concerns of mattering. Impression management is an attempt to influence the definition of the situation in an interaction and see to it that others behave in ways that facilitate the self-monitor's goals. As a consequence, the other is largely an object, an audience for whom the impression is managed in order to attain a goal. On the other hand, as an issue involving relationships, mattering is a question of making a difference to individuals, groups, or institutions. Although self-monitoring may be involved in a person's attempt to matter, it is not itself mattering.

Self-Consciousness

Self-consciousness is the chronic tendency to be the object of one's own attention. The psychologist Alan Fenigstein (Fenigstein, Scheier, & Buss, 1975) identifies two general forms of self-consciousness: *private* (the cognitive awareness of one's own personal characteristics) and *public* (the awareness that one is a stimulus for the behavior of others).

Neither form of self-consciousness replicates the notion of mattering. Private self-consciousness is a dispositional tendency to examine the self. It can include an excessive focus on one's physical characteristics (the teenager's obsession with the blemishes from acne), cognitive characteristics (the continual awareness of one's thought processes or attitudes), and affective characteristics (a keen awareness of one's emotions in any circumstance). Although private self-consciousness can affect one's behavior, it does not involve determining one's relationships to others, even at the basic level called for in mattering.

In a different vein, public self-consciousness concerns the realization that others are using our presence and behavior to help determine their actions in the encounter. Once again, the issue is of the self as an object (this time the issue is of others' scrutiny and not one's own) rather than the self in a potential relationship with others. Public self-consciousness can dispose people to be acutely aware of the impressions they give off to others and encourage them to manage these impressions with great care. One can be publicly self-conscious in the presence of those to whom one does not matter, and people need not necessarily be more or less publicly self-conscious among those to whom they do matter.

Although conceptually distinct from mattering, the above notions need not be independent of it. There are good reasons to expect that mattering is positively associated with each of these constructs. For example, mattering to another should be associated with high levels of self-esteem. If people consider me a significant part in their lives, it must be because I am someone worth attending to; they would not invest their resources in me or seek my advice if I were a deficient person. The fact that I matter to them suggests, to the contrary, that I am worthy of their attention, resources, and requests. Therefore, beliefs that one matters to others can induce higher levels of self-esteem. Indeed, earlier research efforts I have conducted demonstrate a positive link (of varying degrees) between one's placement on the continuum of mattering, on the one hand, and perceived social support, self-esteem, self-consciousness, and self-monitoring, on the other (Elliott, Kao, & Grant, 2004).

Further, statistical analysis reported therein also demonstrate that the items I have constructed to measure mattering exhibit strong *construct* and *discriminant validity* (Nunnally & Bernstein, 1994); that is, they are excellent measures of the concept of mattering, and they do not reflect any of the aforementioned constructs. From these results, we can be confident that mattering, as conceptualized and as actually measured, is a distinct part of our self-understanding.

Of course, other constructs could also be identified. Establishing discriminant validity is an ongoing process. As mattering becomes more integrated into the social-psychological study of the self, it will be necessary and possible to enlarge the range of concepts to which mattering is linked but from which it can be distinguished in a theoretically meaningful way.

A Similar Construct

Research in social psychology has occasionally focused on concepts that appear to be similar to mattering. For example, in addition to his work on self-esteem, Roy Baumeister, with Mark Leary (1995), investigated a concept that appears to be quite close to mattering: the need to belong. They posit that "human beings have a pervasive drive to form and maintain at least a minimum quality of lasting, positive, and significant interpersonal relationships" (Baumeister & Leary, 1995, p. 497). The need to belong is so general that it can be satisfied by connections to *any* person or group. Belonging is characterized by frequent personal contacts with a person or group and the construction of a strong bond between the self and the other.

There are certainly similarities between the need to belong and mattering. For example, both concepts are characterized by *satiation*. Satiation has to do with the number of people to whom one is connected. With each concept, a few relationships will suffice; forming additional connections to others will likely result in diminishing returns. As Baumeister and Leary (1995, p. 520) note, "Having two as opposed to no close relationships may make a world of difference to the person's health and happiness; having eight as opposed to six may have very little consequence." The same is true for mattering. A person does not need to matter to everyone, just to those who are significant in that person's everyday life.

In addition, *substitution* is possible for both the need to belong and mattering. With the need to belong, one might lose an attachment to a particular group but replace it with another satisfactory group. Young people graduating from middle school to high school may lose their "citizenship" in the former but will suffer no undue anxiety if they can secure a sense of belonging in the latter. Similarly, students leaving high school for college may find that they no longer matter to the friends they have left behind, and this might initially lead to some regret. However, once they realize that classmates at college have become aware of them, invest in them, and rely on them, a sense of mattering will be restored. The loss of mattering to former friends may be mourned, but their new friendships ensure that they still make a difference in the lives of others.

Still, there are ways in which the two concepts are different. First, as argued by Baumeister and Leary (1995), the need to belong fosters and requires a psychological attachment to a person or group. Although this can be true for mattering relationships (consider the need to matter to one's family), it is not necessary. A student may matter to a teacher without forming an emotional bond to that teacher. (In the television series *The Wonder Years*, Kevin, the young adolescent who is the focus of the dramas, finds himself disappointed by a teacher he respects. Confronting the teacher, Kevin remonstrates, "I thought you were my friend!" The teacher replies, gently but firmly, "No, Kevin, not your friend; your teacher.") There is a difference between bonding and caring, and only the latter is necessary to signal mattering.

Further, the need to belong can impel a person to initiate the attachment process and work to cement those that take root. In contrast, a sense of mattering is induced in an individual by the attentions, inputs, or needs of others. It generally cannot be forced by the person with a need to matter. Indeed, as I shall point out later, "forced" mattering, in which a person behaves (often outrageously) in order to secure attention, usually arouses negative reactions in others, something not likely to satisfy a need to belong.

Baumeister and Leary (1995) also theorize that the need to belong requires frequent personal contacts or interactions. Their argument suggests that a sense of belonging is a rather fragile awareness that requires continual and clear reaffirmation. On the other hand, reaffirmations of mattering need not be so personal or frequent. For example, contacts by a manager with employees in a firm may not be personal and involve no face-to-face interactions, yet managers can instill a sense of mattering in the employees. Once mattering is established, it is not likely to be questioned, unless circumstances suggest otherwise. Most of us realize that we continue to matter to significant others, even in the absence of continual contact. Fleeting anxiety about making a difference can quickly pass upon reflection about one's history of mattering.

Finally, mattering and the need to belong can be distinguished by the range of behaviors employed to satisfy their demands. In establishing a sense of belonging, most people would avoid socially undesirable behaviors. Untoward actions are not likely to attract a person to others. They would more likely evoke rejection and ostracism rather than an invitation to join the group.

This may not be so with regard to mattering. It is certainly the case that the best experience of mattering comes from being noticed, supported, and relied upon for socially desirable behaviors. But, as I will argue in Chapter 2, the need to matter is so powerful that people will even resort to disapproved actions to call attention to themselves. In the panic and desperation that comes with the failure to matter, they would rather be negatively known than not known at all.

Mattering and the Self as Entity

As I have conceptualized it, mattering is a dimension of the self-concept. The self-concept is an organized representation of the self stored in the mind. Rosenberg (1979, p. 7) defines the self-concept as "the totality of the individual's thoughts and feelings having reference to [the] self as an object." Put simply, the self-concept is a cognitive construction based on an interpretation of the elements of the self. (See Baumeister, 1998, for an extensive discussion of the self and its status as an entity.)

Thinking about the self as an entity reflects a particular perspective on human beings that is derived from Cognitive Social Psychology, one of several paradigms, or scientific perspectives, that inform our understanding of people and their social experiences. (See Isen & Hastorf, 1982, for a thorough discussion of the paradigm.) Its basic assumption is that human beings are rational creatures who think about themselves and the world around them and then make decisions about behaviors based on their cognitions. Rather than react automatically to stimuli from the environment, as do organisms governed by instincts, people's decisions are based on the understanding of their environment, including particular objects and the context in which those objects appear.

Rejecting the simple stimulus–response model of the behaviorists (cf. Watson, 1939, for the classic approach to Behaviorism), cognitive social psychologists assert that the individual intervenes between the stimulus and the response. One interprets the stimulus, assesses its meaning, and chooses a response that is deemed to be appropriate for that meaning. Perception and cognition are no longer seen as passive and dispassionate processes. Instead, they are understood as useful functions for a thinking organism adapting to its environment.

Some have used the analogy of a computer to describe the work of the human information processing: A person perceives stimuli from the environment (input), interprets the information through cognitive processing (the brain is our central processing unit), and decides how to behave in light of this interpretation (output). However, in spite of our attempts to be rational, the processes involved in these appraisals and decisions can be (and often are) influenced by "contaminating" factors (including emotions, motivations, and individual needs) that prevent us from perceiving accurately the meaning of things in our environment.

The attribution of meanings to objects in the environment (including other people) can suffer from a variety of limiting or distorting factors. For example, because our cognitive capacities are not infinite, we cannot attend equally to all of the many stimuli available to us at a given moment; we would be paralyzed by the task of sorting it all out, and behavior would cease. In response, we have learned to be selectively perceptive, deciding which stimuli merit our attention and which can be ignored.

Our choice of what to perceive is often influenced by the motivations underlying our participation in a social encounter. In particular, our feelings and our motivations may lead to a biased understanding of what happened and why. For example, voluminous research has affirmed the existence of a self-serving bias (Pysczynski & Greenberg, 1987), in which people are eager to take credit for success but generally eschew responsibility for failure, unless reality constraints make the claim ludicrous (Elliott, 1989). A central part of the theoretical argument I will present in Chapter 2 for the significance of mattering is that a failure to matter is likely to distort the attributions a person makes and is likely to lead to dysfunctional behavior.

From the Cognitive Social Psychology perspective, then, the self is one of the objects in a person's experience that must be understood. As Rosenberg (1979, p. 8) notes, the self "is an object of perception and reflection, including the emotional responses to that perception and reflection." But the meanings attributed to the many aspects of the self are not a mere agglomeration of elements; rather, they possess a certain structure that organizes our understanding of ourselves into a reasonably coherent whole. For example, the elements of the self can be crudely divided into two categories: *personal identity* (the personal attributes and characteristics that make up the physical, cognitive, and emotional aspects of the self) and *social identity* (the social categories to which one belongs and which are recognized and affirmed by others, such as race, gender, student).

Indeed, the social psychologist Hazel Markus (1977) speaks of self-schemata as interpretive structures that help lend coherence to life experiences. They are the core of a person's self-concept. In general, a schema is defined as a structure of the process of cognition that operates as a framework for organizing and interpreting the social environment. Such a cognitive structure is derived from past experience as familiarity with the concepts they represent grows. Schemata are learned by individuals through the process of socialization, in which significant individuals and social institutions in our lives teach us how to become a human being.

A schema serves several important functions in the cognitive process. First, it influences what information will receive attention and how it will be encoded and organized. Second, it has a selective influence on retention, retrieval, and the organization of memory. Third, it functions as an interpretive framework and so influences evaluations, judgments, predictions, and inferences. Finally, it influences overt behavior.

A self-schema is a cognitive generalization about the self, derived from socialization experiences, which organize and guide the processing of self-relevant information. They represent the way that the self is articulated and differentiated in memory. A self-schema determines what information about the self is attended to, how it is structured, and how much importance is attached to it. It reflects invariances that people discover in their own orientations and behavior and that are categorized and organized.

The self-concept is a set of cognitive structures used to recognize and interpret self-relevant stimuli in the individual's social experience. It influences what stimuli receive attention, how the information is processed, and how one actually responds to these stimuli. In short, the self-concept fits the criteria of the definition of a schema.

Further, some of the elements of the self-concept consist of a continuum over which people are arrayed by dint of the everyday socialization they experience. Placement on this range orients people to themselves and to the world around them in certain ways, and people at different points on the continuum differ in these orientations.

Mattering is one such self-concept dimension, and the extent to which we believe we matter to others is learned in the socialization process that teaches us how to be human beings. Different people, with different socialization experiences, may find themselves at different points along the mattering continuum. Some may believe that they matter a great deal. They have experienced the attention, investment and reliance from others. Others may have learned from the significant others in their lives that they are nearly superfluous in this world. It is the placement along this dimension that helps to account for differences in behavior.

Social and behavioral scientists have identified three major processes by which we construct an understanding of ourselves. The first, *reflected appraisals* (conceptualized by the psychiatrist Harry Stack Sullivan, 1947), asserts that we are deeply influenced in our self-conceptions by the way that others react to us. People are continually communicating to us how they see us, and it is easy, especially when we are children, to incorporate their understandings into our own self-concepts. We internalize the image of ourselves that is communicated to us by others and make it our own. (A public service message about child maltreatment warns parents: "Words hit like a fist. Be careful what you say to your children!")

Reflected appraisals constitute perhaps the strongest source of mattering. The feedback we get from significant others in our lives goes a long way in determining whether we matter. On the one hand, when a parent says, "I know you, and I believe in you," the child is reassured about mattering. On the other hand, by using the condemning phrase "Forget you!" a teenage gang member can let others know that they do not matter at all.

Another way of learning about ourselves is to compare ourselves to some well-defined standard. (Am I a tall person? Am I good at linear algebra?) However, often there is no clear standard by which we can measure our standing in some category or dimension. (Am I a good tennis player? Am I a tolerant person?) In that case, the social psychologist Leon Festinger (1957) argues that we learn about ourselves by comparing ourselves to others. We may do so in order to determine congruence with another (same vs. different) or for evaluative purposes (better or worse). In either case, we often get valuable information about who we are by the process of *social comparison.*

The social comparison process is another way to assess the extent to which one matters to others. Counting the number of friends enjoyed by others or the quality of their relationships in comparison to one's own circle of friends may give a person a relative sense of mattering.

Finally, the psychologist Darryl Bem (1972) holds that one's self-understanding can be based on observations of one's own behavior and the conditions under which it occurs. Just as we are willing to make inferences about others on the basis of observing their behaviors, so we infer elements of our own self-concept by the process of *self-attribution.* We learn something about who we are by paying close attention to what we do.

Self-attributions may be an important way to assess the extent to which one matters to others. Simply recalling the number of times a person responds to a request for emotional support by another can provide convincing evidence about that person's self-perceived mattering.

Proceeding through the life course, one's sense of mattering may change. Encountering a new person (a teacher in school, a coach at play, a mentor in a firm) may impart, for better or worse, a new understanding of the difference one makes in the lives of others. Further, there may be specific times or situations in which a transient turnabout in mattering occurs. Nevertheless, it is possible over time to build a reasonably stable sense of how often and how much other people pay attention to us, encourage and support us, and turn to us when they are in need. Although change in mattering is always possible, we expect it to be an evolutionary change, not characterized by unanticipated seismic shifts.

At the same time, we may find that we matter at different levels of intensity to specific persons, groups, or institutions. The higher the level of mattering across all possible sources, the more secure the self-concept. Yet, as with the need to belong, mentioned above, there are likely to be diminishing returns as the number of people to whom one matters increases. It may be sufficient that one matters greatly only to a few particularly significant others. Indeed, research on resilience (Goldstein & Brooks, 2004; Rubin, 1996) demonstrates that people (adults *and* children) can survive horrific trauma if there is one person who takes a special interest in them. That is, mattering to one person can save a person from a severely damaged self-concept, even in the face of terrifying physical or psychological threats to the self. The most devastating threats to the self-concept arise when an individual matters to no one.

Mattering and the Self as Process

A fundamentally different way of understanding the self emerges from a uniquely sociological paradigm: *Symbolic Interactionism*. First articulated by the sociologist George Herbert Mead (1934) and elaborated by his student Herbert Blumer (1969), Symbolic Interactionism begins with a very different premise from that of Cognitive Social Psychology, a premise that also involves the nature of meaning. Both paradigms assert that human beings react toward objects in their environment according to the meanings that these objects (including other persons) have for them. From this point on, the two paradigms diverge sharply. Whereas Cognitive Social Psychology presumes that meaning is an integral part of the object itself, Symbolic

Interactionism begins with the axiom that all meaning is socially constructed and imposed on objects by those people involved with the object.

The self, then, cannot be an entity, because that would imply that it has a meaning that is internally constructed, albeit changeable. Rather, the symbolic interactionists see the self as a process by which the individual, in concert with others, creates and maintains meanings in a given social interaction. Meanings, unique to the ongoing situation, are created for all elements, including physical objects, gestures, and even the people taking part in the interaction. Successful encounters are possible only when all involved share the meaning that is constructed for the occasion. Without consensus as to meaning, the situation is not well defined, and the interaction is likely to descend into chaos. If things are to proceed, the participants must engage in "remedial work" (Goffman, 1971) to ensure that a common meaning is shared by all. As an example, students who can't agree whether a gathering is a study group or a party will have neither until agreement can be reached.

The process that is the self consists of what Mead (1934) calls a "conversation" between the two parts of the self: the "I" and the "Me." The "I" is the impulsive part of the self, an inclination to react to a stimulus that is prior to any cognitive assessment of it. In the common parlance, we often speak of a "gut reaction," an almost automatic and certainly unorganized predisposition to respond. This is the "I" in action. If there were only the "I" in our selves, we would find the world a chaotic and frustrating place, as each of us, acting impulsively, without awareness of or sensitivity to the needs or behavior of others, finds interactions with others exceedingly difficult.

But Symbolic Interactionists argue that this is not the case. As the "I" goes into play, it is immediately followed by the workings of the "Me." The "Me" is the phase of the self in which a person imaginatively takes the perspective of another to look back at the self. This perspective taking is called by Mead (1934) "taking the role of the other." Its purpose is to understand what meaning might be attached by observers to the many potential responses a person could make to a given stimulus. After consideration of the many possibilities through the operation of the "Me," the person can select the behavioral response whose meaning best fits with the definition of the situation (the meaning of the interaction created and maintained by all participants) and will most likely lead to the goals pursued by the person. When someone greets me on the street, I can consider the various responses before I act. What meanings will the greeter attach to the possible responses I can make? Is a casual "hello" in keeping with the nature of the interaction, or should I be formal in addressing the other?

Initially, children are limited by newly developed cognitive skills to taking the role of specific others in a given interaction. During the pre-adolescent years, they do not have the ability to integrate these distinct (and potentially contradictory) standpoints into a unitary perspective on the self. This skill is attained only as their cognitive capacities mature. The process of cognitive maturation varies across individuals, but by early adolescence (12 years, or so), a person has learned how to take the role of the generalized other, a viewpoint on the self that is an amalgamation of the specific others in one's life to date. When the adolescent can understand how the amorphous "they" would attach meaning to potential behaviors, the "Me" is fully formed, and self as a process is complete.

The "Me" is also a source of self-understanding. In the early days of sociological analysis of the self, Charles Horton Cooley (1922, pp. 183–184) introduced the notion of the "looking-glass self":

> In a very large and interesting class of cases, the social reference takes the form of a somewhat definite imagination of how one's self – that is any idea he [*sic*] appropriates – appears in a particular mind, and the kind of self-feeling that one has is determined by the attitude toward this attributed to that other mind. A social self of this sort might be called the reflected or looking-glass self:
>
> "Each to each a looking-glass
> Reflects the other that doth pass."

The looking glass self is a parallel notion of Sullivan's (1947) reflected appraisals. By understanding the meanings that are attributed to us on the basis of our choices of behaviors, we come to gain a picture of who we are as participants in a given interaction. Symbolic interactionists call this understanding a *situated identity*.

It is the understanding of a person's situated identity that makes possible a sense of mattering. If one is allowed to take part in goal-directed activity, it is easy to infer that one matters, at least with regard to the current interaction. If one is allowed to participate only as a tangential entity or not at all, the message is clear: One does not matter. One important motivation for my claim of a situated identity in an interaction that is significant to me is the need to reassure myself that I matter, that I have a meaningful and necessary part to play in the ongoing interaction. If I fail to do so, I am very likely to abandon the current interaction and seek one that will reinforce my sense of mattering.

Over time, where appropriate, people strive for consistency in their situated identities across interactions. The accumulated memory of aspects of past situated identities is often brought to the current interaction to be included as part of the creation and maintenance of a current situated identity. These regularly recurring aspects of the self are called the *biographical identity* of the person. Gender is a good example of an element of a biographical identity. For most people, the situated identities they claim from one interaction to the next are constrained by the social understandings of gender appropriateness. Any situated identities that might violate gender expectations would likely be denied a person, unless the definition of the situation called for such a contradiction.

It is in the realm of identity that mattering gains full meaning for Symbolic Interactionism. Some followers of this paradigm, notably sociologists George J. McCall and J. L. Simmons (1978) and Sheldon Stryker and Peter J. Burke (2000), identify themselves as Structural Symbolic Interactionists. Structural Symbolic Interactionism, as the name implies, embeds the negotiation of situated identities and the recognition of biographical identities within the context of society's established social institutions. In particular, followers of this paradigm argue that one's locus in the structure of society will constrain the identities available for claiming in a given situation.

Structural Symbolic Interactionists have enlarged the focus on identities to include the notion of *role identity*: "the character and the role that an individual devises for himself [*sic*] as an occupant of a particular social position" (McCall & Simmons, 1978, p. 65). The role identity is a person's "imagination of himself *as he likes to think of himself being and acting* as an occupant of that position" (McCall & Simmons, 1966, p. 65; emphasis in the original). It is the place in the social order, the collection of positions (offspring, sibling, student, co-worker, spouse), that identifies an individual and makes him or her recognizable (meaningful) to others.

Stryker and Burke (2000, p. 286) assert that role identities are "internalized role expectations." We are taught by the socializing agents in our lives to conform to the commonly accepted and shared understandings of what it means to occupy a particular position in the social order. For example, besides gender, we are taught what it means to be a member of a particular race or ethnic group according to the racial projects our society constructs (Omi & Winant, 1994); a particular level of socioeconomic status that determines our value to society (Sennett & Cobb, 1972); and a particular kind of religious belief (or unbelief) (Berger, 1969).

According to Stryker and Burke (2000, p. 286), role identities are "cognitive bases for defining situations, and they increase sensitivity and receptivity to certain cues for behavior." As such, role identities help maintain an acceptable situated identity for each participant in the interaction. And commitment to the role identity, "the degree to which persons' relationships to others in their networks depend on possessing a particular identity" (Stryker & Burke, 2000, p. 286), ensures that a relationship between individuals will stand the test of time. Failing to abide by a role identity's expectations is likely to jeopardize our ability to build and sustain a mutually satisfying relationship with others, as people will not be able to count on us to claim a familiar and easily acceptable situated identity. Adhering to the expectations of a role identity confers on any situated identity a legitimacy that makes us a trustworthy participant in any encounter (Goffman, 1971).

And this is where mattering comes in. First, one's role identity may preclude the possibility of mattering to others in a social gathering. For example, servants, who are relegated to the status of "non-person" on the basis of their place in the social order, will learn very quickly that they do not matter to those whom they serve (Goffman, 1967). They are expected not to participate in any interaction involving their superiors, including any conversation. They are not to offer advice to their "betters," nor show approval or disapproval of what occurs, and in fact, they are not to attend at all to what is going on around them (often more honored in the breach than in observance).

Second, when a role identity allows us to take part in an encounter, we expect that we do matter to the significant others also involved. We do not expect to be ignored; we expect to be noticed. We expect that others will acknowledge the importance of the role we play, by supporting our role enactment. Finally, we expect them to acknowledge their reliance on the role identity we inhabit, so that the encounter can proceed to a successful conclusion.

More particularly, we expect that people with whom we are supposed to have a meaningful, perhaps intimate, relationship will allow us to enact our role identity fully. Failing to matter in this case is a violation of the expectations associated to these role relationships and so is a threat to role identity. To fail to matter means that the others in the relationship do not attend to us, refuse to give even minimal support to us, and deny their need for our place in the interaction. In short, it deprives us of the legitimacy required to assume and maintain that desired role identity.

The more salient the role identity, the more damaging the threat caused by a failure to matter. If you do not matter to an acquaintance, you may be able to avoid the shame or guilt that might otherwise overcome you, because your role identity with respect to the acquaintance is not central to your understanding of your place in the social order. However, a child who does not matter to his (or her) parents gets a powerful message that "I am not who I should be," a violation of the "identity standard" (Stryker & Burke, 2000, p. 287) of the socially prescribed meanings that define a person's identity in a situation and in the family system as a whole.

Ultimately, mattering deals with the possibility of establishing a meaningful connection to the significant others in our lives. When successfully accomplished, we can be confident in our role identities and can take the necessary steps to pursue our aims. Failure raises the terrifying awareness that the desired relationship and its concomitant identity are destroyed. It may be self-produced (due to ineffective attempts to take the role of the other), but it may also be that others simply have no desire to accord us the legitimacy required for the role identity, for reasons known only to them. The point is that success in adopting a role identity is not merely a matter of personal effort or ability. If others do not recognize our claim, it is difficult to force them to do so.

Still, we may yet feel responsible for the loss of the role identity, as we ask ourselves, "What is wrong with me, that I am rejected by those to whom I should be connected?" The classic example of such self-recrimination is found in the case of child neglect, in which the child concludes that he or she somehow deserves to be a non-person within the family (cf. Miller-Perrin & Perrin, 2007, ch. 5).

Both paradigms, then, acknowledge, explicitly or implicitly, mattering as a fundamental motivation within the self. The Cognitive Social Psychologists understand mattering as a dimension of the self-concept, learned from socialization by the significant others in our lives, which exerts a powerful impetus to act in ways that assure we matter to others. The Structural Symbolic Interactionists view mattering as an integral part of the process by which role identities are created and sustained in everyday life. From both perspectives, mattering is a strong element of (and failing to matter is likely to be a strong threat to) a personally and socially integrated self.

Mattering and the Life Course

Whatever the orientation taken on the self, recognition of the importance of mattering is never extinguished. Once we become cognizant of the essential nature of mattering, we never reach a point at which we no longer desire to be meaningfully connected to others. As long as the need is satisfied, the issue of mattering may never rise to the level of consciousness within us. Contrariwise, when threatened with the possibility, contemplation of the loss of mattering is terrifying at any time in a person's life. Then, in our desperation, we quickly realize how necessary mattering is.

Researchers in developmental and social psychology have focused on the importance of connection to others, from the youngest of us to the oldest. The question of attachment to adult caretakers is an important part of the infant's and young child's development (Bowlby, 1969). The degree and kind of attachment surely lays the groundwork for the sense of mattering developed later in life. It is highly likely that those with a secure attachment to their parents (or parent figures) will form the strongest experiences of mattering to their families and will seek such security in other relationships. In contrast, those with ambivalent, avoidant, or disorganized attachments (Ainsworth, Blehar, Waters, & Wall, 1978) will very likely come to believe that they do not matter to their parents.

However, the limited cognitive development of the children involved in these studies means that mattering is not meaningfully operating in their lives as yet. It is as cognitive capacities develop that young people begin to appreciate the centrality of mattering in their lives, and its effects become measurable. From that point on, the question of mattering becomes critical for the individual. Indeed, the research on mattering to date has covered the life span from pre-adolescent youth to the elderly.

In his initial effort (Rosenberg & McCullough, 1981), Rosenberg found that mattering to parents is related to self-esteem and depression among junior and senior high school students. Those who mattered more had higher levels of self-esteem and less depression than those who mattered less. The psychologist Andrea Dixon Rayle, focusing on high school students, found that females believed they mattered to their families more than did males (Rayle, 2005); results from an additional analysis of the same data revealed that mattering is a strong predictor of adolescents' evaluation of their lifestyles (Rayle & Myers, 2004).

Among college students, the psychologists Leanne Mak and Sheila Marshall (2004) investigated romantic relationships. They found that mattering is positively associated with the couple's investment in and satisfaction with the relationship and negatively associated with the perception of the quality of alternatives to the current partner. In studying cadets at West Point, the educational psychologist Jane Myers (Myers & Bechtel, 2004) discovered that mattering is positively correlated with a number of wellness measures, including "life tasks" (such as spirituality, work, leisure, friendship, and love) and "self-direction tasks" (including sense of worth, sense of control, emotional awareness, and stress management).

In the first analysis of data from the adolescents surveyed for this book (Elliott, Colangelo, & Gelles, 2005), I demonstrated that mattering is a powerful predictor of suicide ideation among adolescents, working its effects through self-esteem and, to a lesser extent, depression. That is, a failure to matter reduces self-esteem, and lowered self-esteem increases the likelihood of depression. In turn, both lowered self-esteem and increased depression lead to a higher probability that the adolescent would regularly consider suicide.

The sociologist John Taylor studied the importance of mattering among adults. In one study (Taylor & Turner, 2001), he discovered a gender difference, in that for women (but not men), lower levels of mattering are associated with greater levels of depression. A second study (Scheiman & Taylor, 2001) investigated the link between identity and mattering. Having children, and working at a job that is autonomous, complex, and involves supervising others, leads to an increase in self-perceived mattering. In contrast, mattering decreases with increases in relationship and parenting strains.

Mattering is also central in family relationships for adults. Myers and her associates (Powers, Myers, Tingle, & Powers, 2004) compared married medical residents to the general married population and found (unexpectedly) that the former scored significantly higher on a measure of mattering. In a *post hoc* discussion, they argue that the spouse of a medical resident must deal with family stress caused by the demands of the resident's job. A willingness to do so sends a message that the resident matters, because the stress is taken off his or her shoulders.

Marshall and Lambert (2006) turned the tables in the parent–child relationship by examining self-perceived mattering of parents to their children. Parents were asked to complete an open-ended questionnaire designed to elicit the extent to which they mattered to their children, situations in which mattering would increase or decrease, and the parents' emotional response to their self-perceived level of mattering. Parents reported that mattering is situationally specific, emerging from specific interactions with their children. In addition, it appears that reliance is the form of mattering that parents most consistently cite as determining their judgments as to how much they matter to their children.

Mattering is important for a second identity that is central among adults: *employment.* Counseling psychologist Norman Amundson (1993), focusing on employment counselors and their clients, holds that all three forms of mattering (awareness, importance, and reliance) are critical in establishing an effective counselor–client relationship. Rayle (2006a, 2006b) echoes this significance, finding that elementary school counselors who believed they mattered to others at their schools report greater job satisfaction than those who mattered less.

Business school professors Suzanne Masterson and Christina Stamper (2003) addressed the issue of "perceived organizational membership" for employees of business firms. One factor in this perception is mattering, evinced in the extent to which "the organization provides employees with a level of influence over organizational processes, and the organization communicates to employees that they are valuable members" (Masterson & Stamper, 2003, p. 480). When employers instill a sense of mattering among their employees, they engender a much stronger level of perceived organizational membership.

Older members of our society do not escape the motivation to matter. In an analysis of midlife (39–65) women's narratives of living alone, nursing instructor Mary Margaret Segraves (2004) reveals the disturbing consequences of the loss of connection to others. Some women, feeling excluded by married friends, found it difficult to plan social activities. Others anticipated a future filled with increasing challenges, although they countered this anxiety with a greater sense of their own growth in wisdom. Finally, many averred that society in general had little awareness of the consequences of women's aging alone on their well-being. All of this came from a strong shift of connections, or even disconnections to others caused by the distance from others created by living alone. Although Segraves (2004) does not use the term "mattering," it is clearly implicit in her analysis.

In a similar vein, sociologists Leonard Pearlin and Allen LeBlanc (2001) presented evidence that bereavement following the death of a loved one included a perceived loss of mattering. The fact that people were no longer needed by those whom they had nursed for so long erased a sense of purpose in their lives (reliance). This loss was especially acute for women and spouses, less so for men and adult children. Further, the more a person is self-invested in the role of caretaker and the more intimate the relationship with the deceased, the greater the felt loss of mattering. On the other hand, loss of mattering was mitigated by the presence of emotionally supportive others, especially if the respondent had formed a new intimate relationship. Finally, loss of mattering led to lower self-esteem and a reduced sense of mastery, as well as increased levels of depression.

The research reported above is mainly focused on the antecedents to mattering (death of a loved one, change in social status and role) or the intrapersonal consequences of mattering (depression, self-esteem). If mattering is to be established as a central, motivating dimension of the self-concept, it is necessary to establish empirically the protective role that it plays in everyday doings.

Mattering in Adolescence

Although mattering is a powerful motivation throughout the life course, as revealed above, there are segments in which it is singularly meaningful. In particular, I argue that mattering is critically significant during adolescence.

As sociologists Roberta Simmons, Florence Rosenberg, and Morris Rosenberg (1973) have demonstrated, beginning in early adolescence (generally, ages 12–14), the self is characterized by a great disturbance, resulting from the biological, cognitive, and social structural changes that adolescents undergo in this period. Morris Rosenberg (1979) has elegantly explained the sources of the upheaval in self-understanding that is characteristic of this stage of development.

First, the onset of puberty and its resultant physiological changes upset the rather simple understanding of the self developed before adolescence. The body changes shape in radical ways that inevitably focus attention on the self. Growth spurts create an impression of a discontinuous self, rather than a smoothly developing human being. In the mirror, the adolescent sees a physical self that looks qualitatively different from pre-adolescent days: for females, the emergence of breasts; for males, the ability to sustain an erection; for both, the presence of body hair, especially in the pubic region. In addition, the appearance of newly raging hormones, and their effects on behavior, can be difficult to understand. These changes are powerful and occasionally frightening, especially if the adolescent has not been well prepared by parents or peers for these changes. The consequence is that the confused young teenager may have difficulty making sense of the "new" self.

Second, early adolescence is the period in which most young people experience a significant change in their cognitive capacities. They begin to be able to deal in abstractions. Heretofore, the self has been understood largely in terms of external, concrete attributes (sex, race, height, weight). Now, abstract thought allows one to introspect, and therefore to see the self in very different ways. Adolescents begin to understand themselves as possessing internal and intangible characteristics, such as traits, attitudes, and feelings.

Emotions, especially, can be disconcerting. In his analysis of self-concept development in adolescence, Rosenberg (1979, pp. 213–214) found that beginning in early adolescence, over one-third of young people listed as among their chief deficiencies the inability to deal effectively with their emotions, as compared to one-sixth of the younger children. Being aware of their inner lives, the older children see themselves as struggling to control it, whereas the younger children are largely oblivious to their internal states. It is very difficult for new adolescents to integrate the abstract and the concrete parts into a cohesive whole, and the new image of the self may not be easily understood until they have had some experience in dealing with these feelings and abstract notions.

A second consequence of the newly developed ability to deal with abstractions is that the early adolescent comes to recognize the self as the object of others' scrutiny, as a stimulus for their behavior. Once a child learns to see the self from another's point of view, a new order of complexity in understanding the self is introduced. On the one hand, there are many significant others in a person's life. Each views the adolescent from a unique perspective. Cognitive Social Psychologists would say that it becomes the young person's task to form a stable and consistent understanding of the self by synthesizing all the reflected appraisals into a coherent whole. Symbolic Interactionists would argue that this occurs during the growth in the ability to take the role of the other, from the specific to the generalized. In either paradigm, the message is the same: It is a daunting task to use this new-found capacity to re-form a solid understanding of who one is. Add to all this concern the anxiety that we can never be sure that our attempts to see ourselves from another person's perspective are entirely accurate, and we heighten the difficulty of confidently understanding ourselves.

Finally, structural changes in the young adolescent's life can contribute to self-concept disturbance. For example, the shift from elementary to middle school often means a change in peers. For most children, elementary school consists of a group of students relatively homogeneous along such characteristics as socioeconomic status and (sometimes) race. In contrast, in middle school, the classes are more heterogeneous. The challenges to a coherent understanding of the self are thereby multiplied.

Further, in elementary school, the student faced one or two teachers each day, but in middle school the student has several teachers. As a consequence, the feedback the child gets about itself becomes variegated. From the Cognitive Social Psychology approach, this means that there are more and different reflected appraisals that must be integrated into a coherent image of the self. On the other hand, Structural Symbolic Interactionists would argue that the construction of a role identity becomes more complex, in that it requires validation from a greater number of teachers. Indeed, the teachers may not bother to coordinate their understandings of the student with each other, and it is left to the student to deal with any contradictions or inconsistencies.

In addition, qualitative differences in performance expectations emerge in middle school. The young person must learn new ways of learning. With the newly gained ability to deal in abstractions, the focus begins to turn from rote memorization to an investigation of the concepts and processes that underlie observed phenomena. It is no longer sufficient to know what happens; it is now necessary to understand why or how it happens.

It is not surprising, then, that the confluence of these factors can lead to serious upheaval in the self-concept. In his extensive research on the adolescent self-concept, Rosenberg (1979) has demonstrated that the consequences of this period of disruption include a markedly unstable self-concept, very low self-esteem, and unusually high levels of depression. Adolescents spend the later part of their youth rebuilding the self-concept, and fortunately, most do so successfully. Still, people can recall, wistfully or ruefully, the *sturm und drang* of early adolescence.

The extent of self-concept disturbance and the time it takes to repair the damage will, of course, vary across individuals. Elements of the self may facilitate or inhibit the recovery. In particular, the process of building a qualitatively different understanding of the self may be significantly easier if one matters. Mattering serves as an anchor in the turbulence of adolescent self-concept development. Such a meaningful connection to others provides a reassuring basis for simplifying the redefinition of self necessitated by the normal changes encountered in adolescence. Mattering means that others empathize with what you are going through, reach out to assist you when you are ready, and continue to include you in their lives. Its major service to the adolescent is to promote behaviors that would facilitate the development of a self-concept that would be better able to ride through the confusion of this period of development, and to preclude behaviors that would threaten these goals. In short, mattering offers a haven in which one can more safely work out the challenges of adolescence.

On the other hand, failing to matter means one is alone in facing the qualitative changes experienced by the self. Without a firm basis from which to deal with these changes, the "reconstructed" self is likely to be much less satisfactory and the behavioral consequences may be more dire. The research reported in this book focuses on the protective function of mattering for adolescents and the dysfunctional outcomes too often associated with not mattering.

The Structure of the Book

I explore the relationship between mattering and a wide range of anti-social and self-destructive behaviors and confirm that even when controlling for other theoretically meaningful predictors, mattering plays a powerful role in preventing these behaviors. Chapter 2 provides the theoretical reasoning behind the link between mattering and such negative behaviors. In Chapter 3, I briefly describe the data gathered for the research and explain the plan of analysis used to obtain the results presented herein; for the research-oriented reader, Appendix A contains a more detailed exposition. The next two chapters present the results of empirical analyses that confirm the pivotal role of mattering for anti-social (Chapter 4) and self-destructive (Chapter 5) behaviors.

Finally, in Chapter 6, I discuss the antecedents to mattering. First, I examine some of the personal and structural factors that account for some of the variation in mattering found among the adolescent respondents in my study. For example, differences in mattering can be traced to a person's gender, race, and the family's socioeconomic status and structure. Further, personal factors, such as age and religiosity, also help determine the extent to which adolescents believe they matter.

Second, extending the theories from Cognitive Social Psychology and Structural Symbolic Interactionism, I will discuss the underlying processes that work to inculcate mattering in a young person. As children grow and build an understanding of themselves, there are things that adults (parents, of course; teachers; coaches; and any other significant adult figures in their lives) can do to teach them that they matter. For mattering does not come "naturally." Neither can it be *imposed* on a child. It can, however, be *induced*.

2

Mattering Matters

Mattering as a Motivator for Behavior

> *No more fiendish punishment could be devised, were such a thing physically possible, than that one should be turned loose in society and remain absolutely unnoticed by all the members thereof. If no one turned around when we entered, answered when we spoke, or missed what we did, but if every person we met "cut us dead," and acted as if we were non-existing things, a kind of rage and impotent despair would ere long well up in us, from which the cruelest bodily tortures would be a relief; for these would make us feel that, however bad might be our plight, we had not sunk to such a depth as to be unworthy of attention at all.*
>
> William James, *The principles of psychology*

To understand the importance of mattering in everyday life, I want to return to the paradigms I described in Chapter 1. From Cognitive Social Psychology, Rosenberg (1979) argued persuasively that many of the elements of the self-concept have strong motivational power to them. They spur us to action in order to preserve or improve our understanding of ourselves. Motivational elements of the self-concept are sometimes difficult to recognize in ourselves; nevertheless, they exert a strong influence on our behavioral choices. If motivations are blocked by external constraints or personal will, they do not go away. We will find a way to satisfy the more powerful, fundamental motivating factors.

Symbolic Interactionists also subscribe to the impact of motivations on behavior. They agree with Cognitive Social Psychologists that people are often not aware of the motivations that underlie their behavior, because they are a pre-cognitive part of the process of the self.

For the Structural Symbolic Interactionists, enacting appropriate role identities is a powerful source of motivation. A role identity prescribes the beliefs, orientations, and behaviors appropriate for a person inhabiting a particular position in the social order. For example, a daughter learns quickly what is expected of her from her parents, siblings, and others. She is carefully taught, both formally and informally, from her earliest years the do's and don'ts of her role identity, and to the extent that she internalizes these lessons, she will find herself a legitimate participant in the family's undertakings.

The granting of legitimacy to one's role identity is a necessary condition for successful social interaction, so there is a powerful impetus to perform the role as one understands it. As McCall and Simmons (1978, p. 65; emphasis in the original) elaborate: "Role identities . . . are not simply idle musings and entertaining daydreams; they exert important influences on daily life. . . . In fact they give the very *meaning* to our daily routine." We expect role support from others, and if we do not get it, we are in danger of being an enigma, someone who cannot be appropriately classified and responded to in the interaction. One may try to save face by derogating those who deny one's legitimacy, but this tactic may not remove the anxiety that attends the threat of being deemed illicit.

Stryker and Burke (2000) elaborate the theoretical argument for the motivational properties of role identity by noting that some of our identities involve a great deal more commitment than others, in that the rewards for enacting these roles are greater. For example, most people find a great deal of personal meaning in the role of son or daughter. No matter how contentious the relationship, children recognize, at some level, that life would be much worse without it. They are highly committed to the role identity and would be devastated if it were denied them.

Our everyday experience is filled with the impelling force of a wide variety of internal motivations. One develops, as the social psychologist Constantine Sedikides puts it, a "multiply motivated self" (Sedikides & Strube, 1995, p. 1330). Some are biological (such as the need for nutritional sustenance), but many are social, in that they are inculcated in us through the socialization we receive, especially in our formative years. Consider some important examples of the latter category.

One important motivation lying within the self is the desire for continuity in our understanding of ourselves across time and place (Lecky, 1945). Rosenberg refers to this as self-concept stability. It is comforting to know that we are basically the same person when we meet with different people in different circumstances, even as we recognize that unique aspects of the self may arise. Further, although we expect changes due to maturation, we also expect to look back on our development and see those changes as part of a "natural" progression through the life course. In contrast, to experience the self fundamentally different in different encounters can be disquieting. If you are a significantly different person to different people, then who are you, really?

Indeed, the social psychologist William B. Swann (Swann & Ely, 1984; Swann, Stein-Seroussi, & Giesler, 1992) demonstrated that people actually prefer to be with others who confirm their understanding of who they are. In fact, people even elicit behaviors from others that verify their established understandings of themselves.

We are often aware of our need to be in the company of others. The social psychologist Stanley Schachter (1959) initially demonstrated how simple affiliation serves to assuage fears that can beset us, although later research (Firestone, Kaplan, & Russell, 1973) revealed that the need to affiliate is strong only when we are assured that others face the same fear-inducing threat that we do.

Our society teaches us to achieve all that our talents allow (McClelland, Atkinson, & Clark, 1976), to "be all that you can be," as a past recruitment campaign for the United States Army put it. The need for achievement is a powerful motivator that is drummed into us from our earliest days and throughout the life course. To succeed is to earn personal and social approbation. In our society, nearly everyone likes a winner, and very few pay much attention to a loser. For ourselves, very few of us are content with failure. In fact, we can very cleverly invent accounts that take credit for success and eschew responsibility for failure (Weiner, Frieze, Kukla, Reed, Rest, & Rosenbaum, 1972). Many of us would explain away our failures by loudly declaiming some personal or structural handicap that (temporarily) prevented our succeeding (Jones & Berglas, 1978): "I would have passed the exam if I hadn't had to take care of my sick roommate last night."

We also are motivated to earn the approval of others (Crowne & Marlowe, 1960). Life can be very uncomfortable when it is spent in the company of people who treat us as pariahs. When we were children, we reveled in the approval of our parents. How many of us competed earnestly for the approval of our favorite teacher? The sociologist Erving Goffman (1959) has convincingly described the process through which we often orchestrate our behavior in order to preserve a socially desirable situated identity in a social encounter.

The need to belong, introduced in the previous chapter, has its own motivating influence on behavior. In pursuing this path, Baumeister focused on a possible frustration of the need to belong: social exclusion, the rejection of a person by a formally or informally constituted group. He and his colleagues have cataloged some of the myriad deleterious consequences arising from being spurned by others, including simplistic modes of thinking (Baumeister, Twenge, & Nuss, 2002), numbness to physical pain (DeWall & Baumeister, 2006), and increased aggression (Twenge, Baumeister, Tice, & Stucke, 2001).

In a similar vein, Kipling Williams, a social psychologist, examined the effects of ostracism. In discussing its effects, Williams (2001, p. 1) begs the issue of mattering: "Few events in life are more painful than feeling that others, especially those whom we admire and care about, want nothing to do with us. There may be no better way to communicate this impression than for others to treat you as though you are invisible – like you don't exist." In studying forms of ostracism, from the temporary "silent treatment" one quarreling lover gives another, to the shunning visited upon social norm violators in the military academies and among the Amish, he effectively delineates the anguish that envelopes the target of such rejection.

In the context of my study, social exclusion and ostracism are precursors to the sense that one does not matter. They are two of many triggers that can induce a person to question his or her social significance. However, as Williams (2001) has argued, it is possible to avoid the conclusion that one is a nonentity, if there is an alternative explanation for the rejection. Before the conclusion that one does not matter can be made, two conditions must be met.

First, the affront must be experienced as personally directed and intentional. Otherwise, there is no reason to conclude that one does not matter. For example, if the relegation to obscurity is required by role prescriptions (a police officer is supposed to ignore friends while performing official duties), then one can make the attribution that there is no harm meant. Thereby reassured, the cast-off can continue without experiencing any harm to the self-image.

Second, a single incident of rejection may not be enough to support the inference that one does not matter. It may be that the offender is having a bad day, is preoccupied with a matter of soul-stirring relevance, or is distracted by pressing events at hand.

It is much easier to infer that one does not matter if there is an accumulation of incidents that drive the point home. On the one hand, it may be that continued interactions with a single individual or group result in a feeling of superfluity. In that case, it is easy to conclude that one does not matter to that particular person or group. On the other hand, a much more drastic conclusion is likely if rejection comes in interactions with a wide variety of people and groups. Then, there is the risk of recognizing that one's social invisibility is more nearly universal.

The Motivational Properties of Mattering

In general, mattering to others is an existentially reassuring awareness, and, contrariwise, failing to matter is terrifying. We will do almost anything to gain the former and escape the latter.

First, and most important, mattering affirms that a person is alive. Descartes asserted that simply being aware of our own thought processes should be enough to instill this recognition in us, but those who believe that they do not matter to anyone or anything may wonder if the existence they are experiencing could meaningfully be called "living." The social connections that tell us that we matter also provide us with a life of at least minimal quality, and many people would not settle for less.

Second, mattering signals that we are meaningfully involved in a social web and do not need to navigate life's journey alone. It gives evidence that we are integrated into society, and to know that one is socially integrated provides social and psychological security. Although there are times when people crave isolation, most soon discover that a little solitude goes a long way.

At the individual level, social integration means a feeling of attachment to society. Such an attachment gives a person a sense of purpose and belonging; it frees us and encourages us to seek a meaningful place for ourselves in the world at large. Rosenberg and I (Elliott &

Rosenberg, 1989) have identified several levels of social integration. Interpersonal integration concerns attachments to specific others. These bonds are possibly the strongest connections between an individual and society as a whole. They are how society is experienced on a day-to-day basis. Interpersonal integration is signaled by a friendship, a romantic relationship, or a mentoring relationship between a teacher and a student.

At a more collective level, institutional integration means believing that one is a significant part of a social institution, such as a school, a military unit, or a family. A person who is thus integrated endorses the goals of the institution, promotes its welfare, and achieves a sense of security in being a member. The worker who is thanked for his special contributions to a firm's success recognizes the compliment as a signal of institutional integration and an affirmation of mattering.

Finally, there is normative integration into a community or society. When people enthusiastically endorse and follow the beliefs, goals, and values of a collectivity, they are normatively integrated. Tepid acceptance is insufficient. An individual must enact these norms in everyday behavior, advocate them for others, and condemn their violation. College students who are offended by blatant cheating and earnestly try to persuade others to avoid violating the academic code are normatively integrated into the campus community.

The sociologist Peter Berger has developed the concept of a symbolic universe: a shared tradition of values, norms, and beliefs constructed by members of society. This common orientation integrates the various understandings of a collectivity about itself and gives coherence to a person's daily doings. "[T]he symbolic universe provides the highest levels of integration for the discrepant meanings actualized *within* everyday life in society" (Berger & Luckmann, 1966, p. 98; emphasis in the original). Normatively integrated people internalize the prescriptions and proscriptions of the symbolic universe and make them their own. Social understandings become personal understandings.

Durkheim believed that a society rises or falls with the level of normative integration experienced by its members. In discussing the characteristics of organic solidarity, he asserts: "[C]ohesion is essentially due to a community of beliefs and sentiments" (Durkheim, 1933, p. 123). It is the fundamental connection felt among members that makes possible a division of labor in which people are free to take on different roles, trusting that the work of others will be integrated with their own to produce a vibrant society.

On July 4, we gather to affirm our country's symbolic universe, with parades, cooks-out, and fireworks. But not everyone celebrating the holiday is normatively integrated. In a very real sense, "rituals are cheap," in that they require nothing but time-bounded participation, and too often the principles from the symbolic universe that give rise to the rituals are obscured. Those who work toward the realization of a society's symbolic universe in the other 364 days of the year demonstrate true normative integration.

Mattering is a basic component of social integration. If others are aware of your presence, invest in your welfare, and rely on you in appropriate ways, you are interpersonally integrated. There is a web of connections that provides reassurance against the anxiety that you are alone.

Similarly, to matter to social institutions such as the family means that you have a haven that notices you, supports you and counts on you to contribute in meaningful ways to its success. The family is not the only source of institutional integration. The Beach Boys, in a song written by members Brian Wilson and Mike Love, exhort teenagers to "be true to your school, just like you would to your girl or guy." All of us need to find a place for ourselves in the social order, and being integrated into social institutions helps assure us that we have.

Finally, normative integration signals mattering. To advocate for the symbolic universe is to join with like-minded others, physically present or otherwise. The progressive political and social web site Move On takes great care to convince its participants that they are an important part of a social movement dedicated to the preservation of our society's symbolic universe. It is their commonly shared values, norms, and beliefs that make them a coherent unit.

Third, the motivational power of mattering is due to the fact that one learns the extent to which one matters from the earliest stages in the life course. Beginning in the family and continuing with other social institutions (friendship groups, school, and social organizations for the young such as scouts), children are given strong signals of the extent to which they matter. And in these early years, young people do not have the capacity to understand or critique the reflected appraisals of others. They are very likely to internalize this information about themselves into the self-concept and assume it is valid. As I continually say to my students, "What gets in early gets in deep."

Those who believe they matter will be motivated to maintain this sense of connection to others. They will engage in behaviors that reaffirm, and do not threaten, their status in others' lives. In the "safety net" that is mattering, people are emboldened to pursue productive goals, knowing that others find them worthy of attention, support them, and benefit from their activity. Mattering signals social integration in a profound way and reveals the niche we have carved for ourselves in the social order.

From everyday experience, we gain evidence that mattering is a particularly powerful personal motivation. Our lives are made meaningful only when we make a difference in the lives of others. At its most fundamental level, we appreciate it when others notice us (awareness), and if they regularly do not, we are likely to act in ways that call attention to ourselves. Young children express their need for attention bluntly ("Daddy, look at me!"), but the need is not limited to them.

Most people mature beyond the egocentric stages of early childhood development, but they do not lose the motivation to matter. They eventually learn they cannot be the center of their experiential worlds, and moderate their behavior accordingly. Still, they reveal in their everyday doings the powerful motivational force of mattering as a dimension of the self-concept. Adolescents dye their hair an unusual color or wear outrageous styles of clothing, and who knows how much they are simply attempting to draw attention to themselves? Celebrities hire publicity agents to keep their names (and pictures and videos) in the public eye. Very Important People dress regally and are chauffeured around town in expansive limousines to capture the attention of the "regular folk."

We also appreciate the investment that others make in us (importance), and we sometimes make that investment a public issue. Constituents are favorably impressed when a politician knows something about their personal lives (even if that information is delivered by an aide just prior to the encounter with the citizen). A surprise party demonstrates that someone has exerted a significant amount of energy to make a friend's birthday a joyous one. If not obvious, we may seek out opportunities to demonstrate our importance, as when an employee lets it be known that the boss has inconvenienced him- or herself for the employee's benefit.

Finally, it is reassuring (if sometimes onerous) to know that others depend on us (reliance), and we may orchestrate our behavior in situations to reaffirm our belief that this is true. The continual ring of the ubiquitous cell phone in public signals that someone has need of us.[1] Parents may occasionally remind a child that it is their successes in the workplace that keep the young one in luxurious trappings. A lover sometimes makes sure that a paramour realizes and acknowledges how devastating a solitary life would be.

In all these examples, behaviors are often done not only for the benefit of others but also to reassure ourselves in times of doubt. Although it may be important for our standing in the community that others know we matter, it is essential for our own well-being that we be assured of it. In short, we have both a personal and a social motivation to know that we play a significant part in the lives of others.

When all goes well and we firmly believe that we matter to someone or some institution, the world is a secure place, and we can go on with the pursuit of life's goals. The mattering motivation rests, because it is satisfied. We are acutely aware of our need to make a difference only when we suspect we do not.

In that case, we are faced with a profoundly frightening possibility. We confront the realization that, whatever the truth of our physical presence, we are socially non-existent. It seems that the world not only can but *does* get along without us, and we are truly irrelevant. People cannot bear the realization that they make a difference to no one; the emotional pain and anxiety are literally intolerable. Those who suffer this affliction will be impelled to do almost anything to put an end to this agony. They might well turn to behaviors they would never consider were they convinced that they mattered. In response, two avenues are available.

First, one can "compel" mattering by behaving in ways that demand attention, induce others to see to one's welfare, or make it difficult for others to deny one's role in a relationship. For the adolescent, this is often accomplished by engaging in anti-social behavior. Acting outrageously will make it difficult for the significant others in a young person's life to continue to relegate him or her to "non-person" status.

Second, one can escape from the terror of social invisibility by withdrawing from the world that has provided it. Social isolation may not be a pleasant option, but it is better than being constantly reminded of one's insignificance.

However, this is unlikely to be a satisfactory option in the long run. It does not resolve the problem; rather, it merely moves the failure

[1] Thanks to an anonymous reviewer for this contemporary example.

to matter out of social recognition. Sooner or later, if no progress is made, the unfortunate nonentity may take social isolation to its ultimate extreme: self-destructive behavior. Even when there is no acknowledged intention to contemplate or commit suicide, there is still the realization that one is already "absent" from society in the most fundamental way. It is but a short step to engage in life-threatening behaviors.

Further, these options are not mutually exclusive. It is entirely possible for those who do not matter to explore both avenues of relief simultaneously. If one option does not succeed, perhaps the other will.

In the next segments of this chapter, I discuss each response to a failure to matter. In addition, I present a contemporary social incident that dramatically illustrates the desolation (both physical and psychological) that can be brought to society by someone driven to extremes by the motivation to matter. There is no direct evidence that mattering is involved in either of these incidents, but what is known about the two perpetrators strongly suggests that mattering is an integral precursor to their heinous behavior. Although these are rare events, they illustrate that mattering can have a powerful, detrimental effect on a person. The consequences for the self and others can be devastating.

Anti-Social Behavior

> *If perticuliar care and attention is not paid to the Laidies we are determined to foment a Rebelion, and will not hold ourselves bound by any Laws in which we have no voice, or Representation.*
>
> Abigail Adams, Letter to John Adams

One possible option for those who do not matter is to try to "force" oneself to matter to others. It would undoubtedly be better to matter to others in a positive way, knowing that people see favorable things in us that capture their attention, inspire them to invest in our welfare, or encourage them to seek our assistance in times of need. But if this is not to be, the threat of being irrelevant in one's surroundings may impel a young person to gain attention, a sympathetic ear, or the reliance of others through anti-social behavior. Whatever opprobrium that attached to someone would be overwhelmed by the realization that others could no longer avoid attending to the "unseeable" person, as the undesirable behavior commands a reaction.

And so, the "acting out" of adolescents may frequently be due to the self-perception that they don't matter to the significant others in their lives. They may feel ignored at school by teachers, continually slighted by peers, or invisible to parents who are caught up in their own concerns. For all its bravado, outrageous behavior may speak more to a person's vulnerabilities than to strengths.

Whether it be minor acts of irritating impudence or the horrifying violence of public murder, the drive to be recognized as a person distinguishable from others comes from the terrible anxiety of not mattering. For the adolescent, anti-social behaviors come in a myriad of possibilities.

The survey we conducted provided data on many of them. In Chapter 4, I will discuss prior theory and research on anti-social behavior in adolescence and demonstrate that mattering is an implicit part of what has come before. In my analysis, I will focus on the following anti-social behaviors: delinquency (in the form of truancy, vandalism, and dealing in contraband), theft from one's own family, carrying a weapon, and interpersonal violence.

A Contemporary Example: Timothy McVeigh and the Oklahoma City Bombing

An extreme form of forced mattering can be seen in the bizarrely deviant behaviors of people starving for public attention. Not socially integrated into a network of relationships or recognized by social institutions, they are not of significance to others. From serial killers to mass murderers, we see the desperate desire of nonentities to feel they matter, even if mattering means being abhorred by everyone. For some (perhaps brief) time, their seemingly irrational behavior makes them the center of attention. The criminologist Lonnie Athens implicitly credits failing to matter as being a strong motivation for criminal behavior: "On the one hand, notoriety denotes being well-known for something bad. On the other hand, it is sometimes better to be well-known for something which most people think is bad and few think is good than not to be known for anything at all" (Athens, 1992, pp. 74–75).

Unfortunately, in our society there is no shortage of examples. The sociologist Richard Sennett points out that it is part of our society's teachings that people can matter to society only if they distinguish themselves in some meaningful way. "[T]he uncomfortable feelings about those who do not 'make something of themselves' when they have a chance, come out of an assumption that men can be respected only as they become in some way distinctive, as they stand out from the mass" (Sennett & Cobb, 1972, p. 183). Most of us struggle to distinguish ourselves in a socially acceptable way, but the avenues of distinction are not open to everyone. The sociologist Robert Merton (1938) explains that those without access to approved methods of advancement will develop a belief that the rules of society do not apply to the aggrieved person. A fellow sociologist, Melvin Seaman (1959), calls it "normlessness." In response, he or she will likely turn to socially disapproved means to attain distinction (which Merton labels "innovation"). And so it is with mattering.

Failure to matter to the significant others in a person's life may lead to an attempt to rise above them and be publicly recognized for it, in part showing the insensitive and benighted individuals that they were seriously mistaken in their assessments of him or her. When public recognition is accomplished in socially approved ways (politics, the fine arts, important prizes and awards), few question it. But those who do not matter may not have the wherewithal to achieve this goal. If the desperation born of a failure to matter is sufficiently intense, one may decide to turn to socially undesirable methods.

From all available evidence, with the exception of the time he was in the United States Army, Timothy McVeigh was an invisible presence from his high school days to the moment that he detonated a powerful bomb at the Alfred P. Murrah Federal Building in Oklahoma City. Biographer Richard A. Serrano documents the difficulties that McVeigh faced early in his life. Beginning with the blizzard that kept his mother from coming home for a few days when he was eight years old and culminating in his parents' bitter divorce, Serrano (1998, p. 12) avers: "His teenage years were troubled with the twin angst of abandonment and raw nights alone at home, and so he entered manhood eager to please others while at the same time unsure of how to please himself. He craved attention, and he would find it, but he would never find himself." He was a nondescript student, remembered by few who taught him or learned beside him in high school.

In the military, he was an excellent marksman, finally noticed by his fellow soldiers and those immediately above him in the chain of command. But he failed to qualify for the Special Forces unit because he was too exhausted to pass the endurance requirements. In spite of his combat service during "Operation Desert Storm" (the first Gulf conflict), he returned to civilian life as a nonentity and became a security guard. In their book on Timothy McVeigh, his attorney Stephen Jones and writer Peter Israel report: "He'd led a marginal, quasinomadic existence, working here and there, traveling back and forth across the country" (Jones & Israel, 2001, p. 67). According to a co-worker at one of his many (but brief) jobs, McVeigh found it difficult to connect with his fellow workers. "Most of the time, LeBron felt, McVeigh was just trying to impress him, going for the 'Wow!' factor, saying anything that won him attention" (Serrano, 1998, p. 49).

His rage at being ineffectual became rage at the government, which, he believed, did not care about the "common man" and persecuted those who opposed it. McVeigh saw himself as the person to avenge the wrongs inflicted by the government on those who dared to take extreme action against the government's oppression (such as Randy Weaver, a self-proclaimed "patriot" at Ruby Ridge, Idaho, in 1992, and David Koresh and the Branch Davidians in Waco, Texas, in 1993).

According to the *New York Times*, when McVeigh and his co-conspirators planned the explosion, he seemed convinced that his plans would finally get him noticed: He alerted his sister that "something big is going to happen" (Serrano, 1998, p. 116). But even then, McVeigh did not revel in his notoriety. Captured and tried for multiple counts of homicide, the prosecuting attorney, Mark Gibson, was struck by McVeigh's appearance and demeanor: "It was an eerie calm that McVeigh had. You wouldn't look into his eyes and say, 'There's evil exuding.' You just looked into his eyes and said, 'There's nothing'" (Cable News Network, 1995, p. 2).

When the awful deed was accomplished, McVeigh "was convinced, he said, that federal agents had begun to back down from the deadly tactics used at Ruby Ridge and Waco as a direct result of the Murrah Building attack" (Michel & Herbeck, 2002, p. 450). He believed he had finally made a difference. In a conversation with authors Lou Michel and Dan Herbeck, Timothy McVeigh asserted: "I like the phrase 'shot heard 'round the world,' and I don't think there's any doubt the Oklahoma City blast was heard around the world" (Michel & Herbeck, 2002, p. 454). CourtTV described the build-up to the execution: "And, for the last time, Tim McVeigh will be the center of attention when a select group of invitees will get to watch him die."

Self-Destructive Behavior

> *Farhad Khosrokhavar, a University of Pennsylvania sociologist, calls men like [Zacarias] Moussaoui "the new Martyrs": alienated young working-class Arabs from France who saw themselves as "not existing" – certainly not as Frenchmen or North Africans . . . . Khosrokhavar, who interviewed more than a dozen convicted and would-be terrorists for a book published in France in 2002, depicts young men like Moussaoui as willing to "go to extremes in order to get out of this feeling of being 'less than nothing.'"*
>
> Seymour M. Hersh, *Chain of command*

A more dire possibility is that those who recognize their social invisibility would accept their plight; they come to believe that there is nothing that they can do to induce others to notice them, care for them, or rely on them. In that case, a grim alternative would be to escape the horror. That is, they may find self-destructive behavior as less unthinkable or frightening compared to those who believe they do matter. After all, if no one is aware of us, who would notice if we were gone? If we are important to no one, who would care? If no one relies on us in any way, would we be missed?

A dramatic example of the centrality of mattering that can lead to suicidal behavior can be found in the recent film *Syriana* (2005). Amid the multiple tales that converge to a sensational climax is the recruitment of suicide bombers from the recently dismissed local workers, deemed expendable by the global oil company that exploits their labor. Left to their own devices in a country that provides nothing for them, they are easy targets for those who violently oppose the regime. The film follows one such worker, Wasim Kahn, who gradually succumbs to the inducements of an insurgent terrorist and ultimately rides to his death across the water in an attempt to destroy an oil refinery.

The recruiter deftly grooms the new recruit by assuring him that he matters: "We're all brothers. We're one family," and goes on to promise that the disaffected young man will do important things that will memorialize him among the genuine followers of Islam: "We are a small group, the ones who carry convictions and ambition. And within this group, there is another, smaller group who flee from the worldly life in order to spread the true faith. . . . You're ready."

In fact, mattering provides the social barrier to oblivion that keeps most of us pursuing our everyday goals. Émile Durkheim (1951) believed that the strength of a person's feelings of attachment to society was important, not only for societal survival, but for individual survival as well. A weak feeling of attachment to society, he held, is often a root cause of suicide. When a person comes to experience the condition of egoism, in which one's own goals become preponderant over those of the community, "the bond attaching man to life relaxes because that attaching him to society is slack" (Durkheim, 1951, pp. 214–215). For those who do not matter, there is nothing left but oneself, and egoistic suicide becomes a real possibility.

A strong conviction that one matters to the significant others in one's life does much to stave off considerations of self-destructive behavior. Indeed, most of us take our mattering for granted, and therefore thoughts of self-murder seldom penetrate our daily doings. Although momentary dejections may cause disconsolation and self-doubt, the knowledge that others have invested themselves in our welfare, rely on us in fundamental ways, and would miss us if we were gone is likely to brush away any momentary fantasy of death. It is when the anxiety of not mattering is chronic, a day-to-day awareness that crushes our energy and enthusiasm for life, that one may be more likely to consider giving up altogether.

There are many ways to invite death. The most obvious and direct form is suicide. However, there are other ways of putting one's life in jeopardy that are not as direct. The survey provides evidence for several of them, including binge drinking, illegal substance use (such as cocaine, heroin, and amphetamines), and suicide plans and attempts. In Chapter 5, I will examine the relationship between mattering and these self-destructive behaviors.

A Contemporary Example: Seung-Hui Cho and the Massacre at Virginia Tech

On April 16, 2007, Seung-Hui Cho conducted a shooting rampage on the campus of Virginia Polytechnic Institute and State University (Virginia Tech), located in Blacksburg, Virginia. Between the hours of 7:00 and 9:30 A.M., he murdered 32 and wounded 17 members of the campus community, including students and faculty. There have been many such incidents, at both high schools and colleges, but especially relevant to the issue of self-destructive behaviors are those that end in the perpetrator's suicide (either directly or indirectly, in what has been called "suicide by cop"). Unlike Timothy McVeigh, Seung-Hui Cho never intended to survive the carnage he meted out at Virginia Tech. It appears the killings and self-murder were intended to accomplish two goals: to escape the agony of failing to matter and to do so in a way that expressed the rage he experienced because of it.

Seung-Hui Cho had a difficult childhood. His family immigrated to the United States from South Korea in 1992, settling in a Virginia suburb of Washington, D.C., when he was eight years old. The family socialized little with neighbors, and high school served only to emphasize his social isolation. According to a *New York Times* report on the school shootings, "He was unresponsive in class, and unwilling to speak" (*New York Times*, 2007a, p. 2). He was regularly mocked by fellow students because of his poor command of English. "And so he chose invisibility. . . . When they said hello, he ignored them, as if he were not there" (*New York Times*, 2007a, p. 2). It was as if he responded to their rejection of him by inhabiting an alternate world, knowing that he did not have an acceptable place in this one.

Things only got worse when he matriculated at Virginia Tech. In a report from the British Broadcasting Corporation (BBC), his presence in classes was minimal, so much so that students and professors worried about him. Professor Lucinda Roy described him as "the loneliest person I have ever met in my life," and a fellow student said, "on the first day of a literature class last year the students introduced themselves one by one, but when it was Cho's turn, he did not speak. The professor, she said, looked at the sign-in sheet and wherever everyone else had written their names, Cho had written a question mark," as if he were literally a nonentity (BBC, 2007, p. 1).

MSNBC (2007, p. 2) reported that he "set up his own groups on Facebook with names like 'The Cool Kids' and 'Be Cool,' though he clearly felt he was not. His dorm room was as affectless as he was – no posters or photos, just bare cinder block." He would regularly play a plaintive song titled "Shine," recorded in 1994 by the Georgia alternative rock band Collective Soul:

> Teach me how to speak
> Teach me how to share
> Teach me where to go
> Tell me love will be there
>
> (Lyric provided by Song-Lyrics.net)

The *New York Times* (2007a) adds to the picture of an isolated young man so desperate to be a significant part of another's life that he invents an imaginary girlfriend, named "Jelly," a supermodel. In reality, he was twice warned by the campus police about stalking female students to whom he was attracted.

The most compelling evidence that mattering was a factor in Cho's behavior comes from his "manifesto," consisting of videos and written documents that he sent to NBC News just before he began his attacks on campus. What follows is a number of excerpts culled from these materials (compiled from reports by the BBC, the *New York Times* [*NYT*], and the *Washington Post* [*WP*]) that reveal Cho's anxiety and rage at not being a significant part of life at the university.

I begin with Cho's acknowledgment of his status as a nonentity and the ensuing fury that overwhelms him. It is especially noteworthy that he will not take responsibility for his failure to matter but rather holds his fellow students responsible for his plight:

> You sadistic snobs. I may be nothing but a piece of [expletive]. You have vandalized my heart, raped my soul and torched my conscience. You thought it was one pathetic boy's life you were extinguishing. (BBC)
>
> Are you happy now that you have destroyed my life? Now that you have stolen everything you could from me? (*NYT*)
>
> You forced me into a corner and gave me only one option. The decision was yours. Now you have blood on your hands that will never wash off. (*NYT*)
>
> I could have been great. Ask yourself what you did to me to have made me clean the slate. (*NYT*)

Cho attempts to redeem himself by portraying the lethal violence wreaked upon others as an act of personal honor and social benevolence:

> I didn't have to do this. I could have left, I could have fled, but no, I will no longer run. If not for me, for my children, for my brothers and sisters . . . I did it for them. (*NYT*)
>
> Thanks to you, I die like Jesus Christ, to inspire generations of the weak and the defenseless people. (BBC)

Finally, Cho pleads with the despised others who have relegated him to social invisibility. He "believed that people had no respect for him or others he perceived were like him" (*Washington Post*, 2007, p. 2).

If they would only punish themselves, he would be vindicated; but if they do not, he is honor bound to vindicate himself:

> Kill yourselves or you will never know how the dorky kid that [you] publicly humiliated and spat on will come behind you and slash your throats. . . . Kill yourselves or you will never know the hour the little kid will come with hundreds of rounds of ammunition on his back to shoot you down. (*WP*)

It was not long before clinical professionals examined the materials sent to NBC News for signs of mental illness. Although most were reluctant to make a definitive diagnosis, they all saw clues suggesting a severely troubled individual. In the *New York Times*, Dr. Michael Stone, professor of clinical psychiatry at Columbia University, "saw a man characterized by a feeling of powerlessness. 'For 23 years he was a powerless, impotent cipher,' the professor said, and so, 'for two hours of his life, he was a powerful man' " (*New York Times*, 2007b, p. 1). Similarly, Dr. Theodore Millon, dean and scientific director of the Institute for Advanced Studies in Personality and Psychopathology in Coral Gables, Florida, argued, "Such people feel persecuted, deeply isolated, that the world rejects them" (*New York Times*, 2007b, p. 2).

Cho's behavior apparently was intended to make his mark, to achieve notoriety, if that was the only way he could escape the anguish of being someone not worthy of notice. His suicide accomplished two purposes: It heightened the impact of his attention-demanding actions and assured that he would never again feel the nothingness of failing to matter.

In sum, the cases of Timothy McVeigh and Seung-Hui Cho demonstrate that a failure to matter can lead to extreme versions of anti-social and self-destructive behavior. If such outrageous behaviors were the only consequence of believing that one is a nonentity, it would still be important to understand mattering. Although the incidents of such sensational acts of violence are rare, they are devastating enough to merit attention.

But I will present evidence that the motivational strength of mattering is revealed in other, less dramatic behaviors that make it difficult for the adolescent to affirm the self and relate to others effectively. Further, these less histrionic behaviors are more frequently observed simply because they are less drastic, yet they are nonetheless important in that their greater frequency will have continual and lasting consequences for the individual.

The overarching expectation is that the more adolescents believe that they matter, the less likely they will engage in anti-social and self-destructive behaviors. On the one hand, they will not need to elicit attention, support, or requests for assistance from others, because these are already in place, at least often enough to assure themselves that they do make a difference in their social world. On the other hand, the security of being enmeshed in a web with others will go a long way to obviate any consideration of self-destruction.

In contrast, lower levels of mattering will motivate adolescents to "act out" precisely so that others will no longer be able to ignore them. In addition, they hope that others will feel compelled to invest in them and to invite them to contribute meaningfully to the world around them, once these others recognize that the adolescents do not merit nonentity status. In addition, as contemplating one's social invisibility becomes unbearable, the normally frightening aspects of self-destructive behavior that keep most of us on a safer path lose their effectiveness. Of what use is existence in a world that does not know one is alive? As a consequence, flirting with death becomes less terrifying.

Is either response to a failure to matter likely to be successful? Certainly, it is possible that one may come to recognize a significant (or even non-significant) other upon being confronted with either anti-social or self-destructive behavior on that person's part. The father, rushing to the local jail to provide bail after the son's seemingly irrational display of socially undesirable or self-destructive behavior, may realize with a shock that he has not been a meaningful part of his son's life to this point. If Dad can maintain his own rationality, he may understand his son's behavior as the proverbial "cry for help." Perhaps he will use the occasion to begin to make amends to his son by restructuring his life so that the boy is a significant part of it.

Yet, these dysfunctional behaviors may only make the situation worse. People could very well interpret anti-social behavior as evidence that the perpetrator should remain socially excluded, even ostracized. For example, the military academies can decide to shun a cadet who offends the "honor of the corps" by violating the social and academic codes of the institution. Shunning means rendering the cadet a "non-person," as others on campus will neither give to nor receive communication from the offender. If the guilty party was merely trying to attract attention, the act will have had precisely the opposite effect.

Self-destructive behavior may have even more dire consequences. Complete success ends the issue because there is no further opportunity to matter. Near misses merely emphasize the "otherness" of the poor soul, and the end result may be more pity than mattering. Still, perhaps the goal of self-destructive behavior is to "matter in memory." The invisible person may say to him- or herself, "They'll be sorry when I'm gone. They will finally understand that I am a noteworthy person, but it will be too late."

Nevertheless, desperate people often lose their rationality and enact behaviors that superficially will seem to alleviate their plight. In their despondency, they cannot imagine alternative paths to satisfy the overwhelming motivation to make a difference. Careful consideration of options is a luxury that they cannot afford. Failing to matter is a continual frustration of a most basic human motivation. It must be addressed as soon as possible, because it is unbearable to be a non-person. Therefore, it is no surprise that those who believe they have no social significance will, in their disconsolate state, turn to any action that seemingly would rescue them from a meaningless existence, even if a more sober analysis would reveal its folly.

Public shootings are rare, but not rare enough. In February, 2007, an 18-year-old killed five people and wounded four more in Salt Lake City before the police killed him. And as I write this paragraph, the media are flooded with news about a mass killing at a shopping mall in Omaha, Nebraska. According to the *New York Times* web site (*New York Times*, 2007c), the killer, 19-year-old Robert A. Hawkins, shot eight people to death with an old AK-47 before turning the weapon on himself. The woman who took him into her home because he was estranged from his family described him as "a lost pound puppy that nobody wanted." He left a suicide note in which he apologized in advance for the killings and stated he would no longer be a burden on his family. His last words in the note: "Now I'll be famous."

Elaborating the Relationship: The Mediating Role of Self-Esteem

> *If you know you're worth nothing, only a gamble with death can gratify your vanity.*
>
> Don DeLillo, *Underworld*

But there is more to the story. The arguments I have advanced above are supported by theoretical reasoning, but the process by which mattering works may be more complex. I have asserted that mattering is one of the *fundamental* motivating factors for human behavior. One way of understanding this assertion is to conceive of mattering as first among a variety of important motivators. In other words, the need to matter is so powerful that it activates other motivating elements of the self-concept, which, in turn, have a forceful influence on behavior.

One candidate for such an intervening mechanism is self-esteem. Self-esteem is the global evaluation of one's own personal characteristics and attributes. Although one may differentially value the various aspects of the self, in the end a person somehow integrates all these evaluations into a general understanding of his or her self-worth.

To understand more about self-esteem, it is helpful to consider the two extremes of this self-concept dimension. People with high levels of self-esteem are reasonably satisfied with who they are. Their perceived real self is not a threat to them. They acknowledge that they have faults, but they are not overwhelmed by them. On the central elements of their self-concepts, the characteristics that are to them self-defining, they view themselves positively enough. Where they recognize the need for improvement, they are confident in their abilities to do so. Overall, they are comfortable enough about who they are, even as they remain open to further self-concept development.

In contrast, people who have very low self-esteem are very unhappy about who they are. They consider themselves as deficient, unworthy, or inadequate in important ways. They tend to be low on self-acceptance, self-liking, and self-respect. There is a chronic, impulsive tendency to derogate the self and to refuse to recognize positive qualities in themselves. In the end, they may even feel shame about who they are.

There has been confusion about the notion of self-esteem. For example, in the common parlance, high self-esteem has often been understood to mean that a person has few, if any, personal faults. One is completely self-satisfied because there is no need for any substantial improvement. This is a fundamental misunderstanding that has caused problems in the attempt to foster self-esteem. The state of perfection is unattainable by human beings, and if people are told that they can evaluate themselves positively only if they achieve it (or come very close), no one could have high levels of self-esteem.

In the face of this impossibility, well-meaning people working for the well-being of another have sincerely but mistakenly responded by encouraging selective perception in the other. Great care is taken to avoid any mention of flawed characteristics found within the other. Instead, they enter into an unspoken collusion with the person and act as if the problematic aspects of the self did not exist. It is as if the other is so fragile that knowing about areas needing improvement would be too daunting and render the other hopeless. One might call this the "ignorance is bliss" approach.

However, such avoidance calls forth a campaign to distract people from any threatening awareness of their flawed selves. As the sociologist John P. Hewitt (1998, ch. 6) notes, the popular conception of self-esteem is as an emotion, a reaction to the self that is physiologically based and socially labeled. In that case, the best that one can do for another is to persuade that other to think of him- or herself in positive terms. If people can ensure that the person "feels good" about the self, then it will be possible to avoid "feeling bad." And feeling bad about anything, especially the self, is anathema in our society.

But people (even young children) are not stupid. Even if others carefully avoid bringing up challenging issues about your personal growth and development and smother you with compliments, you know that, in some ways and to some degree, you are flawed. Continually failing to acknowledge your faults does not mean that you are no longer aware of them. Your shortcomings become the unmentionable factor that prevents them from granting you full legitimacy as a social actor.

Facing such a response, you are likely to come to one of two conclusions: Either others do not know you very well, or they are remarkably undiscerning human beings. In either case, why should you believe *anything* they have to say about you? As a consequence, you are very likely to reject the positive feedback they lavish on you, if you give it any consideration at all. The effort to cultivate high self-esteem within you is doomed to failure.

Fortunately for the study of human behavior, social psychologists make a clear distinction between the popular *connotation* and the scientific *denotation* of a concept. For example, Rosenberg argues that "realistic" high self-esteem expresses the feeling that one is "good enough."

> The individual simply feels that he is a person of worth; he respects himself for what he is, but he does not stand in awe of himself nor does he expect others to stand in awe of him. He does *not* necessarily consider himself superior to others. . . . he does not feel that he is the ultimate in perfection but, on the contrary, recognizes his limitations and expects to grow and improve. (1989, p. 31; italics in the original)

With realistically high self-esteem, the individual recognizes his or her imperfections but believes that these imperfections do not overwhelm the positive aspects of themselves; in the final summation, the positive aspects, more seriously considered because they are more central to the self-concept, sufficiently outweigh the negatives. With unrealistically high self-esteem, the person recognizes few, if any, faults in themselves, preferring selectively to perceive only the socially valuable components. ("Last year I was conceited, but now I'm perfect.") As a result, true self-improvement is obviated, because one can't change aspects of the self that one does not acknowledge.

Indeed, those who have unrealistically high self-esteem, in that they profess to have no meaningful imperfections, may not have high self-esteem at all. Rather, such unrealistic self-evaluations may be no more than an attempt to defend against a perception of the self that is problematic. The blanket denial of imperfections generally signals a low level of "real" self-esteem.

The lower end of the self-esteem continuum has also received clarification. Rosenberg (1989) began with the notion that "Low self-esteem, on the other hand, implies self-rejection, self-dissatisfaction, self-contempt. The individual lacks respect for the self he observes. The self-picture is disagreeable, and he wishes it were otherwise" (p. 31).

The social psychologist Roy Baumeister (1993) added to our understanding by showing that people with low self-esteem are more confused about their self-image than they are self-loathing: "What distinguishes people with low self-esteem is not the size of their desire to think well of themselves, but rather some interference with fulfilling that desire" (p. 202). They are blocked by their realization of their limited capacity to do the things that would help them feel better about themselves.

The motivational power of self-esteem comes from the same source as mattering: It is highly reassuring to know that one is a person of worth, and people will work hard to maintain a high level of self-esteem. On the other hand, it is extremely difficult to bear the realization that one is not as worthy as others. People so afflicted will strive to improve themselves, or, failing that, will seek to protect themselves from the shame of self-deficiency, often by withdrawing from others.

The research on self-esteem and its effects on behavior is voluminous. I will postpone until later the documentation of the contributions of self-esteem to the outcomes I analyze in this book. Here, I report some of the research detailing the link between self-esteem and other behaviors.

Rosenberg (1989, chs. 9, 10, 12) found that among adolescents, those with low self-esteem were more awkward in their behavior with others and were reluctant to initiate social interactions, compared to those with realistically high self-esteem. They participated less often in school extracurricular activities. When considering their future, they expressed little desire to land a job requiring leadership qualities or a competitive orientation; at the same time, they preferred work that did not involve supervision by a superior. In short, whereas low self-esteem adolescents were eager not to reveal their inferiority to their fellow workers, those with high self-esteem knew that they would not shrink from jobs that demanded much of them. They believed that they have what it takes to shine.

More recently, researchers (Anthony, Wood, & Holmes, 2007) investigated the link between self-esteem and decision-making. They found that low self-esteem people were eager to join a group making judgments about marketing programs only when their acceptance into the group by other members was described as virtually certain; in contrast, high self-esteem individuals were equally willing to join the group whether acceptance was guaranteed or only relatively likely. When you don't like yourself, you are not eager to be scrutinized by people who might reject you. In related research, high self-esteem made it easier to make a decision regarding issues laden with moral consequences (Dai, Nolan, & White, 2002). A favorable self-evaluation gives a person confidence that one will make wise choices involving difficult issues.

Self-esteem is also involved in the processes of self-presentation. How we choose to orchestrate our behavior to create an impression of ourselves in the minds of others is strongly influenced by how we evaluate ourselves. For example, those who do not like themselves have much to lose in social standing by sharing their deficiencies with others, whereas those who are reasonably satisfied with who they are have less to worry about. Consistent with this argument, in earlier research (Elliott, 1982), I found that adolescents with high levels of self-esteem were not afraid of revealing themselves to others, but with low self-esteem, young people were more likely to hide behind a self-presentational façade. Similarly, low self-esteem leads to a greater likelihood that one would "play dumb" (conceal information, despite having knowledge) or "know it all" (claiming knowledge in spite of one's ignorance) (Thornton, Audesse, Ryckman, & Burckle, 2006). Each tactic is an attempt to obviate discovery of one's failings.

Task performance is also a dangerous area for people with low self-esteem, but little threat for people who are reasonably satisfied with their understanding of themselves. Those with low self-esteem tend to approach a task with an orientation to avoid negative outcomes (glitches in performance, outright failure); in contrast, high self-esteem disposes people to emphasize the positive outcomes (creativity, success) as they attempt a task (Heimpel, Elliot, & Wood, 2006). In fact, low self-esteem leads to more procrastination to avoid doing a task, perhaps due to the anxiety that comes with the belief that one does not possess the ability to perform well (Harrington, 2005). Further, those who do not think well of themselves will go so far as to self-handicap (disable themselves in a way that prevents them from even attempting the task) to prevent the attribution that a poor performance is due to a lack of native ability (Martin & Brawley, 2002). More generally, higher levels of self-esteem give a person the wherewithal to deal more effectively with social problems that arise in everyday life (such as conflict with friends, family, and romantic partners, being exploited, being disappointed in another, betrayal of trust by another) (Crocker & Luhtanen, 2003).

Finally, in line with the focus of self-destructive behavior, self-esteem is a primary predictor of disordered eating (Shea & Pritchard, 2006). Much of the connection is apparently due to our society's prescription (ubiquitous in the mass media) that "you can never be too thin." Those who internalize this impossible standard find themselves wanting, come to loathe themselves, and take drastic action to bring themselves into line with the social norm.

It is now possible to make a more sophisticated prediction about the place of mattering in everyday behavior. In particular, it is possible to elaborate at last part of the process by which mattering affects what we do. My assertion is that at least some of the influence of mattering on behavior will be channeled through self-esteem. That is, mattering influences self-esteem, which in turn influences behavior.

I expect that mattering will have a positive relationship with self-esteem. The more one matters, the higher the self-esteem; the less one matters, the lower the self-esteem. It is not difficult to understand why this should be so. Those who matter can easily conclude that they are worthwhile people. The fact that someone notices them, takes an interest in their welfare, and relies on them reinforces the notion that they are persons of value. It is prima facie evidence that they are worth something, because no one would waste time on a person with severe personal or social deficiencies.

In contrast, someone who does not matter can only wonder why. They may very well attribute their failure to make a difference to others to the fact that they have little or nothing to offer. When others ignore them, invest their personal resources in someone else, or never turn to them in time of need, they may make the self-attribution that they are deficient people. Indeed, Rosenberg (Rosenberg & McCullough, 1981) has already established this link, using an ad hoc series of items cobbled together from his prior studies of young people. I will later affirm the relationship among adolescents using the index I constructed specifically to measure mattering.

Turning to the second link in the chain, I anticipate that self-esteem will be negatively associated with anti-social and self-destructive behaviors. Those with positive evaluations of themselves will eschew socially undesirable behavior because it would threaten the self-image. Thinking reasonably highly of themselves, they would avoid any behaviors that might call into question their self-evaluation and would make a special effort to confine themselves to acts that would affirm it.

In contrast, a person whose self-concept is seriously deficient has very little to lose and ostensibly something to gain by acting in a socially undesirable manner. By thumbing their noses at society, perhaps they will gain back the self-esteem lost by the failure to matter. Baumeister (1993, p. 203) has noted: "Events that threaten to undermine self-worth may therefore bring out defensive and protective reactions among people with low self-esteem." It does no good to point out that these desperate attempts are likely to be unsuccessful. Because self-esteem is also a powerful motivation, the shame that accompanies self-loathing is likely to block a rational assessment of protective behaviors. Further, even if their actions do not ameliorate the situation, they could hardly be worse off, because self-esteem is already low.

Self-esteem will also be negatively related to self-destructive behaviors. As people of worth, those with high self-esteem would see no reason to harm themselves. To do so would destroy all they have successfully constructed over the years. It would make no sense. On the other hand, those who think ill of themselves have very little to lose. They fear death less than others, because their lives do not offer promises of success or happiness in any sense of these words. Their deficiencies mean they do not have much to offer this world. Indeed, they may believe that society would be better without them.

Mattering to Family

> *Cameron:*
> *I dented the shit out of it [his father's Ferrari]. . . . Good. . . . My father will come home; he'll see what I did. I can't hide this. He'll come home, and he'll see what I did. He'll* have *to deal with me.*
>
> John Hughes, *Ferris Bueller's day off*

It matters to whom one matters. In discussing the notion of significant other, Rosenberg (1973) notes that not all candidates are equally influential in the life of a person; the individual makes the choice of which significant others he or she will turn to for support, based on the strong motivation to enjoy high levels of self-esteem.

In a reciprocal vein, not all others in a person's life will be critical sources of mattering. We recognize that we want to matter to certain significant people in our lives, while we care less if we matter to others. The ideal relationship structure is one that balances the notions of mattering and significant other: We matter to persons who matter to us.

Several sources of mattering could be important in a young person's life. Certainly, friends loom large in the world of any adolescent. Friendships are built on reciprocity (Jourard, 1971), and it is the mutual feeling of mattering that is the glue that binds friends to each other. In the search for an autonomous identity, mattering to friends can be especially important, as friends can help each other on this very difficult project.

For some, it is a teacher who inspires them to develop themselves further than they might do on their own. In an after-hours conference about schoolwork, students realize that the teacher is going above and beyond the call of duty to improve their lot.

When a coach encourages a student athlete to work a little bit harder and gives praise for the effort, the athlete will appreciate the exacting standards because they mean that the coach cares enough to demand a bit more. If it were done in a demeaning way, it might merely evince the coach's need to win. But when it is done in a supportive way, the athlete recognizes the investment being made by the coach. Further, such treatment indicates how much the team depends on a successful performance by each team member.

An employer who makes a special effort to integrate the young hireling into a large workforce signals that the youth is not just part of an undifferentiated mass. Even occasional checks on the worker's performance, if done appropriately, may induce a sense of mattering: The boss is impressed with me and wants to make sure I get a chance to "show my stuff" and earn a promotion; not only that, he relies on me to get the job done.

For others, the counseling given by a religious cleric may instill a feeling of mattering. Being able to talk about the mysteries of life with a good listener who wants to know what you believe and wants to help you sort it all out makes a profound difference during the upheaval that occurs during adolescence. Indeed, a large part of the damage done by abusive members of the clergy likely comes from the utter betrayal felt by the young victims. Being used as an object cannot connote mattering; it requires a sincere interest in the life of another.

Among adolescents, the family, especially parents (or parent figures), but siblings as well, serves as a crucial source of mattering. The importance of mattering to one's family cannot be overstated. Parents are, for most children, their chief socializing agents; they are the major sources of reflected appraisals that help form the young person's self-concept. They serve as models for attitudes and behavior. In addition, the growing child is critically dependent on them for subsistence, information, and affirmation. When children know that they matter to their family, they can be confident in their search for autonomy, knowing that however much they define themselves as different from their parents, they are safe. They will not be rejected or ostracized, because their family takes a sincere interest in them.

The popular image of deep hostility between adolescents and parents has been overstated (Arnett, 1999; Steinberg, 1990). The adolescent's search for autonomy does not necessarily involve bad feelings and estrangement from parents, and certainly not *exclusively* bad feelings and estrangement. Children recognize at an emotionally primitive level that they would be lost without a solid understanding that parents are meaningfully involved in their lives. To fail to matter to parents is to realize that those who are most responsible for shaping the self and for the survival of the child to this point do not take this responsibility seriously. The terror that follows this recognition is not easily erased or even ignored.

Research has suggested that most adolescents maintain a strong emotional bond to their parents, even as they carve out a separate identity (Steinberg, 2001), although there are variations across gender (Geuzaine, Debry, & Liesens, 2000) and race/ethnicity (Phinney, Kim-Jo, Osorio, & Vilhjalmsdottir, 2005). The same body of research also shows that adolescents who have a close relationship to their parents are more self-reliant (Steinberg & Silverberg, 1986), learn greater motivational levels and perform better in school (Henderson & Dweck, 1990), and, relevant to our purposes, develop higher levels of self-esteem (Rosenberg, 1979; Harter, 1999). Implicit in this research on parental caring and involvement is the notion of mattering. Children can form a healthy attachment to their parents when they know that they matter to them. Those children who do not matter have no basis for a satisfactory relationship with their parents and are left alone to figure life out for themselves.

Relationships with siblings are also important. Perceived support in adolescent sibling relationships is negatively related to externalizing problems (aggression, delinquency) (Branje, van Lieshout, van Aken, & Haselager, 2004; Criss & Shaw, 2005; Updegraff, Thayer, Whiteman, Denning, & McHale, 2005). In general, the more supportive or otherwise positive the sibling relationship, the less likely an adolescent will engage in anti-social behavior. Further, internalizing problems (involving loneliness, depression, and self-esteem) are reduced with more intimate sibling relationships, even those that involve conflict (Ponzetti & James, 1997; Kim, McHale, Crouter, & Osgood, 2007; Yeh & Lempers, 2004). In short, it appears that mattering to one's sibling goes a long way to make life easier.

Mattering to family is taken for granted by most people. It is a part of a role identity (offspring) that one has not chosen but rather has been ascribed by our society's symbolic universe. Because of the biological and deep emotional connections that a child has with its parents, it is something that usually comes with the role identity. It should not have to be negotiated. As a consequence, it is the most fundamental shock when a child realizes that its parents simply do not attend to, invest in, or rely on him or her. The failure to bond mutually comes from an inability or unwillingness in the parents to play out their ascribed role identity.

Therefore, it should be especially informative to understand the part mattering to family has to play in decisions about anti-social and self-destructive behavior. If the family is indeed a critical source of mattering, then a failure to matter to one's family should have especially dire consequences for the adolescent.

3

Researching Mattering: An Overview

The theoretical arguments advanced in these first two chapters are intended to be sufficiently persuasive that mattering is a primary motivation within the self-concept. But even so, they are merely intellectual games until social or behavioral scientists provide empirical evidence that this theory describes the processes underlying actual human behavior. In this chapter, I briefly elaborate the structure and the process of the research I conducted to answer the questions I have raised about the relationship between mattering and behavior. Those who want a more detailed description should read the Appendix.

Operationalization: The Craft of Measurement

Measuring Mattering and Self-Esteem

So far, I have defined the important motivating concepts (mattering and self-esteem) in precise words. Mattering is the perception that, to some degree and in any of a variety of ways, one is a significant part in the lives of others. Self-esteem is the global evaluation of one's own personal characteristics and attributes. These *conceptualizations* may ring true for most of us, but in order to conduct meaningful, valid, and reliable research it is necessary to develop a measure of the extent to which they are actually experienced by people. With a quantitative measure of each concept, I can examine the patterns of relationships between mattering and self-esteem, on the one hand,

and reported behaviors, on the other. In the language of research, I need an *operationalization* of each of the dimensions of the self-concept.

Unfortunately, heretofore there existed no demonstrably valid and reliable measure for mattering. For example, the instrument used by Rosenberg (Rosenberg & McCullough, 1981) was constructed from two surveys he conducted before he had developed the concept of mattering. As a consequence, he was forced to use items that had not been created to tap this concept and only obliquely reflected it. Further, the questions did not cover all three components of mattering. Other operationalizations (Marshall, 2001; Taylor & Turner, 2001) were similarly limited in scope and therefore lacking what measurement specialists call *content validity*: The extent to which the measure covers the full range of meaning contained in the definition of the concept.

To that end, I had earlier constructed and validated an index to measure mattering that satisfied the three most important criteria of a valid measure: It measured what it was supposed to measure (construct validity); it did not measure other, theoretically meaningful concepts (discriminant validity), and it covered a substantial range of the ways people could matter, using all three components (awareness, importance, and reliance) developed by Rosenberg (content validity). Details about the construction and validation procedure can be found in Elliott, Kao, and Grant (2004).

The analysis yielded 24 items, but this proved too long for the extensive Youth at Risk Survey. Accordingly, I trimmed the list to the 15 best-performing items, subject to the criterion that all three components were sufficiently covered. The items retained for the Youth at Risk Survey are presented in the Appendix.

Finally, the original index items measured self-perceived mattering in general, without any specific focus. For the Youth at Risk survey, I changed the wording such that the items reflected perceived mattering to one's own family. The wording of the items makes it easy to change the focus of mattering without changing the meaning of the item (Elliott, Kao, & Grant, 2004, contains the complete index).

For self-esteem, I used the well-known index developed by Rosenberg (1989). This measure has been around for a long while, with evidence continually building up regarding its effectiveness as a valid and reliable report of a person's self-evaluation. Items from the Self-Esteem Index are also available in the Appendix.

For both indices, respondents indicated the extent to which they agreed with each item as a self-description; the options were Strongly Agree, Agree, Neither Agree nor Disagree, Disagree, and Strongly Disagree. The coding of responses was such that a higher number reflected higher levels of mattering or self-esteem. I calculated a total score for each respondent by summing the scores for all items in the index. A higher total score means greater levels of perceived mattering and self-esteem.

Measuring Behaviors

The Youth at Risk survey included a wide variety of anti-social and self-destructive behaviors. For this book, I selected the following anti-social behaviors for analysis: truancy, vandalism, dealing in contraband, theft from the family, carrying a weapon, and violence against people outside the family. In addition, I examined the following self-destructive behaviors: illicit drug use, binge drinking, planning to commit suicide, and suicide attempts.

Each behavior was represented by one or more specific questions asked of the adolescent respondent. In some cases, responses from several questions were necessary to construct the measure needed; in other cases, responses to a given question had to be combined in a certain way to achieve the appropriate measure. The actual questions and the procedures used to construct the measures can be found in the Appendix.

Because of the heavy skew on these variables (most respondents had not engaged in anti-social or self-destructive behavior), each of the outcome variables is structured as a dichotomy (the respondent either has or has not engaged in the behavior within the given time frame). As a consequence, I will report the results in terms of the probability that a young person has enacted the behavior in question.

Measuring the Control Variables

Many other factors contribute to the likelihood of anti-social and self-destructive behaviors by adolescents. In research parlance, these variables are known as *control variables*, that is, variables whose impact must be accounted for in order to achieve an accurate assessment of the contributions of the theoretical focus variables (in this case, mattering to family and self-esteem). Failure to include the control variables in the analysis will inevitably lead to biased estimates of the roles played by mattering to family and self-esteem. The control variables are no less "important" than the theoretical variables; they are simply not the major focus for my analysis. Indeed, one person's control variable is another person's theoretical variable.

By design, the data from the Youth at Risk study contained many of these variables. Based on the theory and research discussed in Chapters 4 and 5, I selected the following variables:

Sex is often an important discriminator in behaviors, especially in adolescence. The socialization into a gender role identity leads boys and girls into different orientations to their world, with resultant differences in a wide range of behavior.

Race/ethnicity is also a critical factor in social identity. The data allow me to create three categories for this variable: non-Hispanic white, non-Hispanic black, and Hispanic. Unfortunately, there were not enough Asians or Pacific Islanders in the sample to constitute a separate category. As a result, they were included in a catch-all category (labeled "other") that included Native Americans, those who indicated multiple racial identities, and those who named a racial/ethnic identity not included in the listed categories. There can be no meaningful contrasts involving this motley group; it exists only to preserve these adolescents' responses to all other variables used in the analyses.

Socioeconomic status is the third pillar of the sociological perspective. I chose the level of educational attainment of the adult respondent to reflect this powerful contextual factor in an adolescent's life. Families in different levels of socioeconomic status experience the world differently and provide a different crucible for the development of their children's role identities. I created five categories of educational attainment: less than high school, high school diploma (or GED), some college (including vocational training), college degree, and postgraduate education.

Family structure is also an important issue. In recent history, the composition of a family has taken on more forms than the traditional, married two-parent model. Differences in the composition of a family can have a powerful influence on how adolescents come to understand who they are, as well as their everyday behaviors. The questions in the survey allowed me to distinguish among three types of families: two-parent families, either biological or blended, single-parent families in which the head of household was previously married, and single-parent families with never-married heads of household. (There were not enough two-parent families in which the adults were cohabiting [58] to distinguish them from the traditional married model in my analyses, so I was forced to combine them with the married parents.) The number of children in the household is another aspect of family structure that deserves consideration, and I was able to determine this number from questions in the survey.

The *age* of the respondent adolescent is particularly important. Theories of social development of young people, detailed in Chapter 1, argue persuasively for an ability to distinguish respondents according to developmental stage. Age is not a perfect indicator of social maturation, as there are noticeable individual differences in progress within any age level, but it is a reasonable proxy, given that there is no direct measure of development available in the data. In the sample, age ranges from 11 to 18. Because very few of the 11-year-olds engaged in the anti-social and self-destructive behaviors I studied, I combined them with the 12-year-olds.

Finally, research has shown that *religiosity* has much to say about the likelihood of dysfunctional behavior in adolescence. (In this book, I discuss these studies as I focus on each particular dysfunctional behavior.) The question from the survey asks the adolescent, "How important is religion in your life today?" I classified the responses into four categories: not important, fairly important, very important, and extremely important.

Gathering the Sample

The data were gathered under the auspices of a colleague, Richard J. Gelles, Dean of the School of Social Work at the University of Pennsylvania. He designed the Youth at Risk Survey to study a wide variety of anti-social and self-destructive behaviors and invited me to take part.

Gelles enlisted a professional survey firm to conduct a telephone interview with a sample of respondents taken from the population of adolescents in the United States. Using random digit dialing, the interviewers were able to generate a random sample that would most likely be representative of the population of adolescents. The interview included a conversation with the adolescent respondent, as well as a parent or guardian. The adult respondent was interviewed first. When completed, the survey provided data from 2,004 families. Missing data reduced the sample size for each analysis. I report the effective sample size in the tables found in the Appendix.

Plan of the Analysis

Phase 1: The (Total) Relationship of Mattering and Behavior

Each analysis consists of three phases. The aim of the first phase is to determine the effects of mattering on the various anti-social and self-destructive behaviors for the adolescents participating in the study. To accomplish this purpose, I constructed statistical models in which the main independent variable was the score on the mattering index and the dependent variable was the behavior in question.

The analysis also included the control variables, to determine if mattering's role is robust in the presence of other theoretically meaningful predictors of the behavior. If mattering remains a powerful influence on behavior with the control variables in the analysis, one has persuasive evidence that its predictive power is not due to its relationship with any of the other predictors in the model.

Each of the behavior variables was highly skewed, with most respondents not engaging in the behavior in question. Therefore, I dichotomized the variable to discriminate those who did not do the behavior from those who did, to any degree. As a consequence of the dichotomous dependent variable, I conducted Logistic Regressions using the SAS Institute (1999) software package to provide estimates of the coefficients and determine their level of statistical significance.

Phases 2 and 3: Elaborating the Contribution of Mattering

The second and third phases together establish the strength of self-esteem as a mediator between mattering and adolescent behavior. The analytical treatment follows the pattern discussed in Kenny, Kashy, and Bolger (1998). (See Figure 3.1 for a pictorial representation of the elaborated model.)

The objective of the second phase is to determine the relationship of self-esteem to mattering. In a preliminary analysis conducted

Figure 3.1 Mattering, Self-Esteem, and Adolescent Behavior

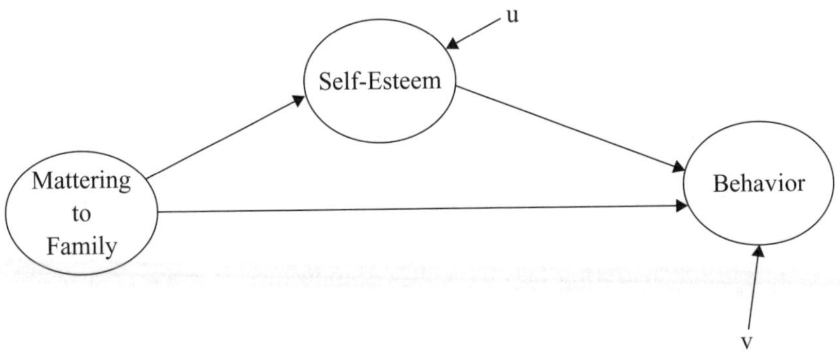

Note: Arrows from sources labeled with a lower case letter represent the contributions from factors not contained in the data (including randomness).

before that of the behavioral outcomes, I determine the extent to which mattering to family and self-esteem are associated. Even if self-esteem has a strong role to play regarding adolescent behavior, if mattering to family is not related to self-esteem, then self-esteem cannot serve as a mediator between mattering to family and behavior. The data will have failed to establish the first link in the chain model, and mattering and self-esteem are independent influences on behavior. Only if there is a significant connection between the two is it possible that self-esteem could intervene between mattering to family and behavior, channeling the contribution of the former to the latter.

To this end, I analyzed self-esteem as a function of mattering and the control variables. Because the dependent variable is measured (by design) at the interval level of measurement, I used Ordinary Least Squares Regression (again, with SAS) to estimate the contribution of mattering to family (and the control variables) to self-esteem. A significant coefficient of mattering on self-esteem, combined with a significant association of self-esteem and behavior in the third phase of analysis, would reveal self-esteem as a meaningful mediator of the relationship between mattering and behavior.

The purpose of the third phase of analysis is to determine the role of mattering and self-esteem together in understanding the adolescent's choices regarding behavior. First, a significant coefficient estimate for self-esteem would mean that it is also an important predictor of the behavior, thereby establishing the second part of the link in the chain model of mattering to self-esteem to behavior depicted in Figure 3.1.

Second, I look to see the extent to which the coefficient estimate for mattering changes in the elaborated model. If it changes only trivially, one must conclude that self-esteem does not channel the contribution of mattering to behavior. If the coefficient for mattering decreases substantially when self-esteem is also in the model, it would suggest that the role played by mattering established in the first phase may be, at least in part, mediated by self-esteem. Further, if the coefficient for mattering fails to achieve significance, it is then reasonable to conclude that the entire influence of mattering on behavior is due to the mediating role played by self-esteem: positive mattering is associated with high self-esteem, which, in turn, is associated with a lower probability of dysfunctional adolescent behavior.

A Caveat

I hasten to add that the relationship between mattering and behavior could be more complex than is addressed by the analyses I have conducted. For example, some might say that parents will decide that their child does not matter to them upon learning of the child's illicit drug use, rather than failing to matter to them contributing to it. Even so, I would make two points.

First, while the parent's reaction may be rejection, usually this does *not* imply a failure to matter. When a child truly does not matter to parents, they would not care if he or she were being self-destructive or anti-social. Except for the inconvenience and public shame involved, the child's behavior means nothing to them. (Occasionally, one hears of a parent saying, "My child is dead to me." If the parent is serious and not merely trying to avoid the pain of the child's misbehavior, then the statement truly signals a failure to matter.) No, the anger in parents' reactions to their child's misbehavior often communicates how much the child actually matters.

Second, if the relationship is truly bi-directional (each factor contributes to the other in a feedback loop), the ability to tease apart the bi-directionality in this relationship awaits one of two developments: a longitudinal study across (at least) two points in time, or the discovery of what statisticians call instrumental variables (two variables, each of which is related to only one of the two variables involved).

Considering the nature of the two variables in question, the second option is a tall order indeed. It is difficult to conceive of a variable that is highly related to mattering to the family that would not also be highly related to any of the behaviors I examine in the following chapters, and the reverse is also true.

Therefore, from these two points, I argue that the models I have set up are the most appropriate, given the state of the art of mattering research. The theory of mattering holds that, as a fundamental motivation for human beings, mattering to family will be a major contribution to the likelihood of anti-social and self-destructive behavior. The reverse possibility is considered less powerful and, in some cases, not theoretically meaningful.

Reporting the Results of the Analyses

The outcome behaviors are analyzed as dichotomies (the adolescent either acknowledges or denies engaging in the behavior). Therefore, I will present the results in terms of the probability of engaging in the behavior for each of several levels of the predictor variables (mattering and self-esteem). When I examine the relationship between mattering and self-esteem, both of which are measured as placement on their respective dimensions, I will present the predicted self-esteem score for a given level of mattering to family.

Because of its negatively skewed distribution (happily, most teenagers believe that they matter to their families to a reasonable degree), I will focus on contrasts across four levels of mattering: the mean, and one, two, and three standard deviations below the mean. In other words, the results I present will show how a diminution in mattering is associated with an increased likelihood of the undesirable behavior in question.

Next, as self-esteem is added to the model, I will describe its independent contribution to these probabilities. I will use the same four-category discriminations that I use for mattering. I will also present the new probabilities for the behavior for levels of mattering, which will have changed due to the addition of self-esteem.

In addition, for each behavior, I present the results of the analysis as they apply to Figure 3.1. I denote with a solid connecting line any relationship involving the major theoretical variables (mattering to family and self-esteem) and the behavior in question that is statistically significant ($p < .05$). I use a dashed line to indicate any relationship that is only marginally significant ($.05 < p < .10$). And when a relationship fails to attain significance, there will be no line connecting the two variables.

Finally, I will describe the part played by the control variables on the probability of engaging in the behavior. Some of the control variables (sex, race) are measured at the nominal level of measurement; the numbers serve only to distinguish one category from another and have no mathematical properties. Other control variables (socioeconomic status, family structure, and religiosity) are measured at the ordinal level of measurement; the numbers delineate the rank ordering of the categories but do not indicate how much of the underlying concept is entailed with each increase from one category to another. For these variables, I have coded the categories so that the odds of engaging in a given behavior *for a particular category* are contrasted with the *overall* odds of engaging in that behavior *collapsed across all categories*. In addition, because of the possibility that age has a non-linear relationship with problematic behavior, I employ the same category scheme for age that I do for the categorical and ordinal variables. The logistic and Ordinary Least Squares Regression analyses are presented in the Appendix, Tables A.3 to A.17.

In addition to determining whether the category odds differ from the overall odds, I report, from analyses not presented herein, the results of tests determining whether each category of a variable differs from all other categories of that variable. Taken together, these two portraits of a control variable will yield a more complete understanding of its contribution to the behavior in question.

Finally, I treat the variable measuring the number of children in the family as the ratio-level variable it is. For more details on these coding protocols, consult the Appendix.

The stage has now been set for analysis of the data. In Chapter 4, I begin by introducing the overall plan of analysis and then present the results for the relationships between mattering, self-esteem, and anti-social behaviors. I examine in Chapter 5 the differences in self-destructive behaviors that can be traced to differences in mattering and self-esteem.

4

Mattering and Anti-Social Behavior

Judy [Natalie Wood]: I don't even know why I do it [delinquent behavior].

Lt. Ray Fremick [Edward Platt]: Maybe you can get back at your dad that way. I mean, if you're not as close to him as you'd like to be. Maybe this is one way of making him pay attention.

Irving Shulman and Stewart Stern, *Rebel without a Cause*

All disciplines within the social and behavioral sciences have an extensive accumulation of theory and research on anti-social behavior, especially in adolescence. Interest in the topic has spread beyond academia, and the mass media contribute to the public fascination with the issue. Popular films from *The Wild One* (1953), starring Marlon Brando as an alienated biker who rebels against everything, to *Boyz N the Hood* (1991), a tale of struggling youth in south central Los Angeles, aimed a bright spotlight at disaffected young people who face or create trouble in their daily lives. In literature, Evan Hunter's (1954) *The Blackboard Jungle* describes the tribulations of a teacher at an inner-city high school, as he tries to instill the love of learning in the rowdy students who, it seems, could not care less. A work of non-fiction, Frank McCourt's (2005) *Teacher Man*, shows that the desperation of disadvantaged students has not abated.

Theories of Anti-Social Behavior

Researchers have used several theoretical approaches to explain why people might engage in anti-social behavior. In the previous chapter, I have alluded to the first, *strain theory*, based on the work of Robert Merton (1938). The essence of strain theory is the conflict between the goals promulgated by our symbolic universe (success, defined by wealth, status, and fame) and the means to these ends. The symbolic universe in United States society encourages everyone to internalize these goals and make them their personal aspirations. If the legitimate means are available to them, they can pursue personal life ambitions and trust to native ability to lead them to the good life.

For example, parents recognize very early on that the path to success for their offspring is highly contingent on which school is available. Indeed, those who are of means often enlist the counsel of experts to help gain an advantage in the education marathon. At the extreme, it is often the case that great anxiety is involved in getting one's child into the "right" pre-kindergarten class.

If a child does not start well, it bodes ill for his or her entire educational career. Those who find themselves in inferior schools or do not do well in high school may find that college is no longer an option, and those careers requiring a bachelor's degree are no longer within reach.

The process is complicated by the fact that the structural inequalities built into our society (such as gender, race/ethnicity, and social class) mean that the socially acceptable paths to success are not available to everyone equally. For example, sociologists have known for a long time that the family's social class plays an important role in a child's access to the educational system (Sewell, Haller, & Portes, 1994). Throughout the educational system, some young people find out that their position in the stratification hierarchy of our society likely means that the socially prescribed path to success is denied to them.

At the same time, the disadvantaged are not discouraged from internalizing these goals. If they can come up with unorthodox, socially disapproved, and, often illegal, means, they may still succeed through a path Merton calls *innovation*. As Merton (1938, p. 679) puts it:

> The lack of high integration between the means-and-end elements of the cultural pattern and the particular class structure combined to favor a heightened frequency of antisocial conduct in groups. . . . Recourse

> to the first of the alternative responses, legitimate effort, is limited by the fact that actual advance toward desired success-symbols through conventional channels is, despite our persisting open-class ideology, relatively rare and difficult for those handicapped by little formal education and few economic resources.

Frustrated by barriers that no one will admit exist, the disadvantaged will not give up the aspirations they have internalized. Because the goals are deemed so important, by both society and the individual, they will be attained by any means necessary, even those condemned by society.

Implicit in Merton's argument is the concept of mattering. Those who are denied by structural barriers the legitimate means to success receive a clear and painful message from our society that they do not matter. They are somehow unworthy of the opportunities the rest of us enjoy. Without affirmations that they matter, those on the lower tiers of our status hierarchy are likely to turn, as Merton argues, to socially disapproved means to the ends that are not formally denied them.

Further, as Sennett and Cobb (1972) argue, our symbolic universe encourages the excluded to assume responsibility for this failure by preaching that our society is a meritocracy: Those with the talent can make it, if they strive hard enough. The only explanation for failure is either a lack of ability or a lack of effort. Those who can't or won't succeed are encouraged to accept the fact that they do not deserve the attention, the investment, or the reliance incumbent on those who do succeed. The structural barriers fade into the background, as the failures among us come to believe that it is simply a matter of not having what it takes. In desperation, to show that they are indeed persons to be reckoned with, they may turn to socially disapproved behavior. At the very least, they will no longer be ignored.

The second theory of anti-social behavior, labeled *control theory*, was first developed by the sociologist Travis Hirschi (1969) and expanded with a colleague, Michael R. Gottfredson (Gottfredson & Hirschi, 1990). The basic premise behind the theory is that anti-social behavior does not come from the denial of long-term aspirations, as Merton had it. Rather, Hirschi followed the lead provided by Durkheim (1951, p. 209), who stated: "The more weakened the groups to which he belongs, the less he depends on them, the more he consequently depends only on himself and recognizes no other rules of conduct than what are founded on his private interests."

Hirschi argues that social integration into society is defined by four criteria: *attachment* through interpersonal and institutional integration, as I elaborated in Chapter 2; *commitment*, developed by a consideration of the costs of detachment; *involvement*, behavioral investment in the social order; and *belief*, an attitude of respect toward the rules of society, which I have called normative integration. As a socially integrated person, the individual internalizes the prescriptions of society and uses them as guides for behavior. There is no need for social control, because the integrated individual practices self-control.

Contrariwise, criminal and delinquent acts result when an individual does not feel a bond to society, defined by Durkheim (1951) as anomie. (Even though as a sociologist, Durkheim's theory of social integration did not depend upon the individual's recognition of anomie, he implicitly acknowledges the effects on behavior by being in this state. I will have more to say about this when I turn my attention in the next chapter to suicide as the ultimate self-destructive behavior.) As Gottfredson and Hirschi argue (1990), people suffering from this form of alienation do not internalize the rules by which society is governed and therefore lack appropriate self-control. As a result, they seek easy and immediate gratification of their desires and are stimulated by the risk involved in the anti-social acts that will do the job.

Self-control is not inborn. It is learned (or not) early in life from significant others, especially within the family and the school. The development of self-control in a young person is an intensive process, requiring much time and effort. When parents, teachers, advisors, and coaches do not take the socializing role seriously, the child is likely to develop anomie.

Once again, implicit in the process described by Hirschi is mattering. To neglect a child nominally in one's care by failing to encourage social integration is to tell a child: "You do not matter to me." The silence that accompanies being ignored sends a very clear message to the young person. It affirms that not all reflected appraisals are verbal. Further, confirmation often follows from the social comparisons the child can easily make. A youngster can't help but see the careful attention paid to others, the investment of time and resources given to them, and the limits set for their own good. What other self-attribution can the child make other than "I don't matter"?

A Symbolic Interactionist perspective on anti-social behavior takes a different tack. The sociologist Ross Matsueda (Matsueda & Heimer, 1997) begins with the premise that social control is accomplished, not in reaction to a unitary series of prescriptions and proscriptions equally applicable to all, but in the context of a multiplicity of social groups (family, friends, teachers at school). Hearkening back to the notion of role identity I presented in the previous chapter (McCall & Simmons, 1978; Stryker & Burke, 2000), they argue that behavior occurs in response to the expectations communicated by particular groups.

In this frame, life is a series of transitions, as people enact identities appropriate to the role that is primarily relevant in the current context. These transitions usually occur within a specific stage of development. A young man enacts the role of son when with his family, and the role of friend when with his buddies. They also occur as a person journeys through the life course. From the day of her wedding, a woman takes on a new role identity (spouse) and qualitatively changes an ongoing role identity (daughter).

From this perspective, a person claims role identities appropriate to the context for ongoing behavior. Young people are channeled into particular role identities by both recruitment and self-selection. On the one hand, parents socialize their children into their role as offspring. On the other hand, young people also make choices about the role identities they want to play and the nature of the role itself. The choice of extra-curricular activities in high school is just one example.

Matsueda concludes that adolescence, a time of important role transitions, is a critical time for development. In particular, he asserts: "In some cases, the meaning given to maturational processes increases the chances for delinquency" (Matsueda & Heimer, 1997, p. 191). If shaping a unique self means rebelling against the status quo, anti-social behavior is likely to follow. How the young person attaches meaning to his or her development is a function of the socialization practices of the most significant others in that growing person's life: parents, friends, and teachers.

Continuing in the Symbolic Interactionist perspective, the social psychologists Nicholas Emler and Stephen Reicher take a somewhat different approach. They argue (Emler & Reicher, 1995) that much of human behavior is influenced by considerations of social reputation. Building on the work of impression management theorists (Goffman, 1959), they argue that people will tailor their self-presentations for the benefit of the particular audience present in a social encounter. Further, in repeated interactions with the same audience or when audiences communicate with each other, memories of past managed impressions will carry over. In ensuring a consistent presented image over time, a person develops a *reputation*, a public image of the self that is shared by a collectivity.

Consistent with Symbolic Interactionist notions of the self (Mead, 1934), Emler and Reicher make it clear that reputation is not bestowed on a person by others. "Self definition, we argue, depends upon the reputations an individual is able to negotiate with significant audiences" (Emler & Reicher, 1995, p. 8). In addition, one needs to have a proffered situated identity accepted by others if a reputation is to be sustained over time. Acceptance is not automatic and may involve some identity bargaining (Blumstein, 1975), in which explicit negotiation involving all participants as to who one is in an encounter is required to yield a mutually acceptable identity.

As a result, much of social behavior involves "reputation management," in which actors take into account the fact that specific behaviors will have effects on identity that extend far beyond the current encounter. In addition, they must recognize that their reputation precedes them (unless the others have neither met nor heard of them) and therefore provides some constraints on impression management. One must act in ways that are consistent with a desired reputation, or risk losing it. On the other hand, a person may find it difficult to persuade others that a pre-existing undesired reputation should be dropped in favor of a proffered, socially desirable alternative.

This argument is especially relevant for adolescents. In the midst of the natural disturbances to the self experienced during this stage of development, one of the adolescent's major concerns is to define a self that is unique. While leaning heavily on others for support, it is crucial to become a person who is clearly distinguishable from them. Many are the labors of young people to convince the self (and others) that they are not simply copies of their parents. Part of the "uniqueness project" that is adolescence involves creating a reputation that will signify a person. For some, the desired reputation sets one apart from the "conformist" adults and solidifies a link with fellow "nonconformists." S. E. Hinton's (1967) novel *The Outsiders* is an excellent example of constructing and dealing with such a reputation.

The implication of this argument for anti-social behavior is interesting. Emler and Reicher hold that delinquency is not merely a label attached to an adolescent because of undesirable behavior. This gives the adolescent far too passive a role in the process. Instead, "[C]omission of, or abstention from, delinquent action is the principal means by which adolescents lay claim to oppositional or conformist identities. Delinquency is a form of self-presentation through which young people manage their public reputations" (Emler & Reicher, 1995, p. 7).

The relevance of mattering to the Symbolic Interactionist perspective on delinquency extends the theory of the motivational power of mattering beyond what I have developed so far. To the extent that adolescents are granted desired role identities (in my focus, offspring), they will know that they matter. And mattering is a strong incentive to behave in ways deemed appropriate to the specific identity in play. In contrast, those denied a claim to a role identity will recognize that they don't matter to those in their social world. Because of its importance to a child's development, being denied the role identity of child is especially threatening. They may then act in outrageous ways to force mattering (as with parents). A boy ignored by his family can put a dent in his father's car in order to command the father's attention. Alternatively, adolescents can attempt to escape this untenable situation by engaging in self-destructive behaviors.

For these reasons, I expect that mattering to family will decrease the likelihood of anti-social behavior. No matter how oppositional an adolescent's behavior is, most do not want to sever all ties (emotional, was well as material) with their parents. Indeed, the sociologist Richard Sennett (1980) contends that rebellion, far from signifying independence from authority, actually reveals one's psychological connection to it. Rebellion is, in fact, one of the "bonds of rejection" by which people create the illusion of freedom while emphasizing the importance of the authority figure in their lives. "The very act of disobeying, with all its confrontations, anxieties, and conflicts, knits people together" (Sennett, 1980, p. 33). Sennett argues that one does not rebel *against* authority, but rather, *within* authority. And so, a child's rebellion against its parents is guided by the realization that their wishes matter most. The young person disobeys, but in most cases, parents regulate the terms of that disobedience (Sennett, 1980, p. 33).

Relevant Research on Anti-Social Behavior

Perhaps the most comprehensive research on anti-social behavior in adolescence was conducted by the sociologist Delbert S. Elliott (Elliott, Huizinga, & Menard, 1989). Interviews with a nationwide sample of adolescents provided data on a wide range of delinquent behaviors; respondents were asked to report on any such behavior that had occurred within the last 12 months. Behaviors included assault, robbery and theft, public disorder, and vandalism (home and school).

Most relevant to the issue of mattering, Delbert Elliott and his colleagues found a positive link between family involvement (the amount of time devoted to family activities) and delinquency. Family involvement is not a measure of mattering, but it is a good proxy indicator for the concept. Parents who are involved in their child's behavior are sending messages of awareness and importance; when they communicate their expectations in appropriate ways, they are signaling their reliance on the child.

Recent research also suggests, albeit implicitly, that mattering to family can have a strong influence on the likelihood of delinquent behaviors. Parental monitoring (the extent to which parents are aware of their adolescents' whereabouts) is strongly related to anti-social behaviors (Barnes, Hoffman, Welte, Farrell, & Dintcheff, 2006). Similar results for parental monitoring were reported for African-American urban youth by Richards, Miller, O'Donnell, Wasserman, and Colder (2004).

Especially relevant to mattering, family studies researchers Brian K. Barber and Cheryl Buehler (1996, p. 433) make an important distinction between family cohesion ("shared affection, support, helpfulness, and caring among family members") and enmeshment ("family patterns that facilitate psychological and emotional fusion among family members"). The former encourages the healthy development of the self and certainly involves feelings of mattering, as it encourages independence without signaling abandonment. The latter is a method of control that works against healthy self-development and more involves manipulation than true mattering; it is an unwillingness of parents to let go of their children in appropriate ways. The researchers' results are what would be predicted by a consideration of mattering: Cohesion reduced acts of delinquency, whereas enmeshment actually increased anti-social behavior.

More generally, researchers Brent G. Goff and H. Wallace Goddard (1999) found that certain "terminal core values," including being well-respected, warm relationships with others, and a sense of belonging, were negatively associated with frequency of delinquency. These core values are made possible by knowing that one matters. When parents respect their children, it is a form of investment in the child. Respect also communicates reliance, as parents promise to let their children be who they are, but with the expectation that they will respect the needs of the family. A warm relationship is impossible without mattering. How can being ignored facilitate intimacy?

Preliminary Analysis: The Relationship between Mattering and Self-Esteem

Remember that scores on the Self-Esteem Index ranged from a possible low of 9 to a potential high of 45 (37 units in all) and scores on the Mattering Index ranged from 15 to 75 (61 units). The average level of self-esteem produced by setting the values of all the predictor variables (including the control variables) at their average is 39.111; that is, overall, the teenagers in the sample have reasonably healthy self-evaluations. This is the number to which the predicted values will be contrasted in calculating the significance for each category of the nominal or ordinal variables (age, sex, race/ethnicity, adult educational attainment, family structure, and religiosity), as well as contrasts made for specific values of the interval or ratio variables (mattering to family and number of children). In addition, note that the average level of mattering to family among the sample of adolescents is 66.688, a rather secure sense of mattering.

In order to establish the efficacy of self-esteem as a mediator of the relationship between mattering and anti-social behavior, I first have to demonstrate that mattering to family has a significant contribution to make with regard to level of self-esteem. This will establish the first link in the chain model: mattering → self-esteem.

Accordingly, I begin by examining a model in which self-esteem is a function of mattering and the control variables, using Ordinary Least Squares Regression. The results show strong support for the relationship.

They are illustrated in the predicted self-esteem scores found in Table 4.1. The differences traceable to mattering to the family are notable. When mattering scores drop from the average to three standard deviations below, self-esteem scores decline over eight units. Given the impact of self-esteem on most of the outcomes I analyze in this book, this betokens a strong performance for mattering to family through self-esteem. That is, because differences in levels of mattering to family are associated with changes in self-esteem scores, the contribution of self-esteem on the likelihood of engaging in a

Table 4.1 Predicted Self-Esteem Scores as a Function of Mattering to Family and the Control Variables

Independent Variable	*Predicted Self-Esteem Score*
Mattering to Family	
Mean (66.7539)	39.111
One Standard Deviation Below	36.396
Two Standard Deviations Below	33.682
Three Standard Deviations Below	30.967
Age	
11–12	38.452
13	38.882
14	38.829
15	38.664
16	39.499
17	39.708
18	39.746
Sex	
Male	39.730
Female	38.492
Race/Ethnicity	
Non-Hispanic White	39.132
Non-Hispanic Black	40.214
Hispanic	38.540
Adult Respondent's Educational Attainment	
Less Than High School	37.970
High School Diploma	39.311
Some College	39.213
College Diploma	39.345
Postgraduate Study	39.718
Family Structure	
Never Married	39.392
Previously Married	38.931
Married	39.011
Importance of Religion	
Not Important	39.096
Fairly Important	39.061
Very Important	39.095
Extremely Important	39.193

Table 4.1 *(cont'd)*

Independent Variable	*Predicted Self-Esteem Score*
Number of Children in Household	
1	41.088
2	41.120
4	41.185
6	41.250
8	41.315

N = 1792

particular behavior will be partly determined by the respondent's feeling of mattering to family.

Incidentally, as expected, most of the control variables also make a difference in self-esteem scores. The youngest children (11–12) have self-esteem levels that are significantly below the average. But it is not until the 17-year-olds that self-esteem levels again deviate from the average, this time rising above. The 18-year-olds are only marginally significant in their increase above the average level of self-esteem.

Turning to contrasts between age groups, the scores for the youngest groups (11–15) do not differ from each other. The older age groups (16–18) differ from the younger, but not from each other. This result reaffirms Rosenberg's (1979) finding that the early adolescents suffer from deficiencies in self-esteem but improve as they reach the later years.

Consistent with past research (Kimmel, 2007), boys evaluate themselves more positively than girls. Interestingly, blacks have higher levels of self-esteem than whites and Hispanics, whereas Hispanics and whites do not differ from each other. This result must be taken with a grain of salt, however, in light of the research by Rosenberg and Simmons (1972), which showed that black–white differences in self-esteem are a function of the social context in which the black child matures. Those blacks living in a consonant social context (neighborhoods and schools populated mostly by blacks) had self-esteem levels at least as high as whites. In contrast, blacks living in a dissonant social context (neighborhoods and schools populated mostly by whites) were harsher judges of themselves than were whites. I am not able to distinguish between consonant and dissonant social contexts, so I cannot know if context is playing a role in adolescent self-esteem in this case.

The family's socioeconomic status also contributes to the self-esteem of the respondents. Compared to the average respondent, those from families with the lowest education level (less than high school diploma) have lower levels of self-esteem, and those from the highest level (post-graduate study) evaluate themselves more positively. When teenagers from different educational levels are compared, those whose parents did not obtain a high school diploma had lower levels of self-esteem than respondents from any other level of attainment. Further, no category of educational attainment differed from any other of the remaining categories. Self-esteem is almost uniformly higher for all other levels of education. This is consistent with past research (Rosenberg, 1989; Rosenberg & Pearlin, 1978).

The structure of the family made no difference in levels of self-esteem, contrary to results found in other studies (Flouri, 2004; Garnefski & Diekstra, 1997; Wallerstein, Lewis, & Blakeslee, 2000). Similarly, number of children in the family did not yield significant differences in self-esteem. Neither did religiosity.

Truancy

> *The Founding Fathers in their wisdom decided that children were an unnatural strain on parents. So they provided jails called schools, equipped with tortures called an education. School is where you go between when your parents can't take you and industry can't take you.*
>
> John Updike, *The centaur*

The first anti-social behavior under consideration involves absenting oneself from the daily high school curriculum. It is a relatively harmless behavior that makes a statement of autonomy, usually without incurring serious legal or social consequences. The classic film depiction of truancy *Ferris Bueller's Day Off* (1986) presents a fun-loving trio who make a day of it in Chicago on a whim. No one is hurt, nothing is ruined, and the "adult" world is no worse off for the adventure (except for the school principal, who adds enjoyment to the truants' day by his futile attempts to catch them in the act). For those who believe they do not matter to their families, it is an easy way of commanding their parents' attention.

The survey contained two questions on this matter. One asked about skipping classes ("During the last four weeks, how often have you gone

Figure 4.1 Mattering, Self-Esteem, and Truancy

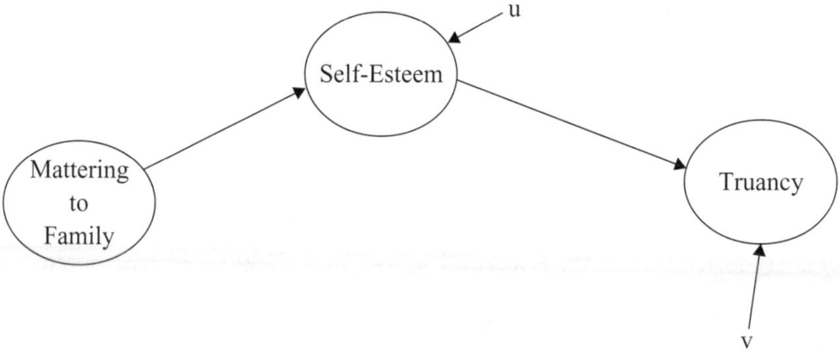

Note: Arrows from sources labeled with a lower case letter represent the contributions from factors not contained in the data (including randomness).

to school, but skipped a class when you weren't supposed to?") and skipping school ("During the last four weeks, how many whole days of school have you missed because you skipped or 'cut'?"). Because the results of the analyses were virtually identical for each variable, I have combined them into a single measure for increased reliability in the analysis. Respondents who *either* skipped classes *or* whole days of school were classified as truants. Those who reported *neither* behavior received a non-truant classification. With all the behavioral outcome variables, I use Logistic Regression to conduct the analysis.

Overall, the probability that a randomly selected adolescent is classified as a truant is not very high (.257), a result that should provide some comfort to parents. The question of import is the extent to which this probability changes when examining specific subgroups of this sample.

Consider first the relationship between mattering and truancy (without taking self-esteem into account). The pictorial representation of these results is given in Figure 4.1, and the estimated probabilities are in Table 4.2.

The first panel of Table 4.2 reveals the differential impact on the overall probability of truancy across variations in mattering to family. The less one matters to one's family, the more one is likely to be a truant. As mattering scores descend from the average to the lowest point in the table, the chances of delinquency rise from about one in four to more than one in three. This ascent in probabilities is statistically significant, so one can say that mattering to family does deter an adolescent from skipping classes or cutting school entirely.

Table 4.2 Probability of School Truancy

	Panel 1 Mattering Only	*Panel 2 Mattering and Self-Esteem*	
Level of Index	*Mattering to Family*	*Mattering to Family*	*Self-Esteem*
Mean	.230	.256	.256
One Standard Deviation Below	.263	.260	.326
Two Standard Deviations Below	.300	.264	.404
Three Standard Deviations Below	.339	.268	.488
Significance Level	$p < .001$	n.s.	$p < .001$

The p-value reported in the Significance Level row is the probability of falsely claiming a significant difference in the likelihood of truancy across levels of the index. (n.s. means the probability is greater than .10).
N = 1758

Now, I will turn to the elaborated model, in which self-esteem is added to the analysis. Panel 2 of Table 4.2 reveals the consequences. First, note that self-esteem is an important factor in the decision to engage in this form of anti-social behavior. As self-esteem decreases, the likelihood of truancy increases sharply. Indeed, almost half the adolescents situated at the lowest level of self-esteem presented in the table can be expected to misbehave in this way.

The second thing to notice is the change in the pattern of probabilities across mattering to family. The differences have shrunk dramatically, so much, in fact, that they are no longer statistically meaningful. With the addition of self-esteem, mattering to family becomes a negligible predictor of truancy.

But wait! This does *not* mean that mattering to family is unimportant for understanding the likelihood of cutting school or classes. Remember from the preliminary analysis that mattering to family is a strong predictor of self-esteem. Combining this result with the outcome that self-esteem as a powerful predictor of truancy, I have now established both links in the chain model: mattering to family → self-esteem → truancy.

In other words, there *is* a strong association between mattering to family and unauthorized school absences in adolescence. Although there is no *direct* relationship between the two, the data evince a substantial *indirect* relationship. This result is entirely consistent with my argument that, as a fundamental motivator within the self, mattering may act on behavior, not directly, but by stimulating another motivator (self-esteem), which in turn will lead to behavior.

Examining the contributions of the control variables to this form of delinquency, I found that age plays an important role. As one gets older, the likelihood of truancy increases, beginning with a low of .064 for the 11- to 12-year-olds. The probability begins to build for those ages 13–17 (.140, 158, .257, .309, and .427, respectively). At 18, it decreases to .316.

The youngest age group is not differentiable from the 13-year-olds but is significantly lower in probability than all other older ages. The 13-year olds are significantly different from all other age groups, except for the 14-year-olds. The ages 15, 16, and 18 differ only from the 17-year-olds, the latter showing a significantly higher probability of truancy than any other age group. These results yield a curvilinear relationship between age and truancy: The probabilities at first increase with age, but after 17, they begin to decrease.

Gender makes no difference in truancy probabilities (males: .278; females: .235). However, race/ethnicity does. Non-Hispanic blacks and whites have negligible differences in cutting classes or school (.166 vs. .191). On the other hand, Hispanics show a significantly greater probability (.344) than either blacks or whites.

Neither socioeconomic status, nor family structure, nor number of children in the household predicts truancy. However, religiosity shows a strong contribution: Those for whom religion is not important have a much greater likelihood of cutting class or school (.343) than the average respondent. The probabilities for the other levels of religiosity do not differ from that of the average teenager in the sample (.246 for Fairly Important; .237 for Very Important; and .208 for Extremely Important). In addition, these probabilities do not differ from each other, even as they are significantly lower than that for the irreligious adolescents.

Overall, then, I conclude that mattering to family is a strong contributor to truancy. The more adolescents believe that they matter to their families, the less likely they are to take unauthorized "vacations" from a single class or school in general. However, this contribution is entirely channeled through self-esteem: Mattering to family leads to higher levels of self-esteem, which in turn decreases the likelihood of truancy.

Vandalism

Killroy was here

Graffito found on many edifices in Europe during World War II, written by American GIs

Vandalism is malicious damage to property that is not one's own. It can take many forms, including graffiti on public buildings, "egging" a car or house, and outright destruction of property. Legal authorities and many of the citizenry of a community decry acts of destruction and want the perpetrators to be severely punished. Even though they may not be identified, the vandals make their mark on the social order and assure themselves that they are people to be noticed.

As with truancy, two questions from the survey were available for the analysis. The first asked about vandalism directed toward family members ("How many times in the last year have you purposely damaged or destroyed property belonging to your parents or other family members?"); the second focused on other targets ("How many times in the last year have you purposely damaged or destroy other property that did not belong to you, your parents, or other family members?"). As before, because the results of the analyses were virtually identical for each variable, I have combined them into a single measure for increased reliability in the analysis. Respondents who damaged *either* their family's *or* another's property were classified as vandals. Those who reported *neither* behavior received a non-vandal classification. Overall, the probability that a randomly selected adolescent is classified as a vandal is .136, a rather low likelihood.

As before, the representation of the relationships involving mattering to family, self-esteem, and vandalism is depicted in Figure 4.2. The probability estimates for vandalism are in Table 4.3.

Beginning with the influence of mattering, the first panel of Table 4.3 provides the probabilities of vandalism for selected levels of mattering. From the table, one can see that mattering to family makes a difference in the probability of vandalism among the adolescents in the sample. Although the increases are not great on an absolute scale,

Figure 4.2 Mattering, Self-Esteem, and Vandalism

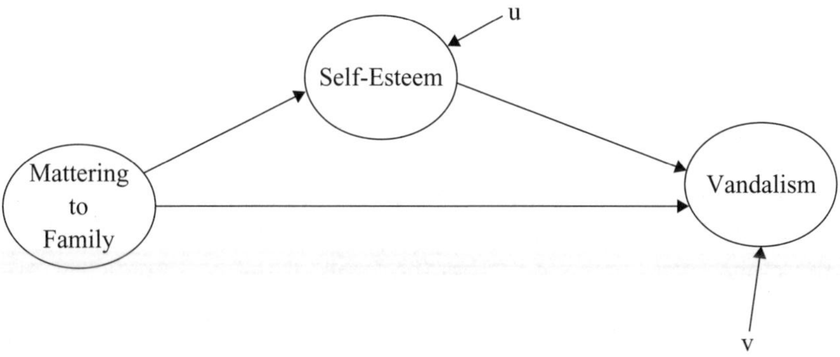

Note: Arrows from sources labeled with a lower case letter represent the contributions from factors not contained in the data (including randomness).

Table 4.3 Probability of Vandalism

	Panel 1 Mattering Only	*Panel 2 Mattering and Self-Esteem*	
Level of Index	*Mattering to Family*	*Mattering to Family*	*Self-Esteem*
Mean	.130	.115	.115
One Standard Deviation Below	.164	.134	.139
Two Standard Deviations Below	.205	.157	.168
Three Standard Deviations Below	.253	.201	.201
Significance Level	$p < .001$	$p < .05$	$p < .01$

The p-value reported in the Significance Level row is the probability of falsely claiming a significant difference in the likelihood of vandalism across levels of the index (n.s. means the probability is greater than .10).
N = 1789

the probability of vandalism nearly doubles in a contrast between those with the average level of mattering to family and those at the lowest level examined.

Adding self-esteem to the analysis reveals its powerful contribution to the probability of vandalism. As self-esteem decreases, the likelihood of vandalism increases. Apparently, the bad feeling that accompanies a poor evaluation of the self is taken out on things that belong to others.

The mediating property of self-esteem in the mattering–vandalism relationship is different from that found for truancy. It is the case that the contribution of mattering to family is reduced when self-esteem is a part of the analysis, but it is not entirely eliminated. There is still a significant increase in the probability of vandalism as mattering to family declines, but the magnitude of that increase is lower. Indeed, the range of probabilities across the levels of the two predictor variables (mattering to family and self-esteem) is identical. The presence of a continuing direct contribution in the face of self-esteem's strong performance indicates that self-esteem only partly intervenes in the relationship between mattering to family and vandalism.

What does this mean? It is not entirely clear. First, it might mean that something in failing to matter to one's family directly triggers the urge to vandalize (even though it did not happen with regard to truancy). Why self-esteem should be a complete mediator for one outcome and not another is also not clear, and if there is a part of mattering that does differentiate between these two delinquent behaviors, we social psychologists have not discovered it yet.

Second, it may be the case that there is another factor, not acknowledged by the current status of theories of the self, which plays a role in the process, if only we would recognize it. It might be an additional intervening variable between mattering and vandalism, an additional precursor to vandalism that stands apart from mattering, or something prior to both mattering and self-esteem. In any case, its absence means that its association with vandalism is at least partly absorbed by the direct relationship segment of the model, thereby giving a false sense of the nature of the mattering–vandalism relationship. Its inclusion in the analysis would sharply reduce, if not erase, the direct component for mattering. If this is the case, until researchers on the self come up with a more complex theory that "sees" it, the direct relationship I found is a glaring admission of ignorance.

The choice between these two possibilities depends on the stance one takes with regard to current theory. A social psychologist can either plumb the depths of the concept, convinced that mattering is even more complex than we have realized to date, or look for other aspects of the self that could step in to erase the direct association between mattering to family and vandalism. The complexity of humans and their behavior with others assures us that there will always be more to know.

There is relatively little explanatory power for vandalism among the control variables. Age has a non-linear relationship with vandalism. The youngest teenagers (11–12) are less likely (.086) than the average adolescent to vandalize property. The 13-year-olds and older (16–18) teenagers do not differ from the average in their propensity for vandalism (13: .124; 16: .094; 17: .107; 18: .092). It is just as the young person is beginning to recover from self-concept disturbance (14 and 15; probabilities: .168 and 155, respectively) that the chances for vandalism rise.

In comparing the age levels to each other, the 14-year-olds, with the highest probability of vandalism, are significantly different from all ages except the 13-year-olds. The next-highest age, 15, is higher in probability than all other age groups, except the 17-year-olds. No other age contrasts are significant.

Another difference is found with sex. All other things being equal, males have more than double the chance of damaging property (.162) compared to females (.080). No other control variable plays a role in distinguishing levels of probability for vandalism.

Once again, mattering to family has much to say as to whether or not an adolescent will engage in anti-social behavior. In this instance, however, self-esteem is only a partial mediator of this relationship. The lower the level of mattering to family, the greater the chances of vandalism, part of it direct and part of it indirect, through self-esteem.

Dealing in Contraband

I'm the son of a preacher man, momma knows I'm thuggin'
And I should of been a chef the way I cook crack up your oven met
Teachers taught us "just say no", I had to hustle though
Even that I stayed broke, didn't want to struggle so
Buy half and eight ball, hit the block runnin'
Thought the world was mine, till I saw the cops coming
And it's too late.

South Park Mexican, Dope house family

A more serious way that adolescents can get into trouble is to deal in illegal or stolen goods. The risk of being apprehended is serious, and the consequences can be more hazardous. The drug gang depicted in the Home Box Office series *The Wire*, created by writer David Simon, is a crew ever on the alert for the police ("5–0"), to say nothing of rival gangs. They constantly make reference to the fact that "real society" cares nothing for them and for those who live in the Baltimore housing projects with them.

They are perfect examples of Merton's (1938) strain theory of deviance. They accept the preaching of our symbolic universe that success, in the form of wealth and respect, is appropriate for all. But they know all too well that the current structures of society do not provide them the means to success. These gangs do not have the wherewithal to change the structures. Rather than reject the universally prescribed goal of success, they are forced to work outside the system.

The wealth is undeniable, but it is the respect that they treasure. The respect is built on fear, and some in the gangs occasionally sense that there could be a better form of respect. Nevertheless, it allows them to feel superior to the "mopes" who matter to no one at all. And, as Richard Sennett (2003, p. 53) notes: "[I]t's the superior whose needs count and who gets recognition."

This is their way of making a name for themselves, feared and abhorred, perhaps, but a name nonetheless. When apprehended, they often act as celebrities, basking in their "fifteen minutes of fame" on the local newscasts. Indeed, I recently heard of a case from a prosecutor (personal communication from S. Lambiase, 2007) in which the defendant beamed with joy upon encountering the assistant district attorney (ADA) prosecuting his case, saying to his friends, "Hey, everybody, that's my ADA!" Even though she was trying to put the youth away for a long time, the prosecutor was paying attention to him. It goes to show that negative mattering is better than not mattering at all.

One study by the sociologists Kathleen Harris, Greg Duncan, and Johanne Boisjoly (2002) is very relevant to questions of mattering and selling drugs. They found that adolescents who had "nothing to lose" (measured as not expecting to live beyond the age of 35) were much more likely to deal in drugs than those who expected to live longer.

Two questions in the survey allow me to examine the relationship between mattering and dealing. First, respondents were asked about dealing in stolen goods ("How many times in the last year have you knowingly bought, sold, or held stolen goods or tried to do any of these things?"). Next, they responded to a similar item regarding illegal

Figure 4.3 Mattering, Self-Esteem, and Dealing in Contraband

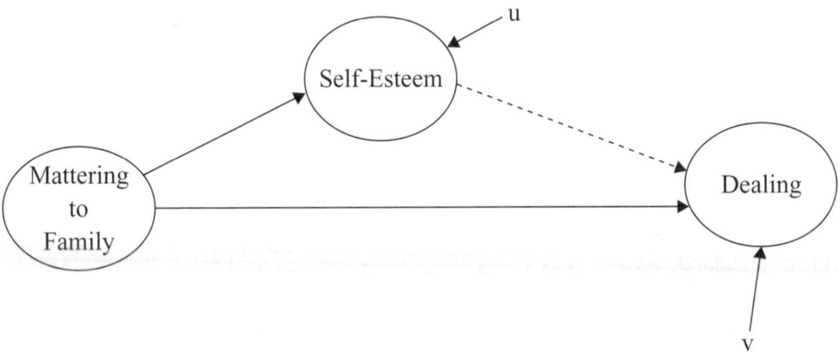

Note: Arrows from sources labeled with a lower case letter represent the contributions from factors not contained in the data (including randomness).

material ("How many times in the last year have you knowingly bought, sold, or held illegal goods, such as drugs, etc.?"). Because these activities are riskier, relatively few respondents engaged in them, especially dealing in stolen goods (60 respondents).

As a result, in order to improve the reliability of the analysis, I combined the two variables into a single measure of dealing. Respondents who dealt in *either* illegal *or* stolen goods were classified as dealers. Those who reported *neither* behavior received a non-dealing classification. In addition, there is a dearth of young people dealing in contraband, so I combined the ages between 11 and 14 into a single category. This produced enough young respondents to make the age contrasts feasible. Overall, the probability that a randomly selected adolescent is classified as a dealer is .098, a quite low likelihood.

Figure 4.3 gives the pictorial representation of the results, whereas Table 4.4 presents the probability estimates from the analysis. As before, mattering to family has a strong and significant impact on the likelihood of dealing, and the pattern is now familiar: The more one makes a difference, the less likely one will deal in contraband. From the mean to the lowest level present in the table, the probability rises from .095 to .195. That is, about two out of ten respondents who matter least can be expected to be dealing, all other things being equal.

When self-esteem is introduced, things don't change all that much. First, as self-esteem declines, the likelihood of dealing increases, from .145 at the mean to .226 at the lowest level presented in the table.

Table 4.4 Probability of Dealing in Contraband

	Panel 1 Mattering Only	*Panel 2 Mattering and Self-Esteem*	
Level of Index	*Mattering to Family*	*Mattering to Family*	*Self-Esteem*
Mean	.095	.145	.145
One Standard Deviation Below	.122	.171	.169
Two Standard Deviations Below	.152	.199	.196
Three Standard Deviations Below	.195	.234	.226
Significance Level	p < .001	p < .05	p < .10

The p-value reported in the Significance Level row is the probability of falsely claiming a significant difference in the likelihood of truancy across levels of the index (n.s. means the probability is greater than .10).
N = 1791

However, the estimate for self-esteem attains only a marginal level of statistical significance.

Second, mattering to family maintains pretty much the same strong relationship with dealing (dropping from .145 at the mean to .234 at the lowest level in the table). Therefore, it appears that self-esteem does not meaningfully mediate the relationship between mattering and dealing in contraband.

Two of the control variables differentiate among those who do and do not deal in contraband. Not surprisingly, age makes a difference. Compared to the average probability, that for the 11- to 14-year-olds is significantly lower (.038), whereas the 16-year-olds are significantly more likely than average to deal in contraband (.224). None of the other probabilities differs from the average.

The contrasts in probabilities between age groups are only significant between the 11–14 category (.038) and all other age groups. When an adolescent reaches the age of 15, the likelihood of dealing in contraband varies very little across age (15: 174; 16: .224; 17: .197; and 18: .213).

Gender is a strong case. Males in the sample are more than one and one-half times as likely to deal in contraband as females (.186 vs. .112), a fact well known to researchers on the topic (Perl, 1992; Hutton, 2005). The adolescent's religiosity also carries much weight. Each category of religiosity differs significantly from the overall average and from each other. The probabilities decrease monotonically as religiosity increases (not important: .260; fairly important: .185; very important: .110; and extremely important: 078). None of the other control variables attains significance.

Therefore, mattering to family diverts an adolescent from dealing in contraband. The role of self-esteem is less clear. Its contribution to dealing is statistically marginal, although the changes in probability are no less impressive than those found for mattering. Because of this, its role as a mediator is questionable. I am in the vexing situation of failing to reject the null hypothesis of no contribution. I cannot conclude that self-esteem is not important, because failure to reject the null does not imply its acceptance. I am in limbo, and answers must wait until further research is conducted.

Theft from the Family

Revenge is sweet but not nourishing.

Mason Cooley, *City aphorisms*

Most people would rate stealing from one's own family as a very serious rejection of the role identity associated with the position of offspring. It is a violation of the trust that parents place in their children, and, if discovered, is likely to lead to grave consequences. Both parents and children realize this, even if it is never articulated within the family. Therefore, if an adolescent does steal, there must be a noteworthy motivation at its root.

Mattering, as the most fundamental motivation seeded within the self, surely fills the bill. As I have argued in Chapter 1, there can be no greater rejection of a young person's role identity as offspring than failing to matter to one's family. Being a non-person in a family is a frightening and enraging experience, and most children will be impelled to redress this grievance. As payback and as a plea for attention, theft from those who have rejected you is one way an adolescent might respond to the ultimate slight. If you are not caught, you have made

Figure 4.4 Mattering, Self-Esteem, and Theft from One's Family

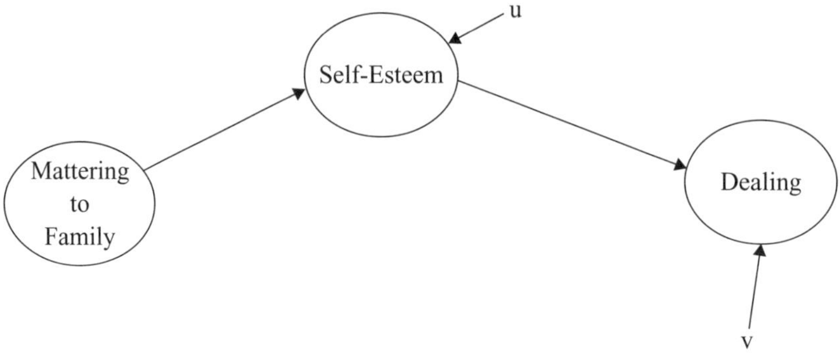

Note: Arrows from sources labeled with a lower case letter represent the contributions from factors not contained in the data (including randomness).

it clear to yourself that you are not to be trifled with, and those who do treat you so badly will pay for their transgressions. If you are caught, you will be successful in capturing the attention of those who usually pay you no mind. In either case, you will have reduced, if only a little, the terrifying recognition that your family cares so little about you. Or so it at least seems to the terrified son or daughter.

In general, it is highly unusual for an adolescent to steal from his or her family. In fact, the data reveal that only about one in twenty (probability: .046) breach the family's trust in this manner. Nevertheless, it is still possible to differentiate among those who do.

Figure 4.4 gives the graphic representation of the results. Table 4.5 offers the probability estimates for Theft from Family.

Mattering to family is a significant predictor of theft from the family. The probability increases almost more than two and one-half times, from .047 at the average level of mattering to family to .115 for teenagers who are at the lowest level given in the table.

When self-esteem enters the analysis, its impact on theft is considerable. The probability of theft is more than two and one-half times as great, rising from .045 at the mean to .121 at the lowest level of self-esteem, three standard deviations below the mean.

In addition, self-esteem fully mediates the relationship between mattering to family and theft from the family. The differences in probabilities across levels of mattering are very small. In other words, mattering protects against theft from the family by raising self-esteem levels, and more self-esteem means less stealing from one's own family.

Table 4.5 Probability of Theft from Family

	Panel 1 *Mattering Only*	*Panel 2* *Mattering and Self-Esteem*	
Level of Index	*Mattering to Family*	*Mattering to Family*	*Self-Esteem*
Mean	.047	.045	.045
One Standard Deviation Below	.064	.052	.063
Two Standard Deviations Below	.086	.059	.088
Three Standard Deviations Below	.115	.068	.121
Significance Level	p < .001	n.s.	p < .001

The p-value reported in the Significance Level row is the probability of falsely claiming a significant difference in the likelihood of truancy across levels of the index (n.s. means the probability is greater than .10).
N = 1779

Interestingly, none of the control variables makes a difference in the likelihood of stealing from the family. Each category for every variable does not differ from the overall probability of theft; nor, for a given predictor variable, do they differ from each other (except for the 15-year-olds).

Physical Violence

Although the anti-social acts studied to this point are strongly disapproved by our symbolic universe, none is likely to bring injury to another person. They may cause annoyance, loss of material goods, and psychological pain to people (and none of these outcomes is to be dismissed), but they are not generally a threat to life and limb. For many in our society, physical violence is the most extreme kind of anti-social behavior, perhaps even in a class by itself, precisely because injury is involved. Aggression may be aimed at the victim, but it also captures the attention of those who witness or learn about it. Again and again, local and national news broadcasts lead with a grisly report of violence. The viewers' attention is captured, if only for a brief time, as the accused is paraded past a string of media reporters, beginning a flirtation with fame. If the violence is heinous enough (such as the shootings in 1999 at Columbine High School), web sites may even be created that inevitably memorialize the perpetrator as well as the victims.

The social psychologist Leonard Berkowitz (1993) made a seminal contribution to our understanding of why people do violence to others. Building on theories formed by the psychologists John Dollard and Neil Miller (Dollard, Doob, Miller, Mowrer, & Sears, 1939), Berkowitz argued that the spur to aggression is frustration, "an external condition that prevents a person from obtaining the pleasures he or she had expected to enjoy" (Berkowitz, 1993, p. 31).

But not every instance of frustration leads to aggression. We all can recall instances in our own lives in which we have been prevented from reaching a desired goal, and we have not injured the person responsible, or anyone else, for that matter. Many college students have been denied requests they made of the registrar's office, but very few have taken violent action against the registrar.

Berkowitz's extension of Dollard and Miller's theory was that only certain kinds of frustration would lead to aggression. Frustrations that are deemed personal, intentional, and arbitrary would do the job.

A personal frustration is aimed at the individual alone and no others. Of all those seeking goals, only this one person is prevented from attaining it. A young woman trying to get into a favorite dance club may see others allowed in freely by the doorman, but she is refused entry. If the insult is serious enough, violence could follow.

Intentional frustrations are not accidents. Every one of us has been kept from a goal because an accident occurred. A road washed out from a thunderstorm's pelting rain keeps a man from making the appointment for a job interview. He may feel disappointment and even anger, but it is highly unlikely that he will aggress against someone. Even when the frustration comes from an accident caused by another person, there is much less likelihood of violence than if it is clear that someone tried to foil one's goal attainment. Another driver who collides with our job seeker in this terrible weather may be considered a clumsy oaf but is not likely to be beaten up because of it.

Finally, frustration more often leads to violence when it is perceived as unfair or arbitrary. Sometimes, the rules of life make frustration inevitable. Waiting in a long line at the Department of Motor Vehicles only to find the service windows closing because it is the end of the workday is very annoying, but we have been taught that service organizations are open for a limited amount of time. Most of us understand that we will be denied our goal in that circumstance, and we do not accost the workers who are leaving. However, when someone seems to single you out for frustration, violence may ensue. A driver who cuts abruptly in front of another may be risking attack, a phenomenon well known as "road rage."

When frustration is perceived to be personal, intentional, and arbitrary, Berkowitz argues that a strong physiological reaction, which he calls negative affect, impels a person to violence. This reaction is primitive and rudimentary and can best be characterized as rage. It is a holdover from our early existence as human beings, before our cognitive capacities had evolved into the more sophisticated stage that we now experience.

The rage that characterizes the arousal of negative affect is not anger, for as the psychologist Stanley Schachter (1964) discovered, anger and other emotions are cognitive constructs, created by a labeling process that follows physiological arousal and helps give a name to it. No, negative affect is a far more primitive response to frustration. It occurs prior to any cognitive activity on our part and is therefore much more difficult to control than a constructed emotion such as anger. When people speak of "seeing red" in reaction to a frustration, they are probably referring to their experience of this negative affect. It causes both the flight and fight responses and triggers behavior before we can think about it. If the circumstances are facilitative, one of those behaviors is aggression. We lash out at the perpetrator of the illegitimate frustration, or anyone who can be even remotely connected to the frustration.

Failing to matter is deeply frustrating, as it keeps a person from taking on role identities that are necessary for social interaction. It is also likely to be understood as a personal frustration, because an individual is being told that he or she is invisible. Even if others are frustrated as well, if they are all targeted because of some common characteristic, then it is possible to see the personal nature of the frustration in the prejudicial treatment of a whole group (including the individual) because of the characteristics that they all share as members of the group. Minorities who are told that it is nothing personal, but "their kind" are not welcome are hardly likely to be reassured. They will take the frustration personally, and the likelihood of aggression increases.

Failing to matter may also be seen as intentional. When another continually flouts a person's legitimate basic claims to a role identity by signaling that he or she doesn't matter, this cannot be construed as an accident. A single instance of being ignored can be attributed to non-malicious intentions, but after a series of interactions in which one perceives a failure to matter, how can a person come to any other conclusion but that it is intentional?

Finally, being continually treated as a non-person is unlikely to be seen as legitimate. In some circumstances, it may be necessary, as when a doctor ignores her patient's family as she tries to help a suffering victim. But more generally, Erving Goffman (1971) has argued that there are ground rules, usually implicit, that cover social encounters, to assure they will be smoothly conducted. As I have argued elsewhere (Elliott, Ziegler, Altman, & Scott, 1982), the first such rule is that any participant's legitimate status in an interaction must not be questioned without cause. When a role identity implies legitimacy, all are expected to honor the person's legitimate status and give that person the benefit of the doubt until evidence suggests that it should be questioned. A son who is "told" he does not matter to his family is denied the legitimacy of his role identity, and therefore his claim on the attention of, investment from, and the opportunity to contribute to his family. This basic and unfair frustration will arouse that primitive negative affect and may very well lead to violence.

The psychiatrist James Gilligan, former medical director of the Bridgewater (Massachusetts) State Hospital for the Criminally Insane and former director of the Center for the Study of Violence at the Harvard Medical School, has added greatly to our understanding of violence by introducing the concept of shame as an essential source of the impulse to do harm. In his book on the subject, Gilligan (1996, p. 11; emphasis in the original) asserts that "*all violence is an attempt to achieve justice*, or what the violent person perceives as justice." The sense that one has been insulted or thwarted evokes a powerful feeling of shame, because our symbolic universe teaches us that people must be in control of their own lives and vulnerable to no one.

Shame is not the same as guilt, although both are reactions to negative self-appraisals. The psychologist Helen B. Lewis (1971, p. 30; emphasis in the original) made a sharp distinction between the two:

> The experience of shame is directly about the *self*, which is the focus of evaluation. In guilt, the self is not the central object of negative

> evaluation, but rather the *thing* done or undone is the focus. In guilt, the self is negatively evaluated in connection with something but is not itself the focus of the experience.

Similarly, the psychologist June Price Tangney (1990, p. 103; emphasis in the original) writes: "[G]uilt involves the perception that one has done something 'bad.' But although the person experiencing guilt may experience it for the moment *as if* he or she is a bad person, his or her self-concept and identity remain exactly the same." In contrast, with shame "the entire self is painfully scrutinized and negatively evaluated."

In other words, guilt is a negative feeling about the self attached to a specific act. One may atone for hurtful behavior and thereby expiate the guilt attached to it. With shame, there is no redemption. Shame means that the entire self is deemed seriously unworthy. Shame is characterological, that is, it puts an indelible "black mark" on the self that can never be erased. Whereas guilt may motivate a person to make amends and reconnect to others, shame broadens the gulf between the offender and all others, not just the offended one.

One source of shame is the failure to matter. To be a non-person, ignored by others is to face the possibility that there is nothing worthy of their attention, nothing for them to invest in, and nothing to offer them. In a society that glorifies the individual and insists that people demonstrate their noteworthiness (Sennett, 2003), having nothing of note to claim for the self is a shameful acknowledgment.

Please note that I do not have the necessary information in the data to test the actual workings of frustration and shame. Then again, neither did Berkowitz and Gilligan, respectively. Berkowitz's (1993) laboratory experiments never assessed the extent to which the frustrations perceived by his subjects were taken as personal, intentional, and arbitrary; he assumed that they were. He also had no way to measure the arousal of negative affect. Similarly, in his discussions with prisoners, Gilligan (1996) inferred the presence of shame from the words they spoke; he did not present them with a specific measure to ascertain it. As they did, I simply lay the conceptual groundwork for the processes that I believe underlie the relationship between perception of mattering and committing violence.

Now imagine the working of both processes (frustration and shame) within the context of the family. Is there any greater frustration for an adolescent than to know that he or she does not matter to the family? The young person's security evaporates, and guidance in life must be sought elsewhere. When parents abandon their role identities and deny that of the child, how is the adolescent supposed to react? Surely, the frustration is experienced as deeply personal. This is *my* parent, who is to care for *me*, support *me*, and teach *me* about being a person. It is also intentional. They didn't "forget" to be my parents; they simply refuse to do it. Finally, it is certainly illegitimate. They are *required by society* to play out the role identity. No matter what I do, or who I am, they are not supposed to abandon me like this. The negative affect aroused by this realization must be especially powerful, for no greater threat to the self is possible, and violence becomes an easy way to relieve the frustration. In contrast, the teenager who matters to his or her family feels none of this devastating frustration, and the possibility of violence is likely to be limited to an occasional fantasy.

Similarly, there must be great shame in being rejected by one's family. No greater statement of social invisibility could be made. Adolescents who do not merit simple attention, investment, or reliance from those ostensibly at the center of their lives would want to keep this a secret from others, but it would be impossible to ignore it themselves. Being a nonentity is shameful in general, but when it is one's own family that considers a person such, it strikes at the core of the self. It would take a great deal of aggression to restore a person's self-image.

In violence research relevant to mattering, Todd Franke (2000), a public policy researcher, found that a secure attachment to family and school militated against aggressive behavior. As I have argued in Chapter 2, absent mattering, people will not form secure attachments, and the attachment is not there to protect the adolescent from violent behavior. Franke's results offer a proxy support for the assertion that mattering will reduce violence.

Next, consider the relationship between self-esteem and violence. For a long time, social psychologists posited an inverse relationship between self-esteem and violence. As Gilligan (1996) asserted, violence is a means to erase shame and restore "pride" in the self. And some prior research (Ali & Toner, 2001; Merwin & Ellis, 2004; Oates & Forrest, 1985) has supported the hypothesis.

Baumeister (Bushman & Baumeister, 1998) disagrees. He posits that it is narcissism, rather than low self-esteem, that facilitates hostile and angry behaviors. According to Baumeister, narcissism is a heightened self-focus that protects an unstable (not consistently negative) evaluation of the self. It is the person who is not sure of his or her self-worth but suspects that it is low who is most defensive and responds to threats by lashing out at others. It should be noted that in the laboratory experiments that supported his argument, aggression consisted of subjecting another to an annoying blast of loud noise. Still, it is an interesting argument that deserves application to more serious forms of aggression.

I argue that if one does not matter, especially to significant others, it is very easy to make the attribution that it is because there is nothing worthwhile in one's self to "earn" mattering. Feeling worthless is perhaps the ultimate frustration; it severely limits the chances for healthy development and future success. Because it is easy to identify the source of the frustration, a target for the violence that follows the negative affect (Berkowitz) and shame (Gilligan) is readily available. If these targets are not accessible, because of physical distance or social constraints, Berkowitz (1993) reminds us that any person who can be connected to the source of frustration by even a trivial link becomes an appropriate target in the mind of the offended person. Therefore, low self-esteem that is induced by a failure to matter will increase the likelihood of aggression.

An Additional Mediator: Attitude toward Violence

> *Mental violence has no potency and injures only the person whose thoughts are violent. It is otherwise with mental non-violence. It has potency which the world does not yet know.*
>
> Mohandas K. Gandhi, *Non-violence in peace and war*

In addition to self-esteem, I propose a second factor that intervenes between mattering and physical violence: one's attitude toward violence. I argue that mattering and self-esteem are related to violence through their associations with attitude toward violence, which in turn is associated with violent behaviour.

Concerning the links involving attitude toward violence, it is easy to understand why mattering might be involved. Those who matter to their families (or others) are not likely to approve of violence as a method of conflict resolution. The protective buffer set up by the knowledge that they matter obviates any favorable evaluation of violence. Instead, they are likely to see violence on their parts as a serious threat to the security provided by mattering, and so they are more likely to hold violence in scorn.

Similarly, youth with low self-esteem are more likely to develop a positive attitude toward violence. People who think ill of themselves, according to Rosenberg (1979), are very much oriented to improving their self-image. When the loss of self-esteem is a product of shame, Gilligan (1996, p. 111) reminds us that violence is an attractive option: "The purpose of violence is to diminish the intensity of shame and replace it as far as possible with its opposite, pride, thus preventing the individual from being overwhelmed by the feeling of shame." The attractiveness of violence implies a favorable orientation to it and a greater willingness to use it to restore one's self-image. This assertion has been supported by empirical research (Merwin & Ellis, 2004).

The relationship between attitude and behavior is one of the earliest issues studied by social psychologists (see Eagly & Chaiken, 1998, for a review). Although research has shown that the relationship between attitude and behavior is not as powerful as some had hoped (median correlation about .30), attitudes nevertheless have been found to be associated with a wide variety of behavioral options.

In the case of attitude toward violence, studies show a positive relationship to delinquency (Landsheer & Hart, 1999), sexual exploitation (Bookwala, Frieze, & Smith, 1992), and dating violence (O'Keefe, 1998). More relevant to the concerns of this book, other researchers have found that attitude toward violence is associated with reports of aggression and fighting behavior (Cotten et al., 1994) and serious violent (drug-related) offending (Kuhns, 2005). Research has also shown that attitude toward violence plays a strong role in the occurrence of domestic violence (Briere, 1987; Markowitz, 2001; Sugarman & Frankel, 1996).

Therefore, the augmented model for analysis is mattering → self-esteem → attitude toward violence → violence. In other words, a low level of mattering is associated with diminished self-esteem; low self-esteem contributes to a positive attitude toward violence, and such a positive attitude encourages violent behavior.

Preliminary Analysis: Mattering and Attitude toward Violence

To establish attitude toward violence as an important intervening variable between mattering and violent behavior, I must first demonstrate that mattering can explain variations in those attitudes. Therefore, as I did with self-esteem, I analyze a model using mattering, self-esteem, and the control variables to predict attitude toward violence. The index used to measure these attitudes appears in Table A.2 of the Appendix. The average level of violent attitude produced by setting the values of all the predictor variables at their average is 28.769; that is, overall, the teenagers in the sample have reasonably low approval of violence as a method of conflict resolution. This is the number to which the predicted values will be contrasted in calculating the significance for each category of the nominal or ordinal variables (age, sex, race/ethnicity, adult educational attainment, family structure, and religiosity), as well as contrasts made for specific values of the interval or ratio variables (mattering to family, self-esteem, and number of children). In addition, the average level of mattering to family and self-esteem among the sample of adolescents is 66.806 and 39.117, a rather healthy state of affairs.

The analysis is a two-stage process: First, I examine the contribution of mattering to family to violent attitudes. This will establish the first link in the chain mattering → attitude toward violence → violent behavior.

Second, I explore the extent to which the mattering–attitude link is channeled by self-esteem. I know from the previous analysis above that mattering is a strong predictor of self-esteem. My interest in the second stage is to confirm that self-esteem plays an important role in forming an attitude toward violence. All analyses include the control variables as predictors.

The results are impressive. To understand the magnitude of the role of each predictor, recall that the potential range of scores for Mattering to Family Index and the Attitude toward Violence index is from 15 to 75; Rosenberg's Self-Esteem Inventory ranges from 9 to 45.

Consider first the direct relationship between mattering to family and attitude toward violence. From the analysis, I found that the relationship is powerful and negative: Mattering more to one's parents means a less favorable view of violence.

Table 4.6 Predicted Attitude toward Violence Scores as a function of Mattering to Family and Self-Esteem

	Predicted Score		
	Mattering Only	*Mattering and Self-Esteem*	
Independent Variable	*Mattering*	*Mattering*	*Self-Esteem*
Mean	27.875	28.769	28.769
One Standard Deviation Below	30.865	30.290	29.913
Two Standard Deviations Below	32.944	31.812	31.057
Three Standard Deviations Below	35.024	33.333	32.202
Age			
11–12	25.438	25.398	
13	27.125	27.703	
14	28.896	28.818	
15	29.896	29.786	
16	29.467	29.524	
17	30.364	30.464	
18	30.309	30.417	
Sex			
Male	30.844	30.950	
Female	26.730	26.587	
Race/Ethnicity			
Non-Hispanic White	27.511	27.499	
Non-Hispanic Black	29.930	30.130	
Hispanic	29.097	28.976	
Adult Respondent's Educational Attainment			
Less Than High School	28.691	28.450	
High School Diploma	29.780	29.802	
Some College	28.947	28.952	
College Diploma	28.356	28.839	
Postgraduate Study	28.152	28.520	
Family Structure			
Never Married	28.570	28.628	
Previously Married	29.459	29.396	
Married	28.327	28.282	
Importance of Religion			
Not Important	29.837	29.854	

Table 4.6 *(cont'd)*

	Predicted Score		
	Panel 1 Mattering Only	*Panel 2 Mattering and Self-Esteem*	
Independent Variable	*Mattering*	*Mattering*	*Self-Esteem*
Fairly Important	28.717	28.721	
Very Important	28.454	28.433	
Extremely Important	28.133	28.158	
Number of Children in Household			
1	28.982	28.965	
2	28.785	28.769	
4	28.392	28.377	
6	27.999	27.985	
8	27.605	27.593	

N = 1773

These results are illustrated in the predicted scores for the Attitude toward Violence Index found in Table 4.6. The differences traceable to mattering to the family are quite pronounced. When mattering scores drop from the average to three standard deviations below average, attitude scores increase nearly five units. That is, because differences in levels of mattering to family are associated with dramatic changes in attitude scores, the latter's contribution to the likelihood of engaging in violence will be partly determined by the respondent's feeling of mattering to family. The link is now firmly established.

To elaborate the link, I examine a model that adds self-esteem as a predictor of attitude toward violence. The results reveal that it is also a strong contributor. When self-esteem falls from the average level to three standard deviations under the average, approval of violence increases nearly four units.

However, it is important to note that the presence of self-esteem reduces the potency of mattering not at all. Indeed, the predicted attitude scores across the four levels of mattering to family (from the average score down to three standard deviations below the mean) show virtually the same range. So, it appears that self-esteem does not mediate the relationship between mattering to family and violence in any meaningful way. Rather, the two factors are separate (and almost equal) predictors of attitude toward violence.

The control variables are strong discriminators in the adolescent's attitude toward violence. As age increases, so does approval of violence. Compared to the average attitude toward violence among all the teenagers in the sample, respondents aged 11–13 and 15 reveal significantly less approval of violence; in contrast, the 17- and 18-year-olds are more positive in their evaluation of violence. Only the 14- and 16-year-olds do not differ from the average attitude.

In assessing the between-group contrasts in favorability of violence, for both age groups 11–12 and 13 each predicted score is significantly different from all others. The 14-year-olds differ in attitude only from the 17- and 18-year olds. Among the 15- to 18-year olds, there are no significant contrasts in attitude toward violence.

Not surprisingly, males approve of violence more than do females. Further, non-Hispanic whites are much lower in their approval of violence than the average teenager, whereas non-Hispanic blacks evince a more favorable attitude. Hispanic attitudes toward violence do not differ significantly from the average.

When I focus on contrasts among racial groups, I find that white attitudes are significantly less positive than both black and Hispanic attitudes. The approval of violence registered by blacks and Hispanics are not distinguishable.

Religiosity is also a predictor of attitude toward violence. When compared to the average attitude, those with no religious conviction are much more favorable. Indeed, in the between-groups analysis, they differ from all other categories of religiosity. None of the other categories is distinguishable from the average attitude; nor do they differ from each other.

Although one of the categories of the SES variable is significantly different from the average score on attitude toward violence, two of the between-category contrasts reach statistical significance. Adolescents living in a family in which the respondent adult earned a high school diploma show significantly more positive attitudes toward violence than those from homes in which the adult respondent received a college degree or went on to postgraduate study.

However, I caution strongly against putting too much faith in this result. Although it is possible in a multi-category variable for no group to differ from the average while some groups differ from each other, it is somewhat unlikely. I would have more confidence in these results if they were replicated.

I can conclude that mattering to family is a strong contributor to one's attitude toward violence. The more teenagers matter to their families, the less approval they turn to violence as a way to settle their conflicts. Further, adding self-esteem to the analysis hardly diminishes mattering's role in the process. Instead, self-esteem joins mattering as an almost equal co-predictor of attitude to violence. It seems that, even as mattering works through self-esteem to influence a teenager's attitude, it still delivers much of its predictive power directly. Perhaps this is testimony to the pervasiveness of violence in the adolescents' daily lives, vicariously via the media if not experientially.

Carrying a Weapon

> *Guns are neat little things, aren't they? They can kill extraordinary people with very little effort.*
>
> Statement introduced by John W. Hinckley's attorney in an insanity defense, attempted assassination of President Ronald Reagan

Before I examine violent behavior in adolescence, I analyze what researchers have determined to be an important concomitant to it: carrying a weapon on a regular basis. Although some carry a weapon for defensive purposes, especially those who have been victimized by violence (Paetsch & Bertrand, 1999), others use it to act against perceived enemies (Webster, Gainer, & Champion, 1993).

Further, carrying a weapon has been empirically linked with physical violence against others (Cotton et al., 1994; Lowry, Powell, Kann, Collins, & Kolbe, 1998). Indeed, Berkowitz (Berkowitz & LePage, 1967) demonstrated that even the mere presence of a weapon, not carried by anyone, can induce greater aggression against an antagonist. Subsequent research (Anderson, Benjamin, & Bartholow, 1998) elaborated on this relationship by showing that the presence of weapons (or even pictures of them) primes aggression-related thoughts, which lead to aggressive behavior.

However, one must be especially careful here. It is not clear whether carrying a weapon leads to violence or whether people who engage in violence are more likely to carry a weapon regularly. It is highly likely that this relationship is bi-directional, that is, each contributes to the likelihood of the other. In that case, it is risky to use one factor to predict the other. Therefore, I will treat each of these behaviors as related but distinct outcomes.

It is not difficult to understand why mattering would be related to the propensity to carry a weapon regularly. A self-perceived non-entity can quickly capture the attention of others by brandishing a weapon or otherwise letting others know that it is available for use. Indeed, when it was introduced, the Colt 45 revolver was hailed as "the great equalizer." People would be more likely to pay heed to men of insignificant reputation if they carried one – and knew how to use it. It is a sign (perhaps only to the carriers themselves) that they are people to be reckoned with. Contrariwise, those who matter to others know they do not require anything dramatic to command the attention of others. They are made confident by the realization that the significant others and institutions in their lives already attend to them, invest in them, and rely on them in appropriate ways.

Similarly, a weapon can be treated as a source of higher self-esteem (if only superficial and transient) for those who consider themselves deficient in important ways. Having little within to command the respect of others, low self-esteem people may believe (however erroneously) that a weapon will do what their own personal characteristics cannot. In contrast, people who think well enough of themselves need no outside affirmation that they are people of worth. Their realistic appraisal of their own strengths (and weaknesses) assures them that they need not compel other people's respect.

Finally, it should be clear that one's attitude toward violence would have much to do with the decision to carry a weapon. Those who oppose violence would more likely eschew any protective device that entails aggression. They would seek to ensure their safety by other, less destructive, measures. Contrariwise, a person who believes that violence is an appropriate way to resolve conflicts may act in accordance with that belief by carrying a weapon. If one expects occasionally to use violence to solve problems, it is best to be well prepared.

Prior research reveals a number of conditions that contribute to the likelihood of carrying a weapon. Cheryl Aspy, PhD, from the Department of Family and Preventive Medicine at the University of

Oklahoma Health Sciences Center, found that gender and race were strong predictors of the likelihood of weapons-carrying (Aspy et al., 2004). Males are much more likely than females to have a weapon on them regularly, and non-Hispanic whites are more likely to carry a weapon than either non-Hispanic blacks or Hispanics.

Health scientist Pamela Orpinas, PhD, found similar gender differences, but in her analysis the contributions of race were different, in that blacks and Hispanics showed a greater propensity to carry a weapon than did whites (Orpinas, Murray, & Kelder, 2007). She and her associates also discovered that adolescents from two-parent families were less likely to carry than those living with one parent.

The psychologists Christine Malecki and Michelle Demaray (2003) focused on carrying a weapon on school grounds. Studying urban, middle school students, they found the familiar gender differences, but their results for race were different again. Hispanics were by far the most likely to carry a weapon while at school, with blacks and whites about equally likely. In addition, children in sixth and seventh grades and from the lower of two socioeconomic status levels carried a weapon to school more often.

Turning to factors that may be related to mattering to family, Aspy and her associates (Aspy et al., 2004) found that good family communication reduced the likelihood of a teenager's carrying a weapon. In a similar vein, parental monitoring diminishes the probability that a weapon will be a part of an adolescent's dress code (Luster & Oh, 2001; Orpinas, Murray, & Kelder, 2007). Family support (emotional, informational, instrumental, and appraisal of the offspring) also means that a teenager is less likely to carry a weapon (Malecki & Demaray, 2003).

Adolescent respondents were asked two questions involving carrying a weapon: "During the past 30 days, on how many days did you carry a weapon such as a knife or a club?" and "During the past 30 days, on how many days did you carry a gun?" Because of the low frequencies of positive responses for each question, I combined them into a single variable. Those who acknowledged carrying in *either* case were classified as having carried a weapon; those who denied it in *both* cases were considered not to have carried a weapon. The overall probability of carrying is .037.

As usual, Figure 4.5 delineates the relationships between mattering, self-esteem, and carrying a weapon. Table 4.7 gives the probability estimates lying behind this representation.

Figure 4.5 Mattering, Self-Esteem, Attitude toward Violence, and Carrying a Weapon

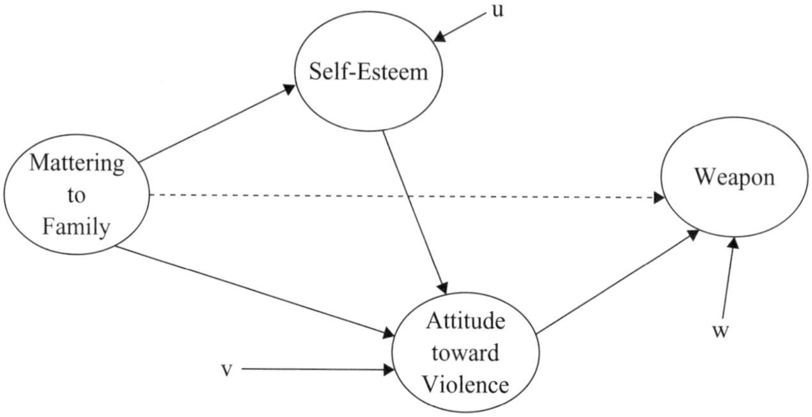

Note: Arrows from sources labeled with a lower case letter represent the contributions from factors not contained in the data (including randomness).

Table 4.7 Probability of Carrying a Weapon

	Panel 1 Mattering Only	*Panel 2 Mattering and Self-Esteem*		*Panel 3 Mattering, Self-Esteem, and Attitude toward Violence*		
Level of Index	*Mattering to Family*	*Mattering to Family*	*Self-Esteem*	*Mattering to Family*	*Self-Esteem*	*Attitude toward Violence*
Mean	.048	.048	.048	.035	.035	.035
One Standard Deviation Below	.067	.066	.051	.042	.031	.075
Two Standard Deviations Below	.092	.088	.053	.051	.028	.153
Three Standard Deviations Below	.126	.118	.055	.061	.025	.286
Significance Level	$p < .001$	$p < .001$	n.s.	$p < .10$	$p < .05$	$p < .001$

The p-value reported in the Significance Level row is the probability of falsely claiming a significant difference in the likelihood of truancy across levels of the index (n.s. means the probability is greater than .10).
N = 1772

Considering first the relationship between mattering to family and the likelihood of carrying a weapon, Panel 1 of Table 4.7 shows it to be strong indeed. The probability at this mean level is somewhat higher than the average probability across all respondents. However, adolescents who matter least to their families are almost twice as likely to carry a weapon as those at the mean level of mattering. Therefore, I can conclude that mattering to family is a powerful disincentive to carry a weapon.

When I add self-esteem to the model, nothing changes. First, contrary to what I argued above, self-esteem contributes virtually nothing to the likelihood of weapon-carrying. The probability in Panel 2 of Table 4.7 changes only trivially as one descends the ladder of self-esteem.

Second, as a consequence, mattering retains most of its role in the decision to carry a weapon. The range of probabilities in Panel 2 is very nearly equal to that found in Panel 1, where mattering is the sole theoretical predictor. Therefore, I must conclude that the relationship between mattering to family and carrying a weapon is essentially unmediated by self-esteem. In the case of violence-related behavior, mattering to family works its protective function without reliance on self-esteem as an intervening mechanism.

When attitude toward violence is added to the mix, things change quite markedly. First, attitude toward violence is a particularly powerful predictor of the propensity to carry a weapon. As Panel 3 of Table 4.7 reveals, teenagers who very strongly advocate violence as a means of conflict resolution are nearly four times as likely to carry as those with only an average amount of support for violence. The latter group's likelihood is about the same as for the average probability across the entire sample.

Next, the contribution of mattering to family drops dramatically. The changes in probability of carrying across levels of mattering are no longer statistically meaningful, although they do reach a marginal level of significance. Nevertheless, I conclude that the relationship between mattering to family and carrying a weapon is almost completely mediated by attitude toward violence. The more teenagers matter to their families, the less likely they are to favor violence as a means of resolving conflicts, and therefore they are much less likely to carry a weapon. Further, only a very small part of this is mediated by self-esteem, by dint of self-esteem's contribution to violent attitudes.

When I consider the control variables, there are two interesting results to report. As found in prior research, there is a dramatic gender difference, with males almost twice as likely (.074) as the average respondent to carry a weapon. This means that female adolescents almost never (.001) carry.

Race, however, has a surprising role to play. In the current sample of adolescents, non-Hispanic whites are much *more* likely (.061) to carry a weapon than the average teenager, whereas non-Hispanic blacks are much *less* likely (.014) to do so. Between-group contrasts reveal that the two racial groups significantly differ from each other. The probability for Hispanics is between the two (.039) and does not significantly differ from either of them, although they do differ from the average likelihood.

In sum, the extent to which one matters to family emerges as a very powerful predictor, in two ways. First, it operates without the mediating assistance of self-esteem, as the latter has virtually no direct relationship with carrying a weapon. Second, because of its strong relationship to attitudes toward violence, it transmits a very strong contribution to the final determination the adolescent makes as to whether or not to carry a weapon. In such a consequential behavior, it is good to know that mattering to family acts as a potent protector.

Violence against Others

> *A society that presumes a norm of violence and celebrates aggression, whether in the subway, on the football field, or in the conduct of its business, cannot help making celebrities of the people who would destroy it.*
>
> Lewis H. Lapham, Citizen Goetz

Teenage violence on the streets and in the schools is a familiar phenomenon these days, and research (Eron, Gentry, & Schlegel, 1994) has revealed a wide range of social and cultural factors that help explain the likelihood of engaging in other-destructive behavior. Differences have been established according to gender (Scherzer & Pinderhughes, 2002; Swaim, Henry, & Kelly, 2006) (males are more violent); race (Blum et al., 2000; Elliott, Huizinga, & Morse, 1986) (blacks and Hispanics); and socioeconomic status (Heimer, 1997) (adolescents from lower status families).

A question in the interview asked: "How many times in the last year have you hit or threatened someone else [outside the family]?" Once again, responses were categorized in a dichotomy of "never" or "ever." Note that the question includes "threaten to hit" as well as hit. The sociologists Murray Straus and Richard Gelles (1995), in their pioneering study of family violence, include the threat of injury, as well as injury itself, in their Conflict Tactics Scale. Often, the threat to do harm is as efficacious as any harm that might actually be done.

In particular, for a study of mattering, including threats is appropriate. People will give you your due (reluctantly, perhaps) if they know that there is always a risk of violent reprisal against them if they do not. Simply being "dissed" is a justification for aggression in troubled neighborhoods, and children learn quickly that respect comes to those who demand it (Sharff, 1998). Threats constitute one way of preempting a show of disrespect from others. Even in more "normal" contexts, the threat of retaliation for not mattering can have severe consequences; a supervisor who does not matter to a worker may not assault the worker, but his or her tenure at the firm may be short. Respect built on fear may be a poor substitute for mattering positively, but it is better than not mattering at all.

The overall probability of violence against others among the adolescents in the sample when all predictor variables are set at their "means" is .245. Analysis of this probability (actually, the odds that produce it) gives rise to Figure 4.6 and Table 4.8. Once again, as revealed in Table 4.8, Panel 1, mattering to family makes a strong difference in the likelihood of violence directed toward others. The probabilities show that from the average level of mattering down to the lowest level, the probability of aggression rises sharply from .290 to .482.

Focus on this result for a moment. Nearly 30 percent of the adolescents with the *average* level of mattering are predicted to engage in violence against others. This is a little greater than the probability for the average for all the respondents. (Recall that all other variables are set at their own means.) When mattering drops below the average, the outcome is frightening. Almost *half* of those with the lowest levels of mattering in the table reported an act (or threat) of violence within the past year.

In contrast with carrying a weapon, self-esteem predicts aggression toward others, although it is not as powerful as the contribution of mattering to family. As Panel 2 of Table 4.8 reveals, decreases in self-esteem from its average value increases the likelihood of violence, as the

Figure 4.6 Mattering, Self-Esteem, Attitude toward Violence, and Violence against Others

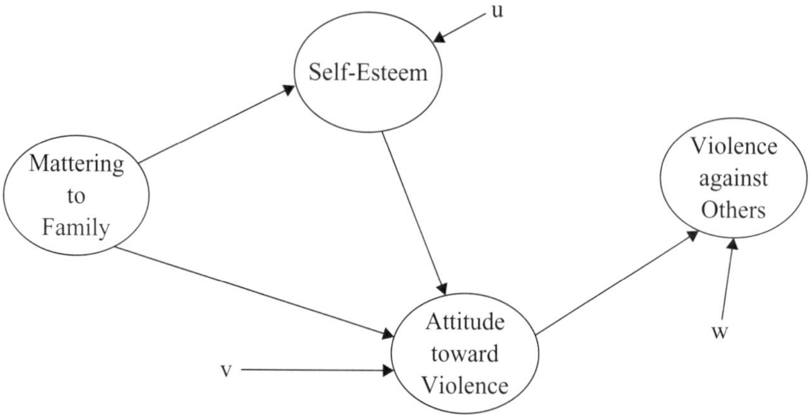

Note: Arrows from sources labeled with a lower case letter represent the contributions from factors not contained in the data (including randomness).

Table 4.8 Probability of Violence against Others

	Panel 1 Mattering Only	*Panel 2 Mattering and Self-Esteem*		*Panel 3 Mattering, Self-Esteem, and Attitude toward Violence*		
Level of Index	*Mattering to Family*	*Mattering to Family*	*Self-Esteem*	*Mattering to Family*	*Self-Esteem*	*Attitude toward Violence*
Mean	.290	.290	.290	.244	.244	.244
One Standard Deviation Below/Above	.350	.336	.318	.255	.243	.470
Two Standard Deviations Below/Above	.414	.384	.347	.266	.242	.709
Three Standard Deviations Below/Above	.482	.436	.378	.278	.241	.870
Significance Level	$p < .001$	$p < .001$	$p < .05$	n.s.	n.s.	$p < .001$

The p-value reported in the Significance Level row is the probability of falsely claiming a significant difference in the likelihood of truancy across levels of the index (n.s. means the probability is greater than .10).
N = 1759

probability rises from .290 to .378. As with mattering to family, barely fewer than 30 percent of the adolescents with the *average* level of self-esteem will engage in violence against someone outside the family; and nearly 40 percent of those at the lowest level of self-esteem will do so.

Adding self-esteem does change the family's influence on the teenager, but only slightly. The relative strength of mattering is as before, although the range of probabilities is somewhat reduced. Therefore, even though self-esteem has its own direct relationship with violence toward others, it does not meaningfully mediate the relationship between mattering to family and violence. In other words, the two elements of the self provide essentially distinct (but not quite equal) contributions to the probability that an adolescent will aggress against someone not in the family.

It is the addition of attitude toward violence that produces a major change in the results. First, its relationship to aggression is powerful. As the attitude becomes more favorable, the probability of violence increases precipitously, until at the most favorable attitude, the likelihood has risen to an astounding .870. For those who view violence as an appropriate and effective means to resolve conflict, almost 9 out of 10 will practice what they believe. In this case, behavior reflects attitude very well indeed!

Second, the contributions of mattering to family and self-esteem to violence are virtually erased. In other words, even though both factors work powerfully to explain attacks on others, their contributions are entirely channeled through their relationships with attitude toward violence, which, as I have demonstrated above, is very potent.

With regard to the controls, it appears that age has a non-linear relationship. On the one hand, compared to the average teenager, the 11- to 12-year-olds are significantly less likely (.189) to engage in violence against others. On the other hand, the 14-year-olds are much more likely (.318) to do so. No other age group differs from the overall average.

When examining between-group contrasts, I find that the youngest age group (.189) differs significantly from the 13- and 14-year-olds (.269 and .318, respectively). Finally, those at age 14 are more likely (.318) to commit violence than the 18-year-olds (.220). All other category contrasts yield no significant differences (15: .249; 16: .241; 17: .232).

As research has demonstrated, all other things being equal, males are significantly more likely (but not much more likely) to engage in physical violence than females (.274 vs. .216). Race also plays its familiar role: Non-Hispanic blacks (.325) report a higher probability of aggression than the average respondent, whereas Hispanics are significantly less likely (.179) than average to be violent. Examining the between-group contrasts, blacks differ in probability of aggression from both whites (.232) and Hispanics. In contrast, the latter two groups do not differ from each other.

A somewhat puzzling result involves religiosity. Only the fairly religious group differs from the overall average level of violence probability, showing a higher propensity to aggress (.296). When I turn to the between-group analysis, the only significant contrast involves the fairly religious and the very religious (.216). Indeed, the probabilities for the irreligious and the extremely religious are virtually identical (.233 and .234, respectively). They fall between the two extremes and do not differ from either.

Finally, for the first time in the analysis, the number of children in the family plays a significant role in the likelihood of violence. As the number of children increases, so does the chance of violence to people outside the family (one child: .224; two children: .244; four children: .287; six children: .334; and eight children: .385).

The likelihood of violence against people not in one's own family reaches the highest levels of probability in the set of anti-social behaviors I examine in this book. Our symbolic universe does implicitly endorse "justified aggression," especially in the face of threat (witness the film *Dirty Harry*, where a "rogue" cop goes to any lengths to bring down the bad guys; *A Time to Kill*, about the trial of a black man accused of killing the two white men who raped his daughter; or *Syriana*, which speculates on how the United States government facilitates the assassination of a foreign leader to make possible a favorable oil policy). Perhaps H. Rap Brown, a Black Panther from the post civil rights struggle in the 1960s, was correct when he said violence "is as American as cherry pie" at a press conference at the Student Nonviolent Coordinating Committee headquarters, Washington, D. C., July 27, 1967, as reported by the *Evening Star*.

And mattering to one's family is an important part of the process by which people turn to aggression to resolve their conflicts, although apparently it takes a superior level of mattering to obviate the attractiveness of violence as an option to resolve conflict. Self-esteem does not reduce the contribution of mattering but plays its own (if somewhat lesser) part. It is the teenager's attitude toward violence that mediates the relationship between mattering to the family and self-esteem, on the one hand, and violence, on the other. Still, because mattering has such a powerful impact on attitude toward violence (and self-esteem), I can conclude that mattering to one's family is a critical protector against adolescent violence.

Mattering and Anti-Social Behavior: Summing it Up

Perhaps we all have an intuitive sense that mattering to family is important. Certainly, the research on social development has given us a reason to believe it. Although, to this point, theorists and researchers have not explicitly referred to mattering, they give hints of it in the terms they use: attachment, parental monitoring, parental involvement, and others. These concepts are not themselves mattering, but mattering is what makes them possible. Without mattering to family, children would have no opportunity to become attached to their parents and siblings. Especially at such an early age, being ignored, lacking parents' investment, and having no parental expectations to respond to imply an insecure attachment (at best). When a child does not matter to its parents, there is no monitoring of its activities, and a *sine qua non* for parental involvement is mattering. Still, until recently, there has been no empirical evidence that mattering even exists, let alone has such powerful motivational impact on people's behavior.

Part of this is due to the fact that mattering is so fundamental and (for most of us) so clearly felt that we easily take it for granted. Indeed, unless specifically prompted to do so, most people probably don't even think of mattering at all. We rarely question whether we matter to our families (or many other individuals, groups, and even institutions) because it seems like a birthright. Unfortunately, as I and others have demonstrated, for a sizable minority of adolescents in our society, mattering is a problematic issue. Adolescents who don't matter are well aware that something is seriously wrong. And for those unfortunate teens life is more than a struggle: It is a continuing, desperate attempt to deny their social invisibility and establish a significant social identity.

One means to this end is to "force" mattering by acting in outrageous and often socially undesirable ways. I have examined a number of them: truancy, vandalism, theft from the family, dealing in contraband, carrying a weapon, and violence against others. In *every* instance, mattering to family makes a strong and significant contribution to the likelihood that an adolescent will engage in these behaviors. As mattering decreases, from the average level expressed by respondents in the sample to an extremely low level (three standard deviations below the average), the probability of doing bad things rises sharply. Even at the average level of mattering, the predicted probability for many of the anti-social behaviors examined in this book is higher than the overall probability found when mattering is not taken into account. In other words, it takes a heap of mattering to lower the chance of doing these behaviors to what would be expected of the average adolescent.

At this point, I want to emphasize an important point about the anti-social behavior revealed in this book. The data do not indicate a pandemic of delinquency in the United States. In general, most of the behaviors that I examined in this chapter are not very likely (a low of .037 for carrying a weapon increasing to .046 for family theft; doubling to .098 for dealing in contraband; a jump to .136 for vandalism; and the highest levels at .236 for violence directed toward others and a peak at .257 for truancy), although even a modest probability for violence is disturbing. These levels are consistent with those found in other research (e.g., A.D. Elliott, Huizinga, & Menard, 1989).

Nevertheless, the results demonstrate that a sizable number of adolescents can be moved to do socially undesirable things. The Office of Juvenile Justice and Delinquency Prevention, a branch of the United States Department of Justice, estimates that "the number of delinquency cases handled by juvenile courts increased 27% between 1990 and 1999" (Stahl, 2003).

The results found in this chapter establish mattering as a fundamental motivator for these behaviors. In Chapter 2, I argued that mattering was such an essential motivation for human beings that it served as a stimulus for other motivations. These other motivations would then pass on the impetus started by mattering to encourage specific behaviors. For mattering to family, self-esteem is such a mediator. Mattering protects against doing most of these behaviors by first raising self-esteem; the greater appreciation of oneself then reduces the motivation to engage in the behavior.

Self-esteem mediates completely the contribution of mattering to truancy and theft from the family. It is largely, but not completely, successful in mediating the relationship with dealing in contraband.

Along with attitude toward violence, self-esteem does mediate the relationship between mattering to family and both carrying a weapon and physical violence against others. Finally, self-esteem does not serve as a mediator at all for vandalism.

It is hard to know why the latter results are so. One thing to note is that vandalism has consequences that are visible to others. A wall covered with graffiti is there for everyone to see (sometimes the vandal will argue that the scrawls and pictures are works of art); overturned gravestones are difficult to ignore; and broken windows in a building capture the attention of passersby. It could very well be that the public nature of the behavior is what makes mattering uniquely powerful. That is, once rendered invisible by your family, the desperate need to matter is strong enough to facilitate directly a public showing that you do matter, to the community, if not at home. You have made your mark for others to see. In addition, in the event that you are caught, your family will now have to recognize you as someone who warrants attention, investment, and expectations. These musings, however, are entirely post hoc and require specific testing before they are accepted as part of the mattering process.

Of course, as I argued earlier, it is also possible that mattering works through some other motivation, one not measured in the Youth at Risk interview survey. If this is the case, it will take more theoretical development of the concept of mattering and its relationship to other elements of the self-concept, as well as further empirical research, to establish the validity of such an assertion. In any case, we can still say with confidence that mattering to one's family has a powerful role (direct, indirect, or both) to play in understanding adolescents' unfortunate and ultimately ill-advised choices.

I say ill-advised, because I believe that anti-social behavior resulting from an attempt to matter to somebody, including one's parents, is not likely to be successful in any permanent way. Once the parents (or siblings) have taken action, thereby signaling that the teenager is worthy of attention in this instance, does this mean that the family will recognize the error of its ways and restore meaningful membership to the youngster? It is possible, of course, but I suspect that more often than not, untoward behavior will only heighten the boundaries between the family and the adolescent perpetrator. Untoward behaviors become just one more reason to keep the child at arm's length and even perhaps out of sight. On occasion, social workers have seen families "cut loose" their misbehaving children, if not during adolescence (which requires official paperwork and can carry a stigma), then when they have reached the nominal age of adulthood.

Still, desperate adolescents (and desperate people in general) don't always stop and think of the long-term consequences of their actions. *Any* behavior that brings a teenager out of the darkness to the spotlight of family attention, investment, or expectations will be preferred to the awful isolation of not mattering. The future costs of anti-social behavior are overwhelmed by the more immediate and bleak prospects of growing up in such lamentable family conditions. The fact that adolescents would do something potentially so detrimental to their futures speaks profoundly about the essential nature of mattering to one's family.

5

Mattering and Self-Destructive Behavior

The life of man is of no greater importance to the universe than that of an oyster.

David Hume, On suicide

Anti-social behavior is at least an annoyance (truancy, vandalism, theft) and occasionally a danger (dealing in contraband, carrying a weapon, violence), but it does not mean a physical loss of self for the perpetrator. There is the possibility of reaching a delinquent adolescent by instilling a sense of mattering, as the literature on resilience (Goldstein & Brooks, 2004; Rubin, 1996) has shown. Sometimes, the continuing presence of one significant other (a parent, a sibling, a teacher, a coach) who tells the teenager "I see something in you. You make a difference in my life" will turn the offender from crime to a more positive way of life. Redemption is always possible, if sometimes seemingly unlikely.

There is a darker side. The one who does not matter may accept social invisibility as his or her lot in life. There seems to be no way to matter meaningfully. Being a nonentity is a terribly heavy burden to bear, and if one cannot alleviate the situation, despair may set in. At this point, alone in agony, a person may seek the only avenue that seems to promise relief: self-destruction. Even the agony of death may be preferable to the agony of life for those who do not matter. Behaviors that can bring death become less frightening when life has such a tenuous grip on the individual.

The great sadness in this "solution" is that it precludes a social rebirth, in which the previously shunned person is able to negotiate a social identity that is integrated into the social order. Risky behavior that can culminate in death is indeed the ultimate social act. Still, as I have said before, desperate people often do very unwise things.

This may be especially true for adolescents who do not matter within their own families. I base this assertion on the life-giving importance of family to an adolescent (Steinberg, 2001). As the most important socializing agent (because it is the earliest), the family is responsible for the basic shaping of the child's self. If, as sociologists assert, we must learn how to be human beings, parents and older siblings are our first teachers. What they impart to us is especially influential in determining who we are.

So imagine the trauma if the basic message from the family is that you are nothing. They act as if you are not there. They do not care what happens to you, your successes or your failures. They do not include you in family discussions or have any expectations regarding your behavior. If your family has continually communicated these understandings to you from your earliest days, you will not always have had the cognitive capacity to critique their reflected appraisals. (Imagine a seven-year-old saying to her mother, "I know you don't mean that, Mom. I know you're just having a bad day.") As a result, the words and behaviors of a parent (or older sibling) have superior staying power. Indeed, a public service advertisement on television some years ago began with a tight shot on a woman's mouth. She begins to speak: "Can't you do anything right?!? What's the matter with you?!? Sometimes I wish you had never been born!" As the scene fades to black, a voice-over intones: "Words hit like a fist. Be careful what you say to your children."

Even knowing you matter to others (say, friends or teachers) may not compensate for the devastating awareness that your family finds you unworthy of their attention. As meaningful and supportive as the other sources may be, they are not the people who were responsible for giving you sustenance and nurturance from birth. This is a hole that cannot easily be filled.

In contrast, the higher the level of perceived mattering to family, the less likely teenagers will be to engage in behaviors that will potentially harm them. Mattering to family is a rock. It will help prevent the despair that drives people to nihilistic acts. Mattering to family (especially in a positive way) makes life worth living. And so, I expect that whatever the adolescents' relationships with anyone else, mattering to family will play a crucial role in their orientation to self-destructive behavior.

There are many ways that people can flirt with death. In earlier research from the Youth at Risk survey data, I have already demonstrated that mattering and self-esteem are each very important in the likelihood of suicide ideation, a combination of thoughts, motivations, and feelings about killing oneself (Elliott, Colangelo, & Gelles, 2005). In this chapter, I will investigate a variety of other potentially self-destructive behavior, including illicit drug use, binge drinking, and suicide plans and attempts.

Theories of Self-Destructive Behavior

Most theoretical approaches have conceptualized the topic in terms of risky behavior. Some theories (Hall, Elias, & Crossley, 2006) are biologically based, focusing on genetic and other physiological factors (e.g., hormones) that may predispose young people to dangerous activity. Research (Marlatt, Baer, Donovan, & Kivlahan, 1988) has shown, for example, that alcohol abuse runs in families, presumably because of a genetically based inclination to imbibe. The sociologist J. Richard Udry has provided much data delineating the importance of biological factors in risky sexual activity in adolescence (Halpern, Campbell, Agnew, Thompson, & Udry, 2002; Udry & Campbell, 1994).

Richard Jessor (1998) and other psychologists have looked to personality to explain risky behavior in adolescence. For example, Marvin Zuckerman (1994) asserts that some people have a physiological need for exciting experiences and so will be more likely to engage in dangerous behavior, such as reckless driving. Although sensation seeking originates in the genetic structure, it is manifested as a personality trait.

In this book, I take a different tack. Remember that the basic orientation underlying the theory and analysis herein is that we must learn how to be human, that there is very little about our species' nature that is innate. Although there is no doubt that genetic factors provide much energy for human behavior, the actual direction for our actions comes from what is learned about the self. Whether we speak about reflected appraisals, social comparison, or self-attribution (Cognitive Social Psychology) or taking the role of the other and creating identity (Symbolic Interactionism), the conclusion is the same: Becoming human is a social process, and our behavior is the result of the way our cognitive processes have been shaped and the resultant decisions we make about what is appropriate for the circumstance.

Mattering, as a strong motivational dimension of the self-concept, bears on the decision-making process. Teenagers who do not matter to their families see the world as a painful and threatening place. If home is no safe haven because they are non-persons there, how much worse is it outside, where there is no social requirement that people pay attention to them, invest in them, or look to them for anything? As a consequence, they are not so cowed by threats to their well-being and may even seek them out, not because they are biologically impelled or because they seek thrills, but because a fatal misstep can take away their agonies. There are worse things than death, and for some people, one of them may be life as a nonentity.

Self-Esteem Again

As with anti-social behavior, I expect that self-esteem will play a mediating role in the relationship between mattering to family and self-destructive behavior. In Chapter 4, I have already established the link between mattering to family and self-esteem in the Youth at Risk data. Here, I will argue that, just as it was with most anti-social behavior, self-esteem is also an excellent predictor of the likelihood of engaging in self-destructive behaviors.

It is not difficult to see why this might be so. People with low self-esteem believe that they are seriously deficient people. Acutely aware that they have little to offer to others, they do not hold out much hope for meaningful relationships with others. If they are condemned to be social isolates, they may very well come to believe that their lives are not worth living. Either directly (suicide) or indirectly (risky behaviors), escape from the painful awareness of their worthless state may be preferable to having to look at themselves in the mirror each day.

In contrast, those who think well enough of themselves have no need to wonder whether each day's existence will be painful. Although they recognize that they have personal deficits, none is so ruinous as to suggest that continuing to live is futile. Instead, the confidence that comes from self-approval and self-acceptance will more likely motivate them toward further self-improvement, not despair.

Illicit Drug Use

> *"When you have a problem, you want the attention, so you keep your problem to make people notice you," Whitney says as she drives across town to a party. "Before drugs, I felt like no one. After my best friend killed himself when I was 13, I took out my betrayal through drugs. I became the girl who did all the hard stuff. People began to know me. I was out there doing stuff no one ever heard of. I was pretty crazy."*
>
> *New York Times*, A Las Vegas juvenile judge finds his test case at home

Potentially lethal drugs are familiar to us all, if not through personal experience, then through the mass media. Local and national newspapers are filled with stories about the illicit drug industry. The entertainment media find drug use a lucrative topic, with films, songs and books galore. In 1956, there was director Otto Preminger's groundbreaking film *The Man with the Golden Arm*, a cautionary tale about heroin addiction. The sixties' freewheeling attitude toward drugs emerged off-Broadway in the 1966 production of the rock musical *Hair*; it quickly moved to Broadway for a long run. Things changed again, as in 1971 Al Pacino portrayed the heartbreak of life as a heroin addict in the film *Panic in Needle Park*. More recently, David Simon's *The Wire* (2002) depicted in painful detail the lost lives of those who dealt in and were addicted to drugs. Few films extol the virtues of drug abuse, but many teenagers have received their vicarious introduction to illicit substances via films like these.

The music industry also cashed in. In the late 1960s and early 1970s, Sly and the Family Stone's *I Want to Take You Higher* (1969), ostensibly about passion, was widely understood to mirror Sly's personal life with drugs. Curtis Mayfield's *Pusherman* (1972) dealt with the "ups and downs" of drug dealing. Hoyt Axton distinguished between recreational drugs, like marijuana, and more serious drugs, like cocaine, in a song recorded by Steppenwolf in 1969, *The Pusher*. Starker images began with the Velvet Underground's *Heroin*, and contemporary songs about drugs are often nihilistic: Buckcherry's *Lit Up* (1999), P. Diddy's *The Future* (2001), Kool Keith's *Drugs* (2001), and Life of Agony's *Heroin Dreams* (2003).

National statistics, provided in the National Household Survey on Drug Use and Health (United States Department of Health and Human Services, Substance Abuse and Mental Health Services Administration, Office of Applied Studies 2004), on the prevalence of illicit drug use (excluding marijuana) reveal the scope of the problem. I used the 2001 wave of the survey because it came as close as possible to the year the Youth at Risk sample was taken. (The 2000 wave of United States Department of Health and Human Services, Substance Abuse and Mental Health Services Administration, Office of Applied Studies did not contain versions of some of the outcome variables I am studying.) Focusing on respondents from ages 12–18, it is unsurprising that substance use monotonically increases as age increases, from a low of 0.7% at age 12 to a high of 3.7% at age 18. Use by gender was nearly identical (males: 1.9%; females: 2.5%). There are also differences traceable to race/ethnicity. Non-Hispanic whites and Hispanics report roughly the same usage (2.3% vs. 2.0%), whereas the percentage for non-Hispanic blacks was lower (1.2%).

Illicit drugs can serve either of two purposes for those who do not matter. First, they can provide an escape from the deeply felt pain that comes from realizing that your family considers you a nobody. A teenager can either soar far above the reality with "uppers" like cocaine and methamphetamines or can descend into the torpor induced by "downers" like heroin and Quaaludes. Either way, reality recedes, and for a little while, you don't have to think of your status (or lack of it) within your family.

Second, if you make a mistake and overdose, what's the difference? Being a non-person means that you are not a part of your own social world anyway, and who would miss you? Without mattering to one's family, one critical restraint on such risky behavior is lessened, if not absent.

There is some related research that highlights the importance of parents' relationships with their children in contributing to their use of illicit drugs. The psychiatrist Daniel Pilowsky and his colleagues found that parental depression and "affectionless control" by parents (measured by a parental bonding instrument) increased a young person's drug use (Pilowsky, Wickramaratne, Nomura, & Weissman, 2006). Depression very likely renders a parent unable to establish a mattering relationship with a child, and affectionless control sounds like a good proxy for the lack of mattering. In addition, the sociologist Grace Barnes and her colleagues discovered that parental monitoring, another proxy for mattering, protects a teenager from serious use of dangerous drugs (Barnes, Hoffman, Welte, Farrell, & Dintcheff, 2006). These studies give some confidence that mattering to family will be an important contributor as well.

Recent research suggests repeatedly that self-esteem has no meaningful association with illicit drug use among young people (Brook, Brook, Gordon, Whiteman, & Cohen, 1990; Kandel, Kessler, & Margulies, 1978; Lopez et al., 2001), although there are exceptions (Kinnier, Metha, Okey, & Keim, 2001). However, for the purpose of comparability with the other analyses in this book, I will include self-esteem as a predictor and intervening variable in the second stage of the analysis.

The number and kinds of illicit substances are many. The Youth at Risk interview contains data on adolescents' use of several: cocaine in any of its forms (powder, crack, and freebase), heroin, methamphetamines, steroids, and inhalants (glue, aerosol, and paint). Because use of these drugs is relatively rare in the sample, I combined these variables into a single drug use measure. Respondents who acknowledged using *any* of the substances above were categorized as a drug user; only if respondents denied using *all* of them were they relegated to the non-user category. The probability of drug use in the Youth at Risk sample, when each of the predictor variables is set at its average value, is quite low: .029.

As in Chapter 4, I present both the calculated probabilities for different levels for mattering, self-esteem, and the control variables (Table 5.1), as well as a visual depiction of the results (Figure 5.1).

Figure 5.1 Mattering, Self-Esteem, and Illicit Drug Use

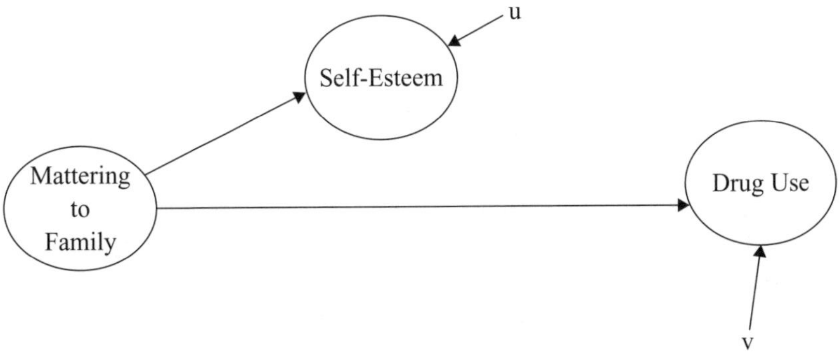

Note: Arrows from sources labeled with a lower case letter represent the contributions from factors not contained in the data (including randomness).

Table 5.1 Probability of Illicit Drug Use

	Panel 1 *Mattering Only*	*Panel 2* *Mattering and Self-Esteem*	
Level of Index	*Mattering to Family*	*Mattering to Family*	*Self-Esteem*
Mean	.028	.028	.028
One Standard Deviation Below	.039	.040	.026
Two Standard Deviations Below	.054	.057	.025
Three Standard Deviations Below	.073	.080	.023
Significance Level	p < .001	p < .05	n.s.

The p-value reported in the Level of Significance row is the probability of falsely claiming a significant difference in the likelihood of illicit drug use across levels of the index (n.s. means the probability is greater than .10).
N = 1792

From Panel 1 of the table, it is clear that mattering to family has a powerful relationship with the likelihood of doing serious drugs. The more one matters to family, the less the chance that one is using. As mattering to family decreases to the lowest level in the table, more than 7 percent of the respondents are predicted to do so.

As prior research has indicated, adding self-esteem to the analysis yields virtually no change in the results. Because the second link in the chain (mattering → self-esteem → drug use) is missing, self-esteem cannot act as a channel for the contribution of mattering, even though its relationship to mattering to family is strong. The second panel of the table depicts the patterns for mattering to family and self-esteem. First, note that the probabilities of drug use across levels of self-esteem change very little. Second, the probability levels across levels of mattering to family are much the same as those found when self-esteem is not included in the model.

Considering the control variables, I find that age makes a difference, but only in the later years of adolescence. In the earlier years, the probabilities do not differ from the average (.017, .022, –.016,

.022, and .030 for 11–12 through 16, respectively). Among 17- and 18-year-olds, the probability of drug use is significantly above average (.057 and .060, respectively).

Turning to the between-groups comparisons, results of the analyses reveal that from 11 through 15 years, the probability of drug use does not differ from one age group to another. However, drug use likelihood in this age range does significantly differ from that for the 17- and 18-year-olds. The two oldest age groups do not differ from each other. Finally, the 16-year-olds occupy a middle position, in that they do not differ from the older or younger adolescents (although the difference with the older groups is marginally significant).

There are no sex differences in illicit drug use. As predicted by prior research, race does make a contribution to drug use patterns. Non-Hispanic blacks are the only race/ethnicity group that differs from the average probability of drug use, being lower than average. Indeed, when contrasting the different groups with each other, blacks are much less likely (.011) to use drugs than Hispanics (.040), but the contrast with whites (.027) is not significant. In addition, whites do not significantly differ from Hispanics.

Finally, those for whom religion is fairly important are more likely than the average adolescent to use drugs (.051), whereas the extremely religious adolescent is less likely (.012) to do so. None of the other contrasts with the average probability is significant (not important: .034; very important: .030). Considering the inter-group contrasts, it is not surprising that the only significant difference in the probability of drug use is between the fairly religious and the extremely religious, (although, that between the extremely religious and the irreligious is marginally significant, as is the case of the contrast between the very and fairly religious categories).

None of the other control variables (gender, family socioeconomic status, family structure, and number of children in the household) even approaches statistical significance.

Therefore, I conclude that mattering to family makes a large difference in the chances that adolescents will use any of a wide range of illicit substances. Because self-esteem is, as expected, not a predictor of drug use, in this analysis, mattering does not depend on self-esteem to mediate its relationship with a behavioral outcome and instead does its protective work alone.

Binge Drinking

All I need is a bottle
And I don't need no friends, no
Wallow in my pain
I swallow as I pretend
To act like I'm happy
When I drink till no end, no
I'm losing all my friends
Am losing in the end
Papa Roach, Binge

Binge drinking among adolescents is increasingly a source of concern for families, teachers, and legal authorities. Binge drinking (sometimes called "heavy episodic drinking") is conceptually defined as the consumption of an inordinate amount of alcohol in a short time period. Because of physiological differences between men and women, it is usually operationalized as the consumption of five or more drinks for men and four or more drinks for women on a single occasion.

United States Department of Health and Human Services, Substance Abuse and Mental Health Services Administration, Office of Applied Studies (2004) estimates that 14% of young people between the ages of 12 and 18 engaged in binge drinking within the last 30 days. Not surprisingly, the percentages increase monotonically from a low of 0.8% at age 12 to a high of 32.4% for 18-year-olds. Gender differences slightly favor the male (15.2%) over the female (12.8%). Non-Hispanic whites (16.2%) have the highest level of binge drinking, followed by Hispanics (12.4%) and non-Hispanic blacks (7.3%).

As with all self-destructive behaviors, I expect that mattering to family will be negatively related to binge drinking. For those who do not matter, binge drinking can serve two functions. On the one hand, as with drugs, excessive alcohol can dull their experience of reality, numbing them to the pain of being ciphers at home. At least for a little while, in their highly inebriated state, they can escape into an alternate reality in which they can pretend that they are somebody.

On the other hand, binge drinking can quickly become lethal. If the drinker is not careful (and becoming drunk gives one license not to be: Heath, 1983), it is easy to consume a lethal quantity of alcohol without realizing it. Those who do not matter may care much less if they commit this error. Unwilling to seek death directly, they act so as to bring it about as a distal outcome of their reckless behavior.

In contrast, those teenagers whose families regularly take note of them, spend time and devote resources to them, and rely on them to be a participating member of the family will find their home a secure foundation. They will have no need of obscuring their understanding of themselves, at least not because of their status within their families. If they do binge drink, it will be for other reasons. Therefore, the probability of binge drinking will decrease as mattering to family increases.

In the early 1990s, researchers at the School of Social Work at the University of Washington examined risk and protective factors for adolescent drinking (Hawkins, Catalano, & Miller, 1992). They cited a number of family practices that facilitated alcohol use and are relevant to the concerns of this book. In particular, the evidence suggests that low bonding to the family (as evinced by lack of reciprocal nurturing and open communication) and poor parenting practices (including failing to monitor children and inconsistent or harsh discipline) greatly increase the likelihood of adolescent alcohol abuse.

Several recent studies found associations between family variables related to this book and binge drinking. The sociologists Stephen Bahr, John Hoffmann, and Xiaoyan Yang (2005) discovered that parental monitoring and attachment to each parent were significant protectors of heavy drinking episodes. Similarly, scholars at the Research Institute on Addictions (Barnes, Reifman, Farrell, & Dintcheff, 2000; Reifman & Watson, 2003) demonstrated that parental support (in a measure of nurturance) and parental monitoring reduced alcohol abuse. Finally, a team of social workers and psychologists (Guillermo-Ramos, Jaccard, Turrisi, & Johansson, 2005), focusing on middle school students, report that parental control has a curvilinear relationship with binge drinking: Too little and too much control increases heavy drinking episodes, whereas a moderate level of control reduces them. In addition, parents who are willing to discuss important issues with their teens find that their children are less likely to binge drink.

Binge drinking may also help low self-esteem people forget how much they do not like themselves. Heavy inebriation erases, if only for the moment, what they know all too well. Tomorrow, they will be sober and still loathe themselves, but tonight they can be someone else or no one. In either case, they are less offensive to their own sensibilities. On the other hand, those with high levels of self-esteem do not have to run away from themselves, because they are reasonably satisfied with who they are. As with drug use, this self-destructive behavior would make no sense.

One study related adolescents' level of self-esteem to binge drinking (Ziyadeh et al., 2007). Social (but not global) self-esteem, defined as the self-appraisal of one's skills at relating to others, predicted binge drinking. The more social self-esteem, the less the odds that a teenager would drink excessively.

The question for binge drinking in the Youth at Risk survey was distinct for male and female respondents, due to the sex differences noted above. Respondents were asked: "During the past two weeks, on how many days did you have [males: 5 / females: 4] or more drinks of alcohol in a row, that is, within a couple of hours?" Respondents who gave any non-zero answer were classified as binge drinkers; those who answered "None" were classified as non-binge-drinkers. The probability of binge drinking when all predictor variables are held at the mean is 0.085. This is slightly lower than the percentage reported in the United States Department of Health and Human Services, Substance Abuse and Mental Health Services Administration, Office of Applied Studies (2004) survey. Because so few of the youngest respondents drank to excess in this manner, I collapsed them into a single age group (11–15).

My analysis reveals that mattering to family is powerfully related to the likelihood of adolescent binge drinking. Figure 5.2 depicts the model of analysis, and Table 5.2 presents the results.

Figure 5.2 Mattering, Self-Esteem, and Binge Drinking

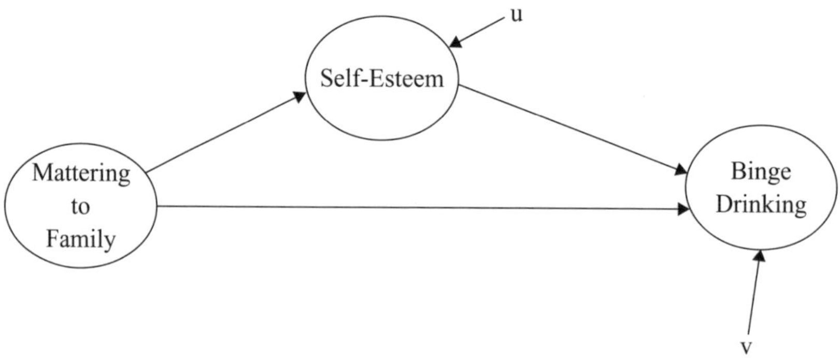

Note: Arrows from sources labeled with a lower case letter represent the contributions from factors not contained in the data (including randomness).

Table 5.2 Probability of Binge Drinking

	Panel 1 *Mattering Only*	*Panel 2* *Mattering and Self-Esteem*	
Level of Index	*Mattering to Family*	*Mattering to Family*	*Self-Esteem*
Mean	.085	.085	.085
One Standard Deviation Below	.113	.103	.106
Two Standard Deviations Below	.149	.124	.132
Three Standard Deviations Below	.195	.149	.162
Significance Level	$p < .001$	$p < .05$	$p < .05$

The p-value reported in the Significance Level row is the probability of falsely claiming a significant difference in the likelihood of binge drinking across levels of the index (n.s. means the probability is greater than .05).
N = 1786

Focusing on Panel 1, when mattering to family falls to three standard deviations below the mean, nearly 20% of these respondents are predicted to drink excessively, more than twice as much as those at the average level of mattering (which probability is the same as that for the sample as a whole).

Adding self-esteem to the analysis reveals it as a significant predictor of adolescents' heavy drinking. As self-esteem increases, the likelihood of binge drinking decreases. Those within the average level of mattering to family are almost half as likely to binge as those at the lowest level of self-esteem presented in the table.

In addition, self-esteem is at best a partial mediator of the mattering to binge-drinking relationship. The changes in probability found for family mattering cover a somewhat shorter range, but there still is an appreciable (and statistically significant) ascent as mattering to family decreases. Therefore, mattering to family and self-esteem channels act as relatively independent (and nearly co-equal) contributors to the likelihood of binge drinking.

With the control variables, as expected, age is a big discriminator. Compared to the probability for the average level of binge drinking

(0.085), those within the youngest age group (11–15) are much *less* likely (0.023) to drink excessively. Contrariwise, the 18-year-olds are much *more* likely (0.185) to binge drink than the average adolescent in the sample. The other age levels do not differ from the average probability (16: 0.098; 17: 0.116). Other researchers (White et al., 2006) have found a disproportionate jump in the last years of adolescence. The authors of this study argue that the change in role identity for many young people at age 18 (e.g., high school student to college student or fully employed worker, or even unemployment) underlies much of the steep increase.

Contrasting the age groups with each other, the 18-year-olds stand out from all the rest in their high probability of binge drinking. The same is true in the opposite direction for the youngest respondents in the sample.

Gender did not discriminate the likelihood of heavy episodic drinking, and race barely did so. Non-Hispanic whites are marginally more likely than average to binge. However, the distinction between whites (0.116) and blacks (0.057) is significant. Hispanics occupy a middle level of probability (0.067) but do not significantly differ from white or blacks. The order is the same as that from the United States Department of Health and Human Services, Substance Abuse and Mental Health Services Administration, Office of Applied Studies (2004) survey.

Finally, religiosity made a difference in binge drinking probabilities. Those in the highest level of religiosity (extremely important: 0.057) were less likely to engage in heavy episodic drinking than the average respondent. In contrast, those who were only fairly religious are more likely than average (0.111). Teenagers in the extremely important category of religiosity are only marginally less likely (0.115) than average, due to the higher standard error for their predicted odds of binge drinking. The very religious do not differ from the average (0.071).

When I contrast several levels of religiosity with each other, I find that the extremely religious are less likely to binge drink than the fairly religious or the irreligious, but not compared to the very religious. The only other between-group contrast to attain statistical significance is that between the very and fairly religious, in which the former are less likely to binge drink than the latter.

In sum, mattering to family works to protect an adolescent against excessive drinking, and most of the relationship is direct. In addition, the analysis establishes, for the first time, the role of self-esteem in the process. Self-esteem's negative relationship with binge drinking qualifies it as a co-predictor but not a strong mediator of the relationship between mattering to family and binge drinking.

Suicidal Behavior

The game of life is hard to play.
I'm gonna lose it anyway.
The losing card, I'll someday lay,
so this is all I have to say.
Suicide is painless.
It brings on many changes,
and I can take or leave it if I please.

Michael Altman and Johnny Mandel, Suicide is painless

It is the ultimate in self-destruction. To end one's life is to preclude the possibility of improving it. Because of its irrevocable nature, suicide is an act born out of despair.

Films have occasionally explored the topic, sometimes with dark humor (Sophia Coppola's *The Virgin Suicides*, 1999), at other times with graphic seriousness (Vadim Perlman's *House of Sand and Fog*, 2003). When the focus is on adolescent suicide, the film can be especially disturbing (Robert Redford's *Ordinary People*, 1980; Peter Weir's *Dead Poet's Society*, 1989).

What could lead an adolescent to such a low point that life no longer seems worth living? It would have to be something that renders life hopeless, offering no promise of rescue. Certainly, on occasion, we hear of adolescents who take their own lives for reasons that may seem foolish to us (failing acceptance at a desired college, the loss of a teenage love), but more often the child contemplating suicide is facing something truly overwhelming.

Baumeister (1990) once again contributes important insights into the issue. He argues that for many, suicide is an "escape from self." When events fall very short of a person's standards and expectations, they are likely to be internalized, in that an individual believes that the disappointments are due to some deficiencies in the self. Consistent with Rosenberg (1979), Baumeister predicts that awareness of such severe inadequacies generates self-degradation, which is too painful to tolerate. Sometimes, it may seem that the only way to relieve the torment is to end one's life.

Failing to matter to one's family is surely such a precipitating element. As I asserted in Chapter 2, children expect that the family will provide a safe haven against an often unfriendly and indifferent world. When all else fails, most of us know that we could return home, where we would be noticed, cared for, and relied upon. Even if the family were occasionally disapproving of us, we would know that we mattered enough for them to say so. Mattering to family helps protect us from an agonizing emptiness that could soon erode our desire to continue. Durkheim (1951, p. 280) recognized this when he wrote:

> One cannot long remain so absorbed in contemplation of emptiness without being increasingly attracted to it. In vain one bestows on it the name of infinity; this does not change its nature. When one feels such pleasure in non-existence, one's inclination can be completely satisfied only by completely ceasing to exist.

The emptiness that arises when one does not matter to one's family must be great, indeed.

Further, in Chapter 4, I argued that failing to matter to one's family is a supremely frustrating experience (personal, intentional, and arbitrary) that will arouse rage and shame within us, and thereby impel us toward violence. And indeed, some children do precisely that, sometimes to a lethal extreme within the family (Heide, 1995).

But if the thought of parricide is overwhelming, it is always possible that the violence will be turned inward. As the psychiatrist Karl Menninger (1968, p. 181; emphasis in the original) puts it: "Is it hard for the reader to believe that suicides are sometimes committed to forestall the committing of murder? There is no doubt of it. . . . It is the choice of the lesser evil, *as it seemed to him.*" Suicide is sometimes what you do when you won't kill the person you're really angry at.

Whatever the underpinnings, mattering to family should be negatively associated with suicidal behavior. The greater the perception of mattering, the less likely adolescents will act to end their own lives. If a teenager knows that home will always be somewhere to go for the attention, care, and reliance that are critically important for making one's way in the world, there will be no need even to contemplate self-destruction (Elliott, Colangelo, & Gelles, 2005), much less bring it about.

There is much research that demonstrates the importance of family connections for suicidal behavior. In a review of factors associated with suicidal phenomena in adolescents, suicide researchers Emma Evans, Keith Hawton, and Karen Rodham (2004, p. 966) found 17 studies that led them to conclude: "Overall, the results from the multivariate analysis indicated that having unsupportive parents is directly associated with suicidal phenomena." And studies keep appearing, reaffirming the relationship (Ackard, Neumark-Sztainer, Story, & Perry, 2006; O'Donnell, O'Donnell, Wardlaw, & Steuve, 2004).

Perhaps the study most relevant to the concerns of this book was conducted by Paul Andrews of the Virginia Institute of Psychiatric and Behavioral Genetics (2006). He distinguished among three motivations underlying suicidal behavior: honest signaling (self-destructive behavior that communicates a real need for assistance), a cry for help (similar to honest signaling, except that it does not always involve seriously self-destructive behavior), and leveraging (risky behavior that manipulates the parents into giving the attention the adolescent seeks).

Each of these options reflects a concern for mattering. Adolescents who do not matter to their families may use self-destructive behavior as an honest signal or a cry for help, if they think that the family will respond in a way that grants them the role identity that they need and cherish. Leveraging, in contrast, suggests that the teenager is more desperate. It is a manipulative ploy used when the family has to be coerced into caring; and if the tactic is discovered, it is likely to backfire. Leveraging may be the last, desperate act of one who is hopeless.

The National Survey on Drug Abuse (2004) asked respondents (17 and under) whether they had received mental health treatment in the past year because of a suicide attempt. The lowest percentage of affirmative responses occurred among the 12-year-olds (9.8%), rising and falling notably from 13 to 16 (16.1%, 20.7%, 16.2%, and 21.1%, respectively), finally dropping to the second-lowest level at 17 (14.0%). Females (19.8%) were more likely to have attempted suicide than males (12.7%). Finally, non-Hispanic whites (17.4%) were followed by non-Hispanic blacks (15.2%), and Hispanics (12.8%).

A good deal of research links suicidal behavior to self-esteem (Overholser, Adams, Lehnert, & Brinkman, 1995; Wild, Flisher, & Lombard, 2004; Yoder, 1999). It is unsurprising to learn that people with low self-esteem are more likely to think seriously about suicide on a regular basis and actually attempt it more than high self-esteem people. On the one hand, if you find yourself a seriously deficient person, you may be disgusted with yourself. You may question the usefulness of life when you are a worthless person. You have little to offer the world, and it just may be better if you leave it.

On the other hand, if you are generally satisfied with who you are, there is no question as to whether life is worth living. Things can always be better, but disappointments are not due to your failings. You are not perfect, but the central aspects of your self are good enough, and you are working on it. Awareness of your deficiencies does not send you into a panic and certainly does not lead you to attempt self-destruction, or even contemplate it seriously.

An Additional Mediator: Depression

> *In depression, faith in deliverance, in ultimate restoration, is absent. The pain is unrelenting, and what makes the condition intolerable is the foreknowledge that no remedy will come – not in a day, an hour, a month, or a minute. . . . It is hopelessness even more than pain that crushes the soul.*
>
> William Styron, *Darkness visible: A memoir of madness*

According to the web site www.NIMH.gov, depression is defined as

> a disease with certain characteristic signs and symptoms that interfere with the ability to work, sleep, eat, and enjoy once pleasurable activities. The characteristic signs and symptoms of major depression include loss of interest in activities that were once interesting or enjoyable, including sex; loss of appetite with weight loss or overeating with weight gain; loss of emotional expression (flat affect); a persistently sad, anxious or empty mood; feelings of hopelessness, pessimism, guilt, worthlessness, or helplessness; social withdrawal; unusual fatigue, low energy level, a feeling of being slowed down; sleep disturbance with insomnia, early-morning awakening, or oversleeping; trouble concentrating, remembering, or making decisions; unusual restlessness or irritability; persistent physical problems such as headaches, digestive disorders, or chronic pain that do not respond to treatment; thoughts of death or suicide or suicide attempts.

Clinical depression must be distinguished from feelings of sadness (often referred to as "the blues") that everyone has endured on occasion. Sooner or later, sadness dissipates as things improve, or one turns one's attention elsewhere to escape the mood.

It is the unrelenting nature of depression that makes it dangerous. It does not go away on its own, and those who suffer from it find it impossible to ignore. The oppressiveness of depression permeates one's entire existence and makes it difficult to carry on.

In my analysis, I posit depression as a second intervening variable, mediating the relationship between self-esteem and suicidal behavior. The elaborated model that results is mattering → self-esteem → depression → suicidal behavior. The chain begins with the assertion (which I have already demonstrated) that mattering to family raises self esteem; self-esteem, in turn, protects one from depression, and without depression, suicidal behavior becomes much less likely.

The argument justifying the insertion of depression into the chain model is straightforward. First, to loathe oneself is depressing. If you are worthless in your own eyes, you are vulnerable to each of the depression symptoms listed above. Second, virtually every theory of suicidal behavior names depression as a major contributing factor. In the throes of depression, death may appear to be a welcome relief from the living hell that one endures every day. Depressed people are desperate to escape the continual pain, and many would trade their lives to do so.

Research has confirmed both links with depression. Depression is a very powerful predictor of suicidal behavior. The review of suicidal behavior by Evans, Hawton, and Rodham (2004), cited earlier, found over 30 studies linking the two. More recent research continues to support the link (Horesh & Apter, 2006; Wild, Flisher, & Lombard, 2004). In addition, self-esteem is strongly linked to depression (Haugen & Lund, 2002; Smith & Betz, 2002; Southall & Roberts, 2002; Watson, Suls, & Haig, 2002), although some have argued that unstable self-esteem is as important as its absolute level (Franck & De Raedt, 2007; Roberts, Shapiro, & Gamble, 1999).

Finally, there is good reason to believe that mattering to family plays an important role in the likelihood of depressive symptoms. When you don't matter to your family, is it unreasonable to expect that you would suffer from hopelessness, a very low energy level, unusual restlessness and irritability, or most of the symptoms listed above? To fail to capture your family's attention, to find your family's resources lavished on others and not yourself, to realize that nothing is required of you by them must be a depressing awareness. On the other hand, adolescents who matter to their families know they have a haven from the world's tribulations. They are saved from the feeling of being alone (psychologically, if not socially), and their families will not be a source of the profound sadness that never goes away.

Empirical research suggests, by implication, that this reasoning is valid. Attachment to parents wards off depression (Kenny & Sirin, 2006), as does knowing that one's parents care and will talk things over (Ackard, Neumark-Sztainer, Story, & Perry, 2006; Field, Diego, & Sanders, 2001). Finally, parental monitoring also reduces the likelihood of depression (Jacobson & Crockett, 2000).

I follow the same procedure I used in Chapter 4, establishing attitude toward violence as an additional intervening variable between mattering to family and violence. First, I examine a model that predicts depression using mattering to family and the control variables. Second, I add self-esteem as an additional predictor of depression. If self-esteem is significant, I will have demonstrated its role as at least a partial mediator, because I have already demonstrated that mattering has a strong relationship with self-esteem. Third, I introduce depression into the model. Given that depression is significantly related to suicidal behavior, the main question is the extent to which the contributions of mattering to family and self-esteem are reduced by its presence. This will determine the mediating properties of depression.

Unfortunately, the Youth at Risk survey does not have a strong measure of depression. Only one question attempted to tap into the adolescent's depressed feelings: "During the past 12 months did you ever feel so sad or hopeless almost every day for two weeks or more in a row that you stopped doing some usual activities?" Respondents who said "Yes" were classified as depressed; those who said "No" were classified as not depressed.

It would have been much better had an index of depression, such as the Beck Depression Inventory (Beck, Ward, Mendelson, Mock, & Erbaugh, 1961) been available. A single item cannot be as valid and reliable as a well-established index. Using the criteria of "two weeks or more in a row" where the respondent feels "sad or hopeless" such that he or she "stopped doing some usual activities" makes it possible that some respondents will be misclassified. For example, respondents who only manifested other serious characteristics of depression will be categorized as not depressed; similarly, those with sub-threshold levels of depression who still manage to get through their daily activities or whose symptoms don't last for two contiguous weeks will not be counted as depressed. The item is also "double-barreled," in that it asks respondents if they felt "sad and hopeless;" both emotions are considered to be essential parts of depression, but a person who felt "merely" hopeless might answer "no" and be classified as not depressed. These problems can obscure the true contribution of depression to the analysis.

Nevertheless, the item is not completely invalid and does capture much of the essence of the concept. It makes explicit reference to several of the symptoms listed above: sad, hopeless, almost every day, ceasing usual activities. Because no other measure is available, it will have to do. And as many researchers using data they did not personally collect have gamely said, it will provide a conservative test of the hypotheses regarding depression.

Based on this measure, the general probability of depression among the Youth at Risk sample is .139. The United States Department of Health and Human Services, Substance Abuse and Mental Health Services Administration, Office of Applied Studies did not ask about depression frequency in the 2001 wave, so I use the 2005 wave (United States Department of Health and Human Services, Substance Abuse and Mental Health Services Administration, Office of Applied Studies, 2006) for comparison purposes. The gap between the two surveys (Youth at Risk and United States Department of Health and Human Services, Substance Abuse and Mental Health Services Administration, Office of Applied Studies) may introduce some degree of non-comparability of the results.

And it turns out that the overall probability of reported depression in United States Department of Health and Human Services, Substance Abuse and Mental Health Services Administration, Office of Applied Studies (2006) is somewhat low (.088) compared to that found in the Youth at Risk data. Not surprisingly, depression is quite unlikely among 12-year-olds (.048), but, in the midst of the time of self-concept disturbance (13 and 14), it begins to rise (.063 and .082, respectively). Finally, in later adolescence, it levels off (15–17: .102, .110, and .114, respectively) and begins to decline at age 18 (.096). Females (.131) are much more likely to be depressed than males (.048). Non-Hispanic blacks (.074) are somewhat less likely than non-Hispanic whites (.090) and Hispanics (.098) to be saddled with depressive affect.

Preliminary Analysis: Mattering to Family and Depression

Mattering to family does indeed play a role in the likelihood of depression. Table 5.3 presents the pattern of probabilities, and Figure 5.3 depicts the results of the full analysis.

Consider the first stage of the analysis, when mattering to family is the sole theoretical predictor of depression (along with the control variables). The probability of depression is almost two and one-half times as great among those with the lowest levels of mattering to family, compared to those at the average level. Even within the average mattering to family, however, about 14% of the respondents can be expected to acknowledge feeling depressed within the last 12 months. Meanwhile, more than one-third of those at the lowest level of mattering to family are in a depressive state. What Rosenberg (1989) documented in the late 1980s still holds true: Adolescents are vulnerable to the crushing weight of depression.

When self-esteem is added, it proves to be very strongly related to depression. About 12 percent of adolescents with average self-esteem levels admit to depression. But when one considers the lowest levels of self-esteem in the table, the results are startling: More than half of these teenagers are depressed, greater than a fourfold increase.

Figure 5.3 Mattering, Self-Esteem, and Depression

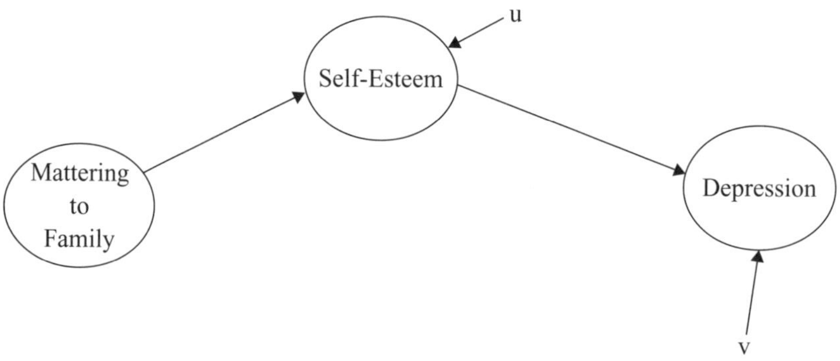

Note: Arrows from sources labeled with a lower case letter represent the contributions from factors not contained in the data (including randomness).

Table 5.3 Probability of Depression

	Panel 1 *Mattering Only*	*Panel 2* *Mattering and Self-Esteem*	
Level of Index	*Mattering to Family*	*Mattering to Family*	*Self-Esteem*
Mean	.137	.123	.123
One Standard Deviation Below	.189	.131	.215
Two Standard Deviations Below	.255	.139	.348
Three Standard Deviations Below	.335	.148	.509
Significance Level	p < .001	n.s.	p < .001

The p-value reported in the Significance Level row is the probability of falsely claiming a significant difference in the likelihood of depression across levels of the index (n.s. means the probability is greater than .05).
N = 1785

In addition, the contribution of mattering to depression is virtually erased. The probability values change very little across levels of mattering to family. As a result, I am confident in saying that the relationship is completely mediated by self-esteem. Mattering to family raises self-esteem, which in turn dramatically lowers the likelihood of depression in these adolescents.

Consider next the control variables. The pattern of probabilities is similar to that from United States Department of Health and Human Services, Substance Abuse and Mental Health Services Administration, Office of Applied Studies (2006). Beginning with age, the youngest members of the sample (11–12) show a lower probability than average (.055 vs. .123, respectively), whereas the oldest (18) have a greater likelihood (.173). All other age groups do not differ significantly from the overall average probability of depression in the sample (13: .147; 14: .119; 15: .126; 16: .119; and 17: .165), although the 17-year-olds' probability is marginally greater than the average. These results contradict Rosenberg's (1989) finding that depression abates at the end of adolescence. Contrasting the age groups to each other,

I find that only the 11- to 12-year-olds show a difference, and their probability is lower than those for all other age groups.

The gender difference in depression probabilities is highly significant, with males (.096) being less likely to suffer the malady than females (.157). The only other difference involving the control variables is found among adolescents in single-parent families in which the parent had previously been married. The likelihood of depression for this group (.161) is higher than average and indeed is significantly different from teenagers whose single parent never married (.109) and teenagers from two-parent families (.106). The latter two groups do not differ from each other.

I have established that high levels of mattering and self-esteem are powerful buffers against depression, with the contribution of mattering channeled completely through its relationship with self-esteem. I can now complete the second step that will demonstrate the mediating capacity of depression: an analysis of the extent to which the direct role of self-esteem on suicidal behavior is transmitted by depression.

Suicidal Behavior: Planning Suicide

Obviously, it is impossible from the current data to determine if mattering is related to successful suicide; those who have taken their leave of this world were not available to participate in the interview. It would take a longitudinal study that followed these adolescents over time to relate earlier scores on mattering to later suicides. (And that assumes that levels of mattering do not meaningfully change across the two time points.)

However, three measures of suicidal behavior are available in the Youth at Risk data. As I mentioned previously, I have already analyzed the first, suicidal ideation (an amalgam of serious thoughts, motivations, and feelings about suicide) in a previously published article (Elliott, Colangelo, & Gelles, 2005). The results reveal that self-esteem and depression completely mediated the relationship between mattering and suicide ideation. Further, self-esteem is a stronger mediator than depression (due possibly to the imperfect nature of the measure of the latter).

The second variable revealed the propensity of the adolescent to formulate an explicit plan of self-destruction. Responses to the item ("During the past 12 months, did you make a plan about how you would attempt suicide?") were dichotomized into those who responded "Yes" and those who said "No." Because only two 11- to 12-year-olds acknowledged planning a suicide, for the analysis, I folded them in with the 13-year-olds. The overall probability of planning a suicide when every variable is set at its "average" value is quite low (.032).

Unfortunately, United States Department of Health and Human Services, Substance Abuse and Mental Health Services Administration, Office of Applied Studies, in any wave, combines suicide planning with suicide ideation, thereby raising the probabilities substantially and eliminating comparability between the Youth at Risk measure of planning alone. As a consequence, I do not report these data.

Despite the low probability, mattering to family still discriminates between those who have and have not planned a suicide within the last 12 months. Table 5.4 gives the probabilities, whereas Figure 5.4 presents the final results of the analysis in graphic form.

Table 5.4 Probability of Planning a Suicide

	Panel 1 Mattering Only	*Panel 2 Mattering and Self-Esteem*		*Panel 3 Mattering, Self-Esteem, and Depression*		
Level of Index	*Mattering to Family*	*Mattering to Family*	*Self-Esteem*	*Mattering to Family*	*Self-Esteem*	*Depression*
Mean	.027	.024	.024	.032	.032	No: .010
One Standard Deviation Below	.042	.029	.042	.038	.044	Yes: .098
Two Standard Deviations Below	.066	.035	.073	.046	.060	
Three Standard Deviations Below	.101	.041	.123	.055	.083	
Significance Level	$p < .001$	n.s.	$p < .001$	n.s.	$p < .01$	$p < .001$

The p-value reported in the Significance Level row is the probability of falsely claiming a significant difference in the likelihood of planning a suicide use across levels of the index (n.s. means the probability is greater than .05).
N = 1784

Figure 5.4 Mattering, Self-Esteem, Depression, and Planning a Suicide

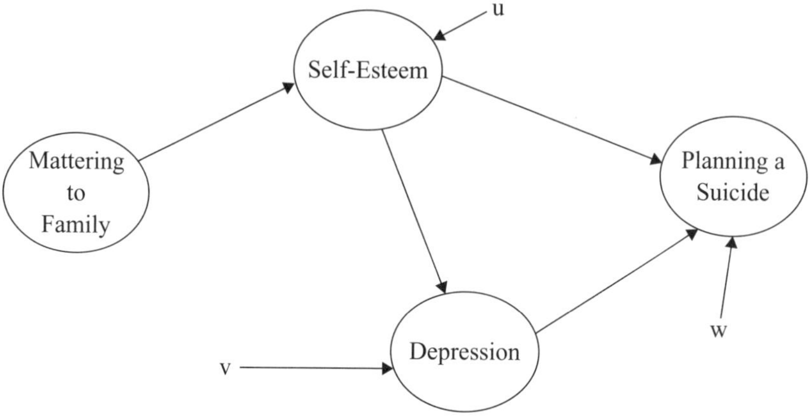

Note: Arrows from sources labeled with a lower case letter represent the contributions from factors not contained in the data (including randomness).

In the first panel of Table 5.4, the results show a powerful change in probabilities. Those with the average level of mattering are relatively unlikely (.027) to plan to kill themselves. However, as mattering to family falls to the lowest level in the table, the probability nearly quadruples: 10 percent admit to making a suicide plan.

Adding self-esteem changes things substantially. The second panel of Table 5.4 shows that self-esteem has taken over as the major contributor to suicide planning. The probability for those at the lowest level of self-esteem is more than five times as great as those at the average level of self-esteem: over 12 percent of the teenagers within this level have planned to end their own lives. In addition, the direct relationship of suicide planning to family mattering has virtually disappeared. As a consequence, the range of probabilities has drastically narrowed. At this point, then, I can say that the relationship between mattering to family and suicide planning is fully mediated by self-esteem.

Finally, as seen in Panel 3 of the table, adding depression as a predictor makes a noticeable difference. First, its contribution to planning a suicide is powerful indeed. The probability is .098 for those who label themselves as depressed, which is nearly ten times as large as that for those who are not depressed.

Second, the mediational power of self-esteem is reduced but not eliminated. There is still a substantial change in the probability of planning a suicide across self-esteem, but the range is constricted. I am willing to assert only a partial mediation (but recall that the measure of depression is far from ideal). Perhaps the relation would be fully mediated by a more reliable and valid measure of the concept.

Because I have shown that the relationship between mattering to family and depression is fully mediated by self-esteem, I can conclude that mattering makes a difference in the likelihood that a teenager will plan a suicide. This contribution comes about through its relationships to self-esteem. As shown in Figure 5.4, mattering to family raises a person's self-esteem, and self-esteem, both directly and in conjunction with its negative relationship to depression, lowers the likelihood of planning a suicide.

The control variables do not contribute much to planning a suicide. Age has a very small effect on suicide planning. Although none of the probabilities for the age categories is different from the average probability of planning a suicide, a check of the between-groups contrasts reveals that the only distinction arises between the 18-year-olds (.053) and the combined 11- to 13-year-olds (.018), but no other age level shows a significant difference from the youngest adolescents. The remaining probabilities vary in a non-monotonic fashion (14: .037; 15: .030; 16: .042; and 17: .023) and do not differ from each other.

In contrast, gender differences are impressive. Females (.069) are more than four times as likely to plan a suicide as are males (.015).

In sum, depression is a powerful predictor of suicide planning among adolescents. But self-esteem holds its own as an additional predictor, even as part of its contribution is channeled through depression. Finally, I have demonstrated that mattering to family begins the chain of associations to suicide planning through its strong association with self-esteem. So, once again, mattering evinces its role as a primary motivation, working through self-esteem together with depression to influence an adolescent's edging closer toward the final step by making plans to commit suicide.

Suicidal Behavior: Attempted Suicide

The second suicide behavior is an actual suicide attempt. It is the last act, and a "success" means that a person has no more opportunity to make his or her life better. The question about attempted suicide was quite direct ("During the last 12 months how many times did you actually attempt suicide?"). It should be obvious that this item includes only those people who were not successful in their attempt. So, this variable would be better labeled as "unsuccessful suicide attempts."

The United States Department of Health and Human Services, Substance Abuse and Mental Health Services Administration, Office of Applied Studies (2004) gives data on those who received mental health treatment because they attempted suicide during the past year. This may very well not include all those who actually tried to kill themselves. Sometimes adolescents' attempts to destroy themselves may go unnoticed. The botched attempt may have had no noticeable consequences or alternative explanations (e.g., a severe stomach ache after swallowing not enough sleeping pills), or parents, afraid to face the reality of their child's plight, may be all too eager to define the attempt as something else (e.g., an accident). In either situation, such adolescents would be unlikely to be sent for mental health treatment, until they get better at the attempt. In addition, the question was asked only for those who were aged 17 and under.

In any case, the overall probability of suicide attempt for those sent to mental health treatment is .166, quite a bit higher than that from the Youth at Risk sample. Age has a curvilinear relationship with attempt (12: .098; 13: 16.1; 14: .207; 15: .162; 16: .211; and 17: .140). The gender difference is not as great as for suicide plans (females: .198; males: .127), nor are the racial differences (non-Hispanic white: .174; non-Hispanic black: .152; Hispanic: .128).

Table 5.5 presents the results of the analysis, and Figure 5.5 depicts the full analytical model. The full sample probability of attempted suicide is .025. Panel 1 shows that the probability of an attempted suicide increases by a factor of almost 5 in moving from the average level of mattering to the lowest level. Although the highest probability is still small, it is a remarkable jump. More than 1 in 20 adolescents at this level of mattering to family can be expected to try to kill themselves. Mattering indeed serves as a protective factor for the ultimate self-destructive act.

As with suicide plans, self-esteem has a strong effect on attempted suicide. The results are presented in Panel 2 of Table 5.5. More than 6 percent of adolescents with the lowest level of self-esteem have made an (unsuccessful) effort to kill themselves.

In addition, unlike with suicide plans, the contribution of mattering to family is only partially mediated by self-esteem. There is still

Table 5.5 Probability of Attempted Suicide

	Panel 1 Mattering Only	*Panel 2 Mattering and Self-Esteem*		*Panel 3 Mattering, Self-Esteem, and Depression*		
Level of Index	*Mattering to Family*	*Mattering to Family*	*Self-Esteem*	*Mattering to Family*	*Self-Esteem*	*Depression*
Mean	.013	.013	.013	.019	.019	No: .008
One Standard Deviation Below	.022	.017	.022	.025	.027	Yes: .045
Two Standard Deviations Below	.037	.022	.037	.033	.038	
Three Standard Deviations Below	.062	.029	.063	.044	.054	
Significance Level	$p < .001$	$p < .05$	$p < .001$	$p < .05$	$p < .01$	$p < .001$

The p-value reported in the Significance Level row is the probability of falsely claiming a significant difference in the likelihood of attempting suicide across levels of the index (n.s. means the probability is greater than .05).
N = 1781

Figure 5.5 Mattering, Self-Esteem, Depression, and Attempted Suicide

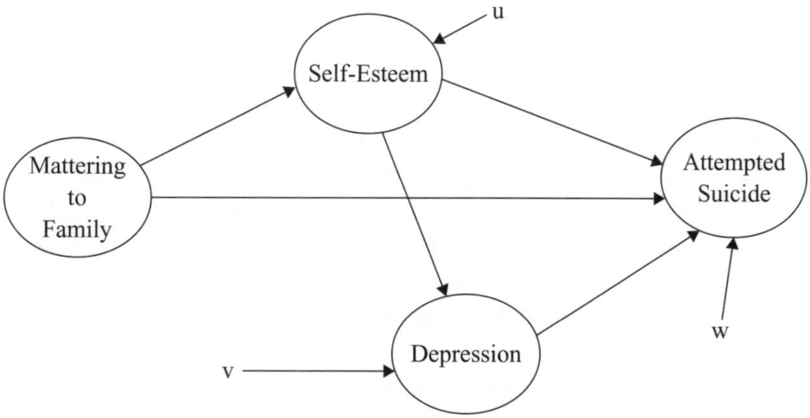

Note: Arrows from sources labeled with a lower case letter represent the contributions from factors not contained in the data (including randomness).

significant variation in probabilities across levels of mattering to family, but it is almost cut in half.

Note the difference between the roles of mattering in the two suicidal behaviors. With respect to planning a suicide, the contribution of mattering is entirely mediated by self-esteem; no direct relationship remains. Turning to attempted suicide, mattering still has a direct contribution, although much of it is transmitted through self-esteem. Self-esteem has the larger direct relationship, indicating that a substantial amount of the relationship between mattering to family and attempted suicide is channeled by self-esteem.

Finally, as seen in Panel 3 of the table, the addition of depression has a very strong impact on the likelihood of an attempted act of self-destruction. First, note that very, very few of those who are not depressed have made a suicide attempt. Second, there is almost a six-fold increase in suicide attempts between those who admit to depressed feelings over the past 12 months and those who do not.

However, depression does not fully mediate the relationship between mattering to family and self-esteem, on the one hand, and suicide attempts, on the other. (Once again, this may be due to the lack of reliability of the measure, occasioned by reliance on a single indicator of depression.) Indeed, both mattering to family and self-esteem have nearly identical contributions to the likelihood of killing oneself. Therefore, even as depression works to lead adolescents to suicide, mattering to family and self-esteem are pulling in the opposite direction, over and above their work accomplished by reducing the likelihood of depression.

Turning to the control variables, gender is the only significant predictor of attempted suicide among adolescents. Females (.042) are about five times as likely to try to kill themselves as males (.008), which is consistent with most research on suicide attempts (Cohen, Spirito, & Brown, 1996). A cautionary word: Women may attempt suicide more often, but there is evidence that they are less serious about it (Nock & Kessler, 2006), especially in adolescence (Lewinsohn, Rohde, Seeley, & Baldwin, 2001). Males succeed more often, principally because they tend to use more lethal methods in their attempts (Spicer & Miller, 2000).

For the direst act of self-destruction, then, mattering to family makes a strong and significant difference, no matter what additional factors enter the picture. Where it counts most, mattering works on its own, independently of self-esteem and depression, as well as through each of them. The family can be a safe haven when things are going badly, if it will be proactive in its dealings with the adolescent. Assuring teenagers that they are noticed, they are important, and they are needed within the family will go a very long way to keep an adolescent from planning or attempting a suicide. This may well be the best thing that mattering does for the young person.

Mattering and Self-Destructive Behavior: Summing it Up

It is comforting to know that mattering to the family protects an adolescent from self-destructive behavior during this stormy period of development. The results of the analyses demonstrate convincingly that teenagers who matter are far less likely to use illicit drugs, binge drink, and plan or attempt suicide.

But mattering to family works in distinct ways for each self-destructive act. With illicit drug use, mattering to family does its work alone, because self-esteem plays no part in the decision. In contrast, self-esteem joins mattering as a distinct contributor to the likelihood of binge drinking, even as it mediates slightly the role played by mattering. In the case of suicide plans, mattering works entirely through self-esteem and then depression. Finally, the probability that an adolescent will actually attempt suicide is strongly related to the level of mattering to one's family, even as self-esteem and depression emerge as important mediators of the relationship.

Mattering can counterbalance the stress brought on by the usual biological, cognitive, and social changes experienced in adolescence. It must be especially frightening to believe that a teenager's parents don't know or care what their offspring is going through and that, therefore, the challenges of development must be met alone. It is perhaps no wonder that adolescents in this plight are more likely to do something from which they may not return.

With self-destructive, as opposed to anti-social, behavior the goal is not to impel mattering, to capture the family's attention by outrageous behavior (unless the act is sufficiently ineffectual so as to be "merely" a cry for help). Those who are desperate enough to engage in nihilistic acts regularly may have given up on the possibility of mattering to their families, or they may be treading down both paths to see which one works first. Perhaps they have already discovered that mattering negatively to the family is, in the long run, unsatisfactory, even if in the moment it is better than not mattering at all.

If the purpose of such a desperate act is, to "matter in memory," as I discussed in Chapter 2, it is mighty cold comfort to know that your family will only realize how significant you are in their lives when you are gone. It is a pyrrhic victory, if indeed it can be called a victory at all.

Further, even more so than with anti-social behaviors, our society does not face an overwhelming number of adolescents who are trying to escape the agony of daily life on a regular basis. The mass media, attracted by the sensational aspects of self-destructive behavior, provide extensive coverage of such acts when they occur, especially when they involve others as well. (Witness the saturation coverage of school shootings followed by the suicide of the perpetrators.) Still, the horrific repercussions of such potentially deadly behavior are surely greater than those for anti-social acts.

And so, the search begins to understand why people would be so careless about their very existence. In this chapter, I have presented evidence for a singularly powerful motivation: mattering to one's family. With it, very few adolescents consider or enact potentially lethal acts; without it, the likelihood of these behaviors, while not momentous, becomes uncomfortably high.

It is then incumbent on families to ensure that their younger members realize without equivocation that they matter. Few households will acknowledge that they have absolutely no interest in doing so, but that does not mean that mattering is automatic, a part of "human nature" or a biologically based certainty. People do not fail to matter because they have a genetic defect or less than fully developed cognitive capacities. Certainly, parents do sometimes reject less-than-perfect children. But others work especially hard to ensure that these children with "special needs" are as aware as possible of how much they matter to their families.

From the sociological perspective on human development, as I detailed in Chapter 1, young people must learn how to be human beings, and one of the things they learn is whether or not they matter to those who are responsible for their upbringing. But few families, if any, are formally trained to accomplish this goal, and the data from the Youth at Risk survey reveal that it is very possible to fail.

In the next chapter, I address this issue. First, I show that there are aspects of the structure of society that influence the extent to which adolescents learn that they matter to their families. The most fundamental institutions constructed over time for us and maintained by us contribute significantly to variations in mattering experienced by individuals. Sociologists recognize and affirm in their empirical research that the social contexts in which a person grows has a powerful influence on the path that development takes and its outcomes as well. In Chapter 6, I demonstrate the impact of such fundamental social institutions as gender, race, socioeconomic status, family structure, as well as the degree of religiosity learned by the adolescent on mattering to the family.

Second, I rely on sociological and psychological theories of human development to offer suggestions as to how mattering can be induced in a young person. In truth, the process of instilling mattering is best begun long before adolescence. By that time, the young person has experienced a great deal of what sociologists call "primary socialization," in which the fundamental shaping of the self is accomplished and the adolescent has the first sophisticated answer to the lifelong question "Who am I?" As I have written before, what gets in early gets in deep.

But the molding of the self is far from completed during adolescence. A person can always gain new understandings about the self, as a consequence of changes in the context of socialization. Even in the teenage years, a youngster can learn for the first time the joy of mattering. The process involves resocialization, in which a person unlearns knowledge about the self that has previously been instilled in favor of a new self-understanding. There is no doubt that resocialization is a much more difficult task than primary socialization. (See Handel, Cahill, & Elkin, 2007 for a thorough discussion of childhood socialization, including adolescence, and Brim & Wheeler, 1966 for a classic treatment of the particular challenges of resocialization.)

Difficult does not mean impossible. It does mean more intensive effort and patience, and perhaps some professional help. Considering the stakes involved, and the protective function of mattering to family, it is well worth it.

6

Inducing Mattering

Our souls are not hungry for fame, comfort, wealth or power. Those rewards create almost as many problems as they solve. Our souls are hungry for meaning, for the sense that we have figured out how to live so that our lives matter, so that the world will be at least a little bit different for our having passed through it.

Rabbi Harold Kushner, *When all you've ever wanted isn't enough*

If mattering is fundamental and necessary in the everyday lives of people, so critical that its absence leads, directly or indirectly, to antisocial and self-destructive behavior, then it raises the question: How does one come to matter? Pursuit of an answer leads back to the original axioms on which this book is based.

Recall that from the sociological perspectives on the self, a person *learns* how to be a human being. If you are a Cognitive Social Psychologist, life is a continuing "seminar" in which reflected appraisals, social comparisons, and self-attributions teach people who they are, both for the moment and for their orientations to the future. One of the things people learn is the extent to which they matter to other individuals, social institutions, and their communities. Awareness of one's placement on the mattering continuum, as I have shown, contributes greatly to the journey through the life course.

If you are a Structural Symbolic Interactionist, the question is one of role identities, the self one is called to be because of the position one inhabits in the social order. Mattering is a necessary condition for people to fulfill these role identities, because these identities are not automatically bestowed on a person. A role identity is a socially negotiated understanding, in which the expectations of all people involved, self and others, must be reconciled into a shared understanding of the identity. Failing to matter ultimately means that a person has little or no input in this negotiation. As a non-person, one is largely excluded from the social process by which society is maintained, from the grandest levels down to interpersonal interactions.

In either case, the extent to which we matter is one of the many things we learn and reaffirm throughout the life course. From our earliest days, people build an understanding of whether and how much they make a difference in the lives of others, and this understanding serves as a frame within which they form aspirations, engage with others, and make decisions about behaviors. Those who matter will act in a way that preserves their favored status. Those who do not will either try to compel mattering, in a (perhaps futile) attempt to capture the attention, investment, and reliance of others, or (and this is the inclusive "or") they will yield to the hopelessness of their situation and engage in self-destructive behavior.

I have argued that mattering to family is especially powerful for adolescents, and the data have supported the argument. Mattering to family constitutes formidable protection against the likelihood that teenagers will lose their way as they assay the difficult construction of an autonomous self. Despite all the popular rhetoric about the conflicted nature of adolescents' relationships with their parents, it turns out that these most basic connections are prepotent to the job.

I want to emphasize at this point that it is mattering to family *as it is perceived by the adolescent* that is at issue. Even though perceptions are the source for understanding and behavior, social psychologists will tell you that they are delicate phenomena. The processes of perceiving everyday life are subject to many influences, from both within the individual (e.g., physiological states, self-interests, cognitive processing flaws) and from the environment (persuasion, coercion, unexpected events). It is up to those involved in a relationship to make clear the extent of mattering involved.

In Chapter 1, I detailed the problems of meaning from both the Cognitive Social Psychology and Symbolic Interactionism paradigms. The conclusions bear restating here: It is the meaning of things, not the things themselves, which motivate human behavior. Whether meaning is perceived (Cognitive Social Psychology) or socially created and imposed (Symbolic Interactionism), it is the source of all human behavior. The "objective" characteristics of elements of the environment, including inanimate things, gestures, and even other people, are merely the source of meaning. If the child does not "see" mattering (whether through perception error or an unfortunate attachment of meaning), then, effectively, it is not there.

Understanding this is critical to what follows. In particular, none of what I present below should be taken as a description of willful behavior on the part of families to deny their children such an important resource for living as mattering to one's family. Instead, as a sociologist, I want to emphasize the importance of social structures in the orientations and activities of family members. These social structures carry with them approaches to life and prescriptions for behavior that can counter inclinations and perspectives that an individual brings to them.

For example, we are all reasonably familiar with the constraints on the self occasioned by our society's understanding and affirmation of gender distinctions. The socialization experiences of boys and girls have some similarities, of course, but the differences are striking. Therefore, as I argue below, there are good reasons to expect differences in the extent to which male and female adolescents matter to their families. This difference is not a statement of relative worthiness, strength, or any other kind of hierarchy. It is simply a reflection of the way we have structured and maintained this part of our society. In short, I beseech the reader to eschew moral judgment in reacting to what follows.

And so it is with the other institutions I consider. If there are racial/ethnic differences in perceived mattering to family, this should not be construed to mean that a particular racial/ethnic group "does" family better or worse than another. Socioeconomic status differences in perceived mattering do not mean that some people are incompetent or evil, whereas others are wise and good. Similarly, differences traceable to family structure variations do not warrant classifying some parents as malicious and others virtuous.

Instead, any variation in mattering to family as a function of social structure would be better interpreted as a consequence of the symbolic universe of our society, the collection of beliefs, norms, attitudes, and values that legitimate the existing social order and the differences contained within it. If one is dismayed by the results that follow, the appropriate reaction is not to condemn the groups that suffer by the contrasts but rather to question how and why our society supports the distinctions that lead to such differences. Can we restructure our understandings of gender, race, and status in ways that minimize the likelihood that some teenagers, because of their memberships in certain categories, will inexorably lack a sense of mattering to family?

The Social-Structural Underpinnings of Mattering

> *That the poor are invisible is one of the most important things about them. They are not simply neglected and forgotten as in the old rhetoric of reform; what is much worse, they are not seen.*
>
> Michael Harrington, *The other america*

In exploring the factors that facilitate mattering to one's family, I focus on two levels of thinking. First, I ask whether there is something about the social structures that we inhabit every day that differentiates mattering among adolescents. All our learning to be a person occurs, not in a vacuum, but in a social context. Each of us occupies a unique position in the social order. A person's gender, race, and socioeconomic status level, for example, present specific opportunities and expectations that influence his or her development through the life course. And a person's life is lived under the prescriptions of the social identities concomitant with that position, as determined by the symbolic universe of our society. Perhaps adolescents differ in their sense of mattering to their families according to the categories they occupy in each of these demographic dimensions. (See Handel, Cahill, & Elkin, 2007, for an excellent review of the differences in socialization experienced by youngsters across gender, race/ethnicity, and socioeconomic status levels.)

To begin with, teenage boys and girls have been treated very differently throughout their youth. Parents (mothers *and* fathers) tend to be more protective of young girls, whereas young boys are more often encouraged to explore their worlds and take risks. In addition, in most families, young girls (rather than boys) are still taught to be keenly aware of the importance of relationships and connections to others. They are also socialized to be nurturers, investing themselves in the welfare of others.

In contrast, young boys are expected to be agentic, to get things done; their behavior is more often instrumental than expressive. As a consequence, they are less in touch with their feelings and are more ignorant of the subtleties and nuances of relationships.

Gender socialization is also heavily reinforced by siblings. Same sex older siblings model the appropriate gender for the child. Opposite sex siblings reaffirm the socially prescribed differences; although they also encourage the development of cross-gender characteristics, they do not reduce the adoption of a gender-appropriate identity. The sociologist Michael Kimmel (2007) presents an excellent description of the fundamental power of gender in the socialization process.

The differences in gender identity might very well be associated with differences in perceived mattering to the family. In the protective nature of parents' and older siblings' relationships to the adolescent female, she might come to understand that she matters a great deal to her family. Contrariwise, the message to the young boy is to learn to stand alone and ultimately depend on no one but himself. Although this may foster ambitious exploratory behavior, it can also raise concerns about the extent to which he matters (especially if there is a sister or two around to bring home the gender differences in relationships to the family). Even if he is in the spotlight, as pressures develop to succeed, he might wonder whether his family really knows who he is or whether they are using him as a proxy for their own experiences. A boy who truly matters to his family will be allowed to shape his own future.

Racial and ethnic differences in the understanding of how a family lives could produce differences in perceived mattering, although I suspect that what varies is not whether a child matters but how that mattering is manifested. There is likely to be more within-group variation in perceived mattering than there is between racial and ethnic groupings. Nevertheless, it is entirely possible that the meaning of "family" and one's place in it varies across race/ethnicity. Therefore, I include race/ethnicity in the analytical model to determine for the first time whether there are racial and ethnic differences in perceived mattering to the family for adolescents.

Socioeconomic status is a different matter. Status is a consequence of a person's standing in a social hierarchy; it is a measure of the respect, deference, and dignity a person has earned by attaining his or her place in the social order. Where social class is captured in the control of scarce and desired resources (initially the means of production [Marx,

1876/1992], more recently, information and technical skills [Reich, 1992]) and is therefore impersonal, status is a measure of social worth, individually earned and therefore a direct indicator of one's character. (See Sennett, 2003, for a full discussion of the personal consequences of status differences.)

The importance of socioeconomic status for this analysis lies in the qualitative differences in socialization that occur between families from the lower-status levels and those from the middle and upper status groups. These differences are likely to lead to variations in perceived mattering to the family.

To substantiate this assertion, I want to turn to the basic understandings of the nature of socialization across status levels. The sociologist Basil Bernstein (1961; Bernstein & Henderson, 1973) pioneered a conceptualization of socioeconomic status as composed of qualitatively different ways of orienting to and understanding the world arising from fundamentally different everyday experiences. The critical socialization differences are those separating the lower end from the rest of the status hierarchy. Between these two broadly defined groups are notable differences in cognitive processing that affect a person's orientation to and behavior in the world. In particular, I argue that these dissimilarities can produce noticeable differences in an adolescent's mattering to the family. (What follows owes much to the discussion of Bernstein's theory provided by the developmental psychologists Robert Hess and Virginia Shipman, 1965.)

The key to status variations in cognitive functioning is language. Bernstein posits that there are variations in the relative orientation of different status groups toward the use of language in social contexts, as well as toward the different areas of meaning that may be explored within a given use. These variations call forth qualitatively different understandings and behaviors from the youngsters who are the target of communication. As a result, language profoundly shapes the child's learning experience early in life and sets the boundaries within which future learning takes place.

Bernstein identifies two forms of communication styles that are responsible for much of the differences in the functions of language. Restricted codes of communication are extremely limited; discourse is condensed, lacking in specificity and precision. In consequence, conceptualization cannot be as rigorous, and fewer differentiations are made. Sentences are short and simple, often filled with clichés and stereotypes. "It is a language of implicit meaning, easily understood and commonly shared. . . . The basic quality of this mode is to limit the range of detail of concept and information involved" (Hess & Shipman, 1965, p. 871). Examples of the restricted code include: "Do as I say!" or "Big boys don't cry!"

The restricted code depends upon closely shared identifications between communicators and so reinforces a group orientation. A sense of social unity emerges, at the cost of uniquely personal experience. But this connection is purely functional; its only goal is to secure compliance. It does not recognize the individuality of the other, nor does it facilitate an attachment to the family. It is as if the child is a nameless, de-individuated entity whose only purpose is to facilitate the smooth running of the "organization" that is the family. Therefore, restricted codes are unlikely to persuade children that they matter a great deal to their families. (I *do not* mean to say that such children do not matter at all. As long as children are not ignored within the family, they will have at least a rudimentary understanding that they matter. I *do* mean to say that the level of mattering induced in the child will be relatively shallow, compared to children reared with elaborated codes of communication. I will have more to say about this in the second segment of this chapter.)

With elaborated codes, communication is specific to the situation and the person at hand. The language used is more precise, allowing a rigorous distinction between related concepts. Use of elaborated codes encourages a more complex thought process that allows a greater differentiation between communicators; the individual is more the focus than the groups to which he or she belongs. An example of the use of elaborated code is given by the following: "Please stop making that noise; when you make such a racket, I can't concentrate."

Because the uniqueness of people is more recognized, their intentions cannot be taken for granted; it is necessary to be more careful and precise in conveying whatever meaning is deemed appropriate to the situation. Use of an elaborated code encourages the recognition of subtle distinctions in the nature of situations and people; it acknowledges the multiplicity of roles that exist in a complex society characterized by a sophisticated division of labor. More relevant to the purpose of this book, it also communicates to the child an appreciation of his or her idiosyncrasies and a willingness to deal with them in all things.

According to Bernstein, these two codes of communication lead to two very different types of social control, first experienced as a child within the family. Status-oriented control, associated with restricted codes, operates through appeals to role expectations. General norms for behavior are deemed applicable to all who take on a given role; there is little or no room for the personal characteristics of the individual to influence social interaction. The status of the person giving the rules for behavior is sufficient to command obedience, even if only with reluctance. There is no sense of the uniqueness of the other when a restricted code is used. As a consequence, restricted codes of communication are unlikely to foster a strong sense of mattering in children.

In contrast, elaborated codes of communication are usually coupled with controls that are person-oriented. With person-oriented control, expectations for behavior take into account the particularities of the person and situation at hand. Although role prescriptions are still important general guides for social interaction, the unique characteristics of the person filling the role may lead to variations in the way the role is enacted; in addition, situational contingencies can modify role requirements. The upshot is that decisions about behavior must be tailored to the realities of the moment.

Parents (and other family members) who have learned elaborated codes of communication within their own family have internalized a way of dealing with a child that is likely to inculcate a deeper sense of mattering. Children quickly understand that they are able to attract meaningful attention from their parents (and older siblings); they appreciate the lengthier and more personal investment that elaborated codes imply; and they understand (even if reluctant to admit it) that the limits imposed by those superior to them in authority are not arbitrary and are tailored to their own personal characteristics, because elaborated codes provide that information to them.

Because I focus on mattering to family, the structure of a person's family may also be more or less conducive to developing a sense that one matters. Does a child within a large family get lost in the crowd? What happens to adolescents who live in single-parent families? It is not only the larger social context that shapes the individual. On the one hand, children in blended families (with at most one biological parent) may find themselves at sea in the family's arrangements. The "yours, mine, and ours" situation can raise the question of their place in the scheme of things, resulting in a reduced sense of mattering. On the other hand, children in single-parent families may be victims of the parent's lack of opportunity to provide a strong sense of mattering.

Because a large number of one-parent families are near or even below the poverty line (Waite & Gallagher, 2000), the overwhelmed parent (most often the mother) may not be able to demonstrate how much the child matters. Indeed, the sociologists Sara McLanahan and Gary Sandefur (1994) have documented the damages to a child's well-being that often comes from life in a single-parent family. Failing to matter may be one more cost the child must endure.

Finally, I also examine the relationship between an adolescent's religiosity and sense of mattering to family. The psychologist William James (1902) long ago recognized that religious belief is for many a supportive factor in making sense of the self. Gordon Allport (1953, p. 95), another prominent psychologist, argued that sincere religious belief contributes to well-being by facilitating "insight, a knowledge of one's values, a clear picture of one's assets and liabilities."

More recently, the psychologist Bruce Blaine (Blaine, Trevedi, & Eshelman, 1998) has uncovered a link between religiosity and well-being (including satisfaction with life, hopelessness, self-esteem, and depression), partially mediated by self-concept "positivity" (the extent to which one's personal characteristics were attributed as positive), although another study showed that this was true only for blacks (Blaine & Crocker, 1995). The psychologists Michael Steger and Patricia Frazier (2005) found that personal meaning in life is a strong mediator of the religiousness to well-being relationship. Finally, from a statistical review of past studies of the relationship between religiosity and mental health, Charles Hackney and Glenn Sanders (2003) remind us that the exact nature of this relationship depends both on how religiosity is defined and assessed and what aspects of well-being are examined.

Implicit in this relationship is the notion of mattering, especially to family. First, almost every form of religious belief emphasizes the importance of the Deity's love for humankind. No matter what else occurs, sincere believers are confident that they matter to the Creator.

Second, if family members are living with the same sincere fervor, they understand how important it is to live out the promise of mattering for each other. They will instill a sense of mattering in a child as an obligation of their faith (one hopes a willing one) and a fulfillment of their own spiritual journey. Therefore, I expect that children who have internalized a deep sense of religious faith will believe that they matter to their family more than those whose faith is nonexistent or only perfunctory.

Table 6.1 Predicted Scores on the Mattering to Family Index

Predictor	*Estimated Score*
Age:	
11–12	64.853
13	65.195
14	65.322
15	64.989
16	65.458
17	65.941
18	66.178
Sex:	
Male	65.024
Female	65.813
Race/Ethnicity:	
Non-Hispanic White	66.244
Non-Hispanic Black	65.914
Hispanic	65.094
Parent's Education:	
Less Than High School	64.345
High School	65.627
Some College	65.752
College Diploma	66.063
Postgraduate Study	65.305
Family Structure:	
Never Married	64.456
Previously Married	65.749
Traditional	66.104
Religion Important:	
Not at All	63.180
Fairly	65.445
Very	66.582
Extremely	66.467
Number of Children:	
1	65.560
2	65.418
4	65.136
6	64.853
8	64.571

Note: Number of Children is fixed at 2 for all other comparisons
N = 1820

Accordingly, I analyzed a model in which level of mattering to family is predicted by each of the control variables. Table 6.1 presents the predicted scores on the Mattering to Family Index. The parameter estimates that yielded these scores are in the Appendix, Table A.16.

In considering the results, it is important to remember that the scores on the Mattering to Family Index are highly skewed. Fortunately for our society, most adolescents in the sample profess a fairly strong degree of mattering to their families. The measures of central tendency describe the location of scores on the number line: mean: 66.688; median: 69; mode: 71; skew: –1.705). (Recall that possible scores on the index ranged from a minimum of 15 to a maximum of 75.)

Note that the median is higher than the mean, and the mode is even higher than the median. This pattern describes the shape of the distribution. As indicated by the median, half the respondents have a very strong sense of mattering to their families. The mode shows that the most frequent score on the index is 71, a very high score. The skew reflects the fact that although scores range all the way down to the minimum (15), only a minority (38%) fall below the average.

Therefore, I transformed the distribution of scores to reduce the skew. I examined several possible mathematical transformations, including squaring the variable and exponentiation applied to the variable. Irrespective of the transformation used, the pattern of results and significance levels were virtually identical to those I found using the untransformed variable. For ease of presentation and discussion, I will discuss the analysis in terms of the untransformed variable.

The results show that all but two of the control variables play a role in the extent to which teenagers perceive that they matter to their families. Although mattering generally increases with age, none of the scores differs significantly from the average level found when all predictor variables are set to their "average" score (65.729). (Table 6.1 shows the particular values for each age, as well as for categories of all other control variables.) When I turn to the between-group contrasts, I do find that the youngest (11–12) and oldest (18) respondents do differ significantly (64.853 vs. 66.178). However, because of the lack of significance in the first analysis and the low threshold of significance ($p < .05$) in the second, it may be wise to be skeptical about this result.

In addition, the number of children fails to discriminate levels of mattering to the family. Although the pattern is in the expected direction (as family size increases, mattering to the family falls), the estimates do not come close to differing across age.

As I expected, gender does play a part in distinguishing mattering scores. Female adolescents (65.813) have a significantly greater average score on the Mattering to Family Index than do males (65.024).

Surprisingly, there are racial differences in mattering to one's family. Non-Hispanic whites (66.244) score higher on the mattering index than the average respondent. Neither minority racial/ethnic group differs from the average. In contrasting the three categories, I find the only significant difference arises between the non-Hispanic white and Hispanic (65.094). Non-Hispanic blacks (65.914) lie between them and do not differ significantly from either in mattering scores.

The analysis reveals a strong relationship between Mattering to Family Index scores and socioeconomic status, as measured by the adult respondent's highest level of educational attainment. Mattering scores for adolescents from families whose adult respondents have not received a high school diploma (64.345) are significantly lower than average, although none of the other educational attainment levels is distinguishable from the overall average (high school diploma: 65.627; some college: 65.752; college diploma: 66.063; and postgraduate study: 65.305). So, Bernstein (1961; Bernstein & Henderson, 1973) appears to be correct. Teenagers from the lowest level of socioeconomic status may indeed be handicapped by the cognitive processing and communication issues that prevent parents from clearly teaching their children that they matter.

Interestingly, the contrasts between groups reveal a non-linear pattern. Adolescent respondents from families with the lowest educational attainment believe they matter less than those from families whose adult respondent had earned a college diploma, but not compared to those who come from families whose adult respondents had completed high school or had some postgraduate study. The former lack of difference can be understood, in that the two educational attainment levels are consecutive. It is more curious that families attaining the highest level of education instill no more sense of mattering in their children than do those who have not made it through high school.

I must mention that the survey collected data on educational attainment from only the adult respondent. In two-parent families, the missing adult might have achieved a different level of education. However, I hasten to add that research by the sociologist Robert Mare (1991) shows that most people in the United States tend to marry people very close to them in levels of educational attainment.

Therefore, I do not expect the absence of data on education from a partner to be a serious problem for this analysis.

Next, the structure of the family contributes a great deal to the adolescent's sense of mattering. Here it is children from single-parent families who suffer. Those who come from two-parent families (married or cohabiting; remember, it is impossible to distinguish them in the survey) scored higher than average on the Mattering to Family Index. In contrast, those from single-parent families in which the parent was formerly married did not differ from the average. Finally, those with never-married single parents showed a marginal tendency to have lower than average scores.

In fact, it is only the contrast between teenagers from two-parent families (66.104) and single parent, never married, families (64.456) that achieves significance. Those who come from families in which a single parent had previously been married have a middling sense of mattering (65.749) that does not differ from the other two family structures. This result adds to the understanding of the benefits of growing up in a two-parent family presented by McLanahan and Sandefur (1994).

Finally, mattering to family is strongly predicted by the adolescent's religiosity. All categories of the importance of religion but one are different from the average mattering score. Those whose religion is extremely (66.467) or very (66.582) important to them are higher than average in mattering scores. In contrast, the irreligious believe they matter significantly less (63.180) than the average respondent. Those for whom religion is only fairly important (65.445) do not differ from the average mattering score.

The between-group contrasts elaborate on this pattern. The non-religious respondents significantly differ from every other religiosity category, as do the fairly religious. In contrast, the very religious and extremely religious do not differ from each other, although both believe they matter more than the two lower-religiosity categories.

As a consequence of the skew in the distribution of scores, highly significant coefficient estimates for the control variables will not yield a very large increase in mattering scores, because of a "ceiling effect." Predicted scores are constrained by the fact that most scores are fairly near the maximum value. This does not mean that the contributions from the control variables are trivial, however. Recall that in Chapters 4 and 5, mattering to family was consistently a strong predictor of each outcome variable under analysis. Therefore even a small change in mattering scores will produce sizable changes in the probability of engaging in an anti-social or self-destructive behavior.

One more point: In the analyses presented in Chapters 4 and 5, many of the control variables often failed to discriminate significantly the likelihood of engaging in the anti-social and self-destructive behaviors. One might be tempted to say that these variables are not important and should be discarded from the analyses.

But once again, this would be a hasty and ill-advised decision. It is more precise to say that they share no *direct* relationship with the outcome variables. However, by contributing to family mattering, these social context variables evince a strong *indirect* relationship with them. The fact that all but two of the control variables (age and number of children in the family) are significantly related to scores on the Mattering to Family Index gives evidence that they do, indeed, make a difference in the behavioral outcomes. Their relationships are simply mediated by mattering to family: Social Context → Mattering to Family → Behavioral Outcome.

A Different Perspective

Another way of examining the impact of the predictor variables is to ask whether they influence the extent to which scores on the index fall above or below certain thresholds of the distribution. The analysis in the previous section reveal those control variables that contribute to the likelihood that an adolescent's score on the Mattering to Family Index will be above or below the average score for the entire sample. For example, religiosity emerges as a significant predictor. This means, among other things, that irreligious adolescents are much more likely to fall below the average mattering score than are females. What about farther down the distribution? Does religiosity discriminate those who fall below one or two standard deviations below the mean? The farther along the distribution the variable discriminates, the more powerful its contribution to scores on the Mattering to Family Index.

Accordingly, I examined models in which the control variables predicted whether a respondent's score on the Mattering to Family Index would fall below each of two thresholds on the distribution of scores: one standard deviation below the mean (59.486), and two standard deviations below the mean (52.174). The results of the analysis are presented in the Appendix, Table A.17, and the changes in the probability of falling below each threshold can be found in Table 6.2. I will present the results for the significant control variables at each level of placement on the mattering to family continuum. The overall probability of being one standard deviation below the mean for the entire sample is .171, and that for being two standard deviations below the mean is .056.

The analysis reveals two control variables that work to place respondents at more extreme lower levels of the continuum. Inspection of Table 6.2 shows that race/ethnicity makes a difference for placement at both levels, but in very different ways. On the one hand, non-Hispanic whites are *less* likely than the average respondent to be found more than one standard deviation below the mean of Mattering to Family Index scores. The other two groups do not differ from the mean probability. On the other hand, when considering placement at the more extreme part of the dimension (two standard deviations below the mean), it is the Hispanics who stand out. They are *more* likely than the average teenager to fall below the lowest cutoff.

In short, being of the racial/ethnic majority keeps a teenager out of the middling low category of mattering, but not the extremely low one, when compared to the overall average. In contrast, Hispanics are relatively wanting for mattering. Although they are not more likely than the average adolescent to fall below the mean or even one standard deviation lower, they are more likely to be found within the lowest level.

Second, the adolescent's religiosity plays a very strong part in the probability that one's mattering score falls into the lower levels of mattering to one's family. Again from Table 6.2, it is clear that those for whom religion is unimportant are much *more* likely to report low mattering scores at both one and two standard deviations below the mean. Further, those for whom religion is very important are *less* likely to fall below both of these levels. On the other hand, when religion is very or extremely important to the teenager, the mattering scores are likely to be *above* the average for the sample.

Examining the between-group contrasts, it is the irreligious teenagers who emerge as different. At both one and two standard deviations below the mean, they are more likely than any other level of religiosity to be found at these levels. The other levels of religiosity do not differ from each other in the propensity to inhabit the low levels of the mattering continuum.

Summing it up, almost every control variable differentiates between those who fall above and below the overall average Mattering to Family

Table 6.2 Placement on the Mattering to Family Continuum as a Function of the Control Variables

Predictor	*Below One Standard Deviation Less than the Mean*	*Below Two Standard Deviations Less than the Mean*
Age		
11–12	.176	.041
13	.184	.057
14	.159	.050
15	.209	.050
16	.146	.063
17	.142	.066
18	.184	.075
Gender		
Male	.177	.056
Female	.165	.056
Race		
Non-Hispanic White	.135	.046
Non-Hispanic Black	.159	.056
Hispanic	.209	.097
Parent Respondent's Educational Attainment		
Less than High School	.190	.061
High School Diploma	.188	.061
Some College	.163	.058
College Diploma	.139	.041
Postgraduate Study	.179	.065
Family Structure		
Single-Parent, Never Married	.192	.066
Single-Parent, Previously Married	.158	.065
Married	.164	.042
Importance of Religion		
Not Important	.287	.130
Fairly Important	.160	.047
Very Important	.123	.030
Extremely Important	.144	.052
Number of Children		
1	.164	.055
2	.171	.056
4	.186	.059
6	.202	.062
8	.219	.064

N = 1821

Index score, with the exception of age and the number of children in the family. Males are more likely to be disadvantaged with respect to mattering than females. Non-Hispanic whites are privileged compared to minorities. Those from families at the lowest levels of socioeconomic status are relatively lacking, in contrast to those at any other social status. Adolescents from two-parent families are more convinced that they matter to that family than are teenagers from single-parent families. The extremely and very religious enjoy a great deal of perceived mattering, whereas those for whom religion is unimportant feel deprived of the resource.

But two control variables do even more damage. Race and religiosity can consign some teenagers to the extremely low end of the mattering to family continuum. Whites are not only less likely to find themselves below the mean; they are also underrepresented at one standard deviation below the mean (although not at the lowest level). Hispanics are not disadvantaged until one examines those who are two standard deviations below the mean; here, they are disproportionately found.

Religiosity is especially powerful, because those who are not religious are more likely to find themselves at very low levels of mattering to their families. It does not matter at which level one focuses. The irreligious are there in greater numbers than one would expect if placement on the continuum were random. A family that does not instill a religious foundation in its children, whether by intent or by neglect, is also in many cases leading those children to believe that they do not matter.

However one looks at it, there are structural and personal factors that stack the deck, positively or negatively, regarding mattering to one's family. This can be somewhat daunting, in that those on the disfavored sides of the fence may believe that their plight is hopeless. And indeed, fighting the processes that underlie the "doing" of gender, socioeconomic status, and family structure in our society is difficult. But not impossible. To be sure, there are often social costs to defying the prescriptions and proscriptions of our symbolic universe regarding the role identities associated with each of these structures. However, mattering to family is not a biological or genetic phenomenon, lying deep within the child and only awaiting some social trigger to emerge. It must be learned, and cannot be self-taught. These lessons come from the parents and older siblings, not the adolescents.

It does not require total destruction of gender to let your son know that he matters as much as your daughter, even if the particulars of mattering are different. Reducing differences in mattering across socioeconomic status levels may be more difficult, considering the deep-seated qualitative differences in communication with children found in the restricted codes of lower-status families (Bernstein & Henderson, 1973). The overwhelming pressure of single-parenting may also stifle efforts at letting teenagers know that they matter to the family. And how likely will families that do not have a religious or spiritual component to them consider reversing themselves in order to find the impetus to increase their children's sense of mattering?

Of course, changes in our symbolic universe could make things easier. If we understood how our current understandings of masculinity and femininity disadvantage both boys and girls, we might be motivated collectively to change them. If we, as a society, encouraged families to broaden communications between members, lower-status families might not stunt the growth of perceived mattering in their children. And if we offered relief to the oppressed single parents in our nation, they might have the time to assure their children that they do matter. But these changes will not come easily. They cannot merely be mandated. We will have to learn that they are necessary to improve the lot of our children, not just in mattering but in many other ways as well.

Teaching Children That They Matter

> *– Do you ever look into your eyes, Henry?*
>
> *– No, Mister Connolly.*
>
> *– You should, son. There's intelligence in there, I can see it sparkling. And creativity and anything else you want. They're all in there. And my daughter tells me you're a good-looking lad. Look into your eyes every morning, son. It'll do you good.*
>
> *And I did. Every morning. And I saw what he'd seen, smouldering away, knocking to get out. He'd fed me, given me clothes, he let me sleep in the Hall. He made me read. He let me know that he liked me. He explained why we were poor and why we didn't have to be. He told me that I was right to be angry. He was always busy and distant but there was always a wink or a grin as he looked up from his work or passed me. He wanted me there.*
>
> Roddy Doyle, *A star called Henry*

In the midst of all the structural contexts are adults trying to inculcate a sense of mattering within their children. With or without society's assistance, most parents want their offspring to know that they make a difference to the family, and they often enlist the help of older siblings in this task. At some level, they recognize the essential nature of mattering, even if they cannot articulate it, and they do the best they can to cultivate it in their children.

Still, it would be helpful if there existed specific principles and guidelines for this most important aspect of socialization. In the remainder of this chapter, I want to examine some of the particulars of mattering and how they may be actualized by parents, siblings, or any others with responsibility for a growing person (extended family, teachers, coaches). I will be making reference to a number of facets of each form of mattering that I identified when I constructed the index to measure mattering as a dimension of the self-concept (Elliott, Kao, & Grant, 2004); these facets were the basis for items in the Mattering Index. In addition, I will be distinguishing effective and misguided behaviors that one might consider when teaching a child that he or she matters. Finally, I will discuss some of the theoretical perspectives on parenting and delineate the essential place of mattering in the processes they use to explain good parenting.

I should add that these techniques are more effective when started early in the young person's life. Under the principle "What gets in early gets in deep," presented in Chapter 2, when a younger child realizes a healthy level of mattering to family, the foundation is set for a connection that will carry through the life course. Adolescents who have been secure with regard to mattering to family are very likely to accept new evidence that this is so without suspicion or skepticism. It *is* possible to convince teenagers who heretofore believed they did not matter that they, in fact, do. But it takes much more effort to be persuasive.

Awareness

Awareness is the realization that others know we exist. When people attend to us at appropriate times and in appropriate ways, we know that we matter to them. In our complex and busy society, attention can be a hard thing to come by. People are faced with so many role expectations that being given someone's undivided attention is a real gift. Most of us appreciate it when someone attends to us and feel uncomfortable when someone does not. Even the smallest slights can have serious repercussions, especially for a young person.

What does this mean in everyday doings? One thing it means is that others explicitly take notice of us when we are in their presence. Young people involved in an interaction within the family may begin to feel invisible if no one looks at them, addresses them, or pays attention to what they say. It can begin with a simple recognition specifically acknowledging their presence; calling a person by name is a very effective way to let others know that they have been noticed.

When people relate to us in a familiar way, showing that they can distinguish us from the other people involved in the encounter, it also signals that we matter. Most of us are pleased when others make public note of the unique (positive) aspects of our selves, and if they also know our faults, they at least have not consigned us to the undifferentiated masses.

Sometimes it is appropriate to focus one's attention solely on one child, at least for a little while. When young children (or adolescents) are begging for attention, family members can on occasion grant the child's wish to be noticed, even to the exclusion of all others. It takes a wise parent to discern when the request should be honored, but when done well, it warms the young person's heart.

Implied in each of these little acts is the obverse: Do not ignore those under your care. There is no greater blow to other people than to act as if they were not present. Few can bear feeling like a literal nonentity. If full attention cannot be paid, surely something can be done to acknowledge the young person's presence. Even if the message must be "I can't right now, but I will as soon as I can," the disappointed child will still appreciate the short acknowledgment that he or she is present.

The answers seem simple, but sometimes the simplest things are overlooked or incorrectly applied. For example, there can be such a thing as too much attention paid to a child. Parents who allow a child to have dominant or even exclusive access to their attention are not instilling a sense of mattering in the child. They are, rather, giving the child an inordinate amount of control over the parents. They are contributing to the egocentricity that is innate in a newborn child. The developmental psychologist William Damon (1995, p. 78) said it very well:

> When children learn to place themselves first, they learn to care more about their own personal experience than about the feelings and

> reactions of others. They come to ignore the guidance and feedback of others, because they have not learned to value it. They fail to establish a firm basis for respecting others, including even the important adults in their lives.

It is good for children, who, of biological necessity, are born egocentric to learn that there are limits to their power to bend others to their will. Indeed, children who are given unlimited control over their environment tend to be less, not more secure. They recognize at some deep level that they cannot handle such power and feel better (even if they do not admit it) when parents set reasonable limits on them.

At the same time, the aphorism "Children should be seen and not heard" takes a reasonable concern to the other extreme. Although children should not be able to command at will their parents' attention, they do need to know, by behavior, that their parents are mindful of them. Just a little attention, appropriately placed by the parents, can underscore the fact that the young person does indeed matter.

Importance

Importance is established by investing one's resources in another. Whether it be time, energy, or material goods, when people believe that they are the object of another's concern, they know they matter. There are many ways that a family can assure younger members that they matter in this critical way.

One of the simplest techniques is for parents to listen, *really listen*, when talking with their children. It is not only annoying to realize that someone is not listening; it is a grievous slight to the self. When a person's gaze wanders around the room while speaking of something of obvious importance to another, it is as if the person is looking for someone or something else to invest in. Apparently, the poor soul is not someone important enough to deal with seriously.

There are many resources parents (and older siblings) can provide to their children. The most obvious is financial, but it may not be as important as the provision of intangible things. Parents who buy all the latest toys, electronic and otherwise, for a child may believe that this signals how much a young person matters to them, but the child may not perceive it that way.

The child may be happier if the parent provides emotional support during times of trial. To know that someone in the family is concerned when things are going badly is to be assured that one is not superfluous to the family. A kind word or an affectionate hug will go a long way to communicate the extent to which mattering cements their relationship.

Parents who take pride in their children's accomplishments are working the other side of the street in communicating how much their children matter to them. However, the praise offered for good works must be carefully focused. In order to be effective, praise must be focused on the specific accomplishment and sufficiently detailed to demonstrate a familiarity with the challenges faced and the effort expended to succeed. ("I really like your use of contrasting colors in this painting. It sets off the two characters you are portraying" is much better than "Oh, what a grand painting!")

Vague, general proclamations that their kids are wonderful won't do it. First, even young children realize that they are not nearly perfect, and suggesting that they are smacks of insincerity and pandering. Second, children may make the attribution that if another can't see their imperfections, the person must be biased or imperceptive.

A parent who promotes the welfare of his or her child is doing much to demonstrate mattering. Urging young people to take advantage of available opportunities and providing appropriate assistance will do the job. Of course, the motivation behind the promotion is all-important. Parents truly interested in the welfare of their child will offer support even if the choice is not one the parent would wish for. This issue arises often in the choice of a college major. Parents often worry when their child chooses a "useless" major, but if the child really matters to them, they will bite their tongues.

In other cases, parents' support is not freely given, because they are trying to live vicariously through their children. Perhaps it is to make up for their own self-perceived failures: "My kid is going to take advantage of the opportunities I never had, or I'll know the reason why!" Or, it could be that the parent insists that the child keep up the standards set in the family. How many "pre-med" students begin their studies because their parents and even their grandparents are doctors, and they are expected to continue the family tradition? And how many see it through? If the motivation to follow a certain career path is not one's own, perhaps it is better not followed.

Much of parenting involves teaching. A great deal of what young people learn about themselves and how to be in the world comes from the explicit or implicit lessons given by their families. Explicit teaching takes time and effort, but they are not often wasted, if done with sensitivity to the needs and readiness of the child. The implicit part comes through modeling, and sometimes taking time to show how a thing is done can do even more to make it clear that the child matters. Instead of reading the newspaper, talking on the telephone with friends, or diving into the work brought home from the office, the parent who teaches his or her son how to ride a bicycle is saying, "You are important to me." And the child gets the message.

A surefire signal that a child matters is when members of the family inconvenience themselves on the child's behalf. Forsaking their own plans in order to support a young person's efforts means a great deal, and most will appreciate it. When an older sibling drives a child to a significant event, mattering is being signaled. The "soccer moms (and dads)" may find it difficult to make the playoff game, but if they trade their own tasks for cheering on their young athlete, it reveals the importance attached to the child. And yet, casual observation of some little-league baseball games can be frightening, when overinvolved parents scream at the umpires or, worse, at their children in order to achieve a better outcome. The focus must be on the child's chance to growth by participation in activity, not on the need to acquit oneself well.

Recognizing and providing for their children's needs (not necessarily wants) for successful maturation is another way to live out the claim that they matter. Although the youngster may not discriminate between needs and wants, it is essential for the parents to do so. A child's needs, such as physical health, a secure self-concept, and opportunities for emotional and psychological growth, must be met, and families that do so are showing how important their children are to them. In contrast, parents who frantically see that their children get everything they want are actually preventing them from maturing adequately. Although it is sometimes difficult to say "No," the word has its place in the parenting lexicon.

When the want is age-inappropriate, satisfying it will likely overwhelm the child and encourage what some have called the "hurried child syndrome" (Elkind, 2007). Hurried children are encouraged to take on roles and allowed to enact behaviors for which they have not been adequately prepared. In this case, saying "No" is a way to set appropriate limits. In dealing with limits, the child learns its way out of the egocentric perspective and into an outlook that better appreciates the mutual obligations that people have toward each other.

Limits can be sent gently or harshly, but it is only the former that communicates the importance of the child to the family. The latter may teach children that the parent must be obeyed, but such children will come to understand that it is the parental interests, not theirs, that are the force behind the command.

One example of limit-setting arises when parents regularly insist on knowing their teenager's whereabouts and activities. It will perhaps not be appreciated at the moment, but when friends discuss how their parents don't care about what they do, the adolescent may come to understand that limits are not set simply to irritate. Caring what their children do and with whom they do it is a subtle but important way for parents to tell their children that they are important to the family.

Another subtle form of mattering occurs when members of the family provide *constructive* suggestions for personal improvement. Given the egocentric nature of most adolescents, this is very difficult to do effectively. Perhaps the best way to make the effort is to proffer questions rather than declarative sentences. ("How do you think you will feel if you don't call Grandma?" "What are the pros and cons of not taking that course in economics?") The task is to convince the youngster that the parent's motivation is to help create an autonomous individual who can make efficacious decisions. The importance of this approach was made clear to me by the statement made by a Catholic priest, Reverend Robert Randall (personal communication, 1989), who said to the teenagers in his parish: "I love you just as you are, but I love you too much not to see you improve."

Warning: It is important not to substitute one's own inclination for that of the child. There lies manipulation, not mattering. Adolescents, and even young children, are not stupid (even if they sometimes seem to be crazy). It will not take them long to see through the façade that the child's welfare is what is important and to recognize that they are being used to further someone else's agenda. In that case, it is very likely that psychological reactance (Brehm, 1966) will set in. Reactance occurs when people suspect that the range of options for behavior is being narrowed by someone else. The ensuing frustration is likely to lead to more, not less, effort to do precisely what is being forbidden. The goal must be to show support for the child's welfare, not their own.

And the effort will work only if no exchange contract (explicit or implicit) is being negotiated. If the child "owes" the parents for their inconvenience, there is nothing special about the sacrifice, and no feeling of importance can be gleaned from the exchange.

Reliance

Reliance is the extent to which others look to an individual when they are in need. At first blush, it may seem that reliance is not a very significant part of mattering to one's family. But a deeper consideration of the term suggests otherwise. It is certainly true that parents should make the major decisions regarding the family's welfare. Very few parents seek their children's advice when deciding on a mortgage plan for the home.

But this does not mean that children must be excluded from family deliberation altogether. When parents seek input from their children in appropriate circumstances, they are telling them that their insights are important, even if the decision does not go the children's way. For example, parents can invite suggestions for the next vacation plans, while making the final decisions themselves. And who knows? Sometimes children do have good ideas.

Another way of allowing participation is to proffer options for a child's behavior. When children make decisions that are appropriate for their age and stage of development, they are learning to become functional members of the social order, but they are also learning that their desires count. Although parents may not allow a youngster to make a breakfast choice ("I want chocolate cake!"), they may proffer a number of acceptable options ("Would you prefer eggs or cereal this morning?"). They are signaling their reliance on the child to take charge where it is proper. As the child matures, the kind and number of decisions expand concurrently until the child has learned to become a functioning member of society.

The family also signals mattering by more direct reliance, again when it is fitting. There are times when advice from children, especially older children, is warranted. When buying a birthday gift for an adolescent's brother or sister, it may be a good idea to solicit some advice from the teenager as to how the sibling will react to certain options.

The family can also seek support from adolescents in its functioning, by assigning chores or other activities. Damon (1995, p. 36) speaks to the essential nature of such a requirement: "Performing serious service confers a sense of personal competence and a sense of personal responsibility. These virtues are central to the child's character development. The earlier that children begin acquiring them, the more surely they will flourish."

Part of that flourishing is realizing that they do make a difference in the world around them. Although teenagers may occasionally resent the "opportunity" to participate, they know, somewhere in their consciousness, that by doing so they matter. Children who are not required to participate in the maintenance and progress of the family are missing something, and, amidst their superficial glee at ducking responsibility, they know it. After a time, a child may begin to wonder at being left out of family routines and wonder about the extent to which he or she matters to the family.

What I am saying here is that mattering as reliance comes from enacting the role identity expected of children. Role identities contain not only rights and privileges but also commitments and obligations. There has been some loss of understanding of this important principle in parenting, as the tendency has become not to demand too much from children, lest they suffer. As Damon (1995, pp. 36–37) puts it:

> In our society, middle-class parents offer three reasons why they refrain from requesting service of their children. First, they say that it is more trouble [to] get children to do something right than simply to do it oneself. Second, they worry that their children are already overwhelmed with activities and 'stressed out' from all the demands of modern life. . . . Third, they believe that children have a 'right' to their own time. . . . Today's concerns revolve around the parent's convenience, the child's emotional comfort, and the shared sense among parents and children that fairness demands fully respecting children's time prerogatives. The concerns do not include worries about the child's future growth prospects.

When parents relieve their children of the "burdens" of role identity, they also relieve them of a sense that they matter to the family.

Parenting Styles and Mattering to Family

The suggestions I have advanced are illustrative of parenting tactics that can induce a sense of mattering to the family, but one must look beyond the collection (incomplete, at best) and ask if there is an overall style of parenting that is more likely to accomplish the task. There are many "guides" to parenting (Dinkmeyer & McKay, 1973;

Ginott, Ginott, & Goddard, 2003; Gordon, 1975; Popkin, 1983) with many strategies, but I will focus on a general perspective first presented by the developmental psychologist Diana Baumrind (1966, 1971).

Baumrind begins by distinguishing between two styles of parenting often discussed in the professional and popular literature. On the one hand, *authoritarian* parenting

> attempts to shape, control, and evaluate the behavior and attitudes of the child in accordance with a set standard of conduct, usually an absolute standard, theologically motivated and formulated by a higher authority. . . . [The parent] values obedience as a virtue and favors punitive, forceful measures to curb self-will at points where the child's actions or beliefs conflict with . . . right conduct. (Baumrind, 1966, p. 890)

There is no discussion about what is required of the child; simple obedience will suffice. The rules are enforced rigidly, even though they are not always clearly articulated. And if there are problems with obedience, "spare the rod and spoil the child" is a motto that fits well the authoritarian style of parenting. As a consequence, parental behavior toward the child evinces very little warmth and often is characterized by exasperation and anger. Authoritarian parenting can be characterized roughly as "high standards enforced harshly."

Authoritarian parenting is not well designed to instill a sense of mattering to the family (although it is not the worst form for that purpose). It is most facilitated by a restricted code of communication (Bernstein & Henderson, 1973), and as I described earlier, the restricted code denies the individuality of the child in the desire to have an efficiently functioning unit. The child, therefore, matters only to the extent that he or she does what is expected, with no questions asked. This might be reasonably expected with very young children, but in adolescence it almost invites rebellion.

At the opposite pole in the common-sense understanding of parenting is the *permissive* parent. The permissive parent

> makes few demands for household responsibility and orderly behavior. She [*sic*] presents herself to the child as a resource for him [*sic*] to use as he wishes, not as an ideal for him to emulate, nor as an active agent responsible for shaping or altering his ongoing or future behavior. She allows the child to regulate his own activities as much as possible, avoids the exercise of control, and does not encourage him to obey externally defined standards. (Baumrind, 1966, p. 889)

There is no need to communicate rules clearly, because the parent will never enforce them.

Permissive parenting can be divided into two subgroups: *permissive-indulgent* and *permissive-indifferent*. Permissive-indulgent parents do not enforce the rules because they do not want to "inhibit" the growth of their child. They are anxious that saying "No" may traumatize the child, so they set very few, if any, limits. Children soon learn the manipulative power this orientation offers them, and most are willing to use it. Whining and crying children are likely to be quite successful in getting their way, because the parent does not want to be "accused" of holding the child back or making the child unhappy. As a result, discipline is inconsistent, and the child does not learn that its behavior may be inappropriate.

On the other hand, permissive-indifferent parents take a laissez-faire approach to parenting. They set no limits because they do not want to be bothered with enforcing them. As long as their children do not inconvenience the parents with bad behavior, the children are assured a free reign, and young children are all too ready to ratify this pact. Freed of the albatross of parental responsibility, parents can pursue their own interests, distracted only when their children fail to police themselves accordingly.

Is there any doubt about the low sense of mattering to the family that is encouraged by permissive parenting? In the first case, the young person at first may appreciate the freedom and resources that indulgence supplies. But sooner or later, the child will realize that some challenges and opportunities require guidance. From their parents' coddling, they will come to sense a power within themselves that they know, intuitively, is beyond their ability to handle effectively. When the world is overwhelming, as it can often seem to teenagers experiencing the disruption of the self that accompanies this stage of development, they may long for the direction the indulgent parent has failed to provide. The feeling of betrayal that follows comes from the realization by the teenager that he or she did not matter enough to receive the necessary guidance.

With indifference, the consequence may be even worse. After all, children facing this parenting style learn very quickly that they are an encumbrance on their parents' freedom. They are surplus to the family, as far as they can tell. Their parents do not rely on them, will not invest in them, and hardly even notice they are around – lacking all three aspects of mattering in one source. Can there be a more desolating awareness for a teenager? It is the epitome of not mattering.

But Baumrind conceived of an alternative to the popularly understood parenting styles that she called *authoritative* parenting:

> The authoritative parent attempts to direct the child's activities in a rational, issues-oriented manner. She [*sic*] encourages verbal give and take, shares with the child the reasoning behind her policy and solicits his [*sic*] objections when he refuses to conform. Both autonomous self-will and disciplined conformity are valued by the authoritative parent. . . . She enforces her own perspective as an adult, but recognizes the child's individual interests and special ways. The authoritative parent affirms the child's present qualities, but also sets standards for future conduct. (Baumrind, 1966, p. 891)

The authoritative parent communicates expectations clearly and enforces them firmly. Children do have input into the process by communicating wants and wishes, and the parent sincerely listens to them, but in the end, the parent makes all decisions. If the child is to be disappointed, the parent will explain the reasons for the decision but will remain unmoved by attempts at coercion or any pleading by the child. The important point is that discipline is non-judgmental of the child's character. Undesirable behavior evokes an expectation of remorse and change; desirable behavior is greeted by pleasure and encouragement. Authoritative parenting can be roughly described as "high standards, enforced with warmth."

Authoritative parenting looks like a prescription for the elaborated code of communication discussed by sociolinguist Basil Bernstein (Bernstein & Henderson, 1973). The recognition of the idiosyncrasies of the child and the situation, the sharing of reasoning, and the verbal give and take are all accomplished through elaborated codes. Further, the whole process of parenting is structured to instill a sense of mattering. The recognition of the child's uniqueness betokens an awareness of who the child is. Although the exact nature of the reasoning used by parents must be appropriate to the current stage of development attained by the child, it will send a strong message of the child's importance to the family. The negotiation signals reliance (even though the child will not be making the decision), as the parents want to know the child's point of view.

I turn again to Damon (1995, p. 49) for elaboration of the importance of parenting style as a precursor to mattering. He discusses the importance of "respectful engagement" by the parent with the child. Its elements include the recognition of common interests; structuring the interaction so that the child comes to understand the parent's agenda; encouraging the child to participate actively and communicate his or her own beliefs and wants; and expressing the parent's own perspective in ways accessible to the child. These criteria are entirely consistent with the process of authoritative parenting and communicate that the child matters.

Empirical evidence reveals the effectiveness of authoritative parenting in furthering the child's well-being, relative to authoritarian and permissive parenting. Much as I have found with respect to mattering, Baumrind (1991) discovered that adolescents reared with authoritative parenting were less likely to use problem drugs than those experiencing other types of parenting styles. In addition, they were more likely to score higher on indices of "competence" (e.g., measures of maturity, resilience, and self-esteem).

Others have expanded the range of findings. Authoritative parenting increases the likelihood of secure attachment to the mother (Karavasilis, Doyle, & Merkiewicz, 2003) and emotional adjustment (Kaufmann et al., 2000). Generativity, developed and defined by the child psychologist Erik Erikson (1950) as the capacity to care for others, is increased by authoritative parenting (Frensch, Pratt, & Norris, 2007), as is Maslow's (1970) notion of self-actualization (Dominguez & Carton, 1997).

Behaviors are also affected by parenting style. Children reared with authoritative parenting do better and act out less in school, compared to children facing all other parenting styles (Lamborn, Mounts, Steinberg, & Dornbusch, 1991). Authoritative parenting also reduces the likelihood of adolescent smoking (Castrucci & Gerlach, 2006) and, more generally, delinquency (Simons, Simons, Burt, Brody, & Cutrona, 2005).

Mattering lies (implicitly) in all of these results. In a sense, they are affirmations of the relationships I report in this book. Authoritative parenting is an effective way to inculcate a strong sense of mattering to the family in children and adolescents. In taking into account the child's individuality, the parent is signaling awareness. The child's importance is involved in discussing the issues and explaining the decision. And reliance is emphasized when parents insist that the child meet the standards appropriate to its age and stage of development.

Begun early enough in the life course, the child can ride through the disturbance of the self in early adolescence and emerge as a young adult ready to take on the challenge of carving a place in the social order. Indeed, with adaptations geared to the age and stage of the child, the process begins in infancy. As the child's cognitive skills develop, parents can continue to teach their children how they matter to the family. Children who matter to their families have a firm foundation that protects them from so many of the pitfalls to which youth in our society are exposed.

Parenting: It's Not About the Parent

An important observation: The success of any parenting style, I have learned both academically and personally, depends ultimately on one very important skill, easy to articulate and difficult to employ: *Keep the "ego" out of it.*

I do *not* mean by this that the child should be the center of the family, allowed to act on whatever whim arises. This is indulgent, not authoritative, parenting. I *do* mean that parents must recognize that they need to balance their own legitimate needs as directors of the family with the child's need to learn how to be a human being who is both autonomous and socially integrated with other individuals, social institutions, and society as a whole.

No doubt, parenting can sometimes be a very exasperating experience. But it is useful to recall Leonard Berkowitz's (1993) finding that frustrations perceived as personal, intentional, and arbitrary are most likely to lead to violence, both physical and psychological. Parents who can distance themselves from the frustrations thrown at them by their adolescents can understand the annoying and sometimes insulting behaviors as the struggles brought on by the self-concept disturbance and subsequent reconstruction of the self that afflicts all teenagers to some degree.

It is easier said than done, primarily because of the strong emotional link between most parents and their children. Ironically, the love that connects parents to an offspring makes them especially vulnerable to manipulation by the very target of their love. Children recognize, even if only in an intuitive way, how much they matter to their parents and, in the egocentricity that characterizes youth, they are often very willing to use it to gain the advantage.

No matter how infuriating children (and especially adolescents) can be, it is important for parents to recognize that parenting is not about the parents; it is about producing a decent, healthy, and responsible human being. This is, perhaps, the most difficult task a human being can face, and it takes great effort. To be truly successful, parenting demands that children matter to their parents. And the best evidence of mattering goes well beyond mere awareness. It necessitates the sincere investment of time and energy, so that children will know they are important to the family. It requires reliance, in the form of parental expectations about appropriate standards of behavior and contributions to the family's well-being, enforced with love. All this is possible, if parents can keep their sense of self-worth and social evaluation out of it. Children are autonomous individuals, awaiting the guidance of someone who cares enough about them to allow them to become their own persons even as they remain linked to the family as a critical foundation for their development.

Parents who focus less on their own psychological and emotional needs are free to employ the precepts of authoritative parenting, offering direction, discipline, and support for the adolescent and, importantly, giving the adolescent the sense of mattering that is essential for human development. For mattering provides the foundation and reassurance necessary for adolescents to begin in earnest the shaping of an autonomous self, strong enough to seek out growth-inducing challenges and secure enough to be connected to others.

There is another way to look at the results of the analyses I have presented in this book. Parents should be encouraged, not daunted, by the overwhelming evidence that mattering to family is such an important protective factor in the lives of adolescents. In a very real sense, the implication is that most children need their families as much as their families need them. Parents can take advantage of that knowledge lovingly, knowing that if they act in ways that signal that their children matter, those children are likely to respond appropriately and enthusiastically. It is not manipulative to play on the need to matter to the family to help instill it in the young person. If parents recognize how much their children need to matter to the family, they may be less intimidated by the hard work necessary to ensure it.

Finally, as a sociologist I would be remiss if I did not note that individual effort at inducing mattering is conditioned by one's locus in the social order. The fact that there are structural sources for differences in levels of mattering among adolescents means that collectively we have much to do if this fundamental motivator is to be inculcated within all young people in our society. It would be a grave error to assume that people stuck in disadvantaged positions in our society are simply incapable of teaching their children that they matter.

The sociologist C. Wright Mills (1959, p. 8) long ago made the important distinction between *personal troubles* that "occur within the character of the individual and within the range of his [*sic*] immediate relations with others" and *public issues* that "have to do with matters that transcend these local environments of the individual. . . . They have to do with the organization of many such milieux into the institutional society as a whole." In short, mattering is as much a structural as a personal problem.

To be specific, gender differences in mattering argue that we must, as a society, re-examine our understandings of what it means to be a boy or a girl. Is there anything inherent in females that entitles them to enjoy a greater degree of mattering than experienced by males? It may be related to the notion that relationships are somehow worth more to females, and that the appropriate focus for males is on instrumental, efficacious behavior. When we realize that boys' unfamiliarity with relationships and the emotions that are involved with them is not biological but is socially taught, and when we are ready to teach them there is more to life than success and independence, then we may take greater care to make sure that boys realize how much they matter to their families.

Racial differences in mattering are more troubling. Still, if we understand that the distinctions in race and ethnicity are not biologically based but are socially constructed (Omi & Winant, 1994), we can think about how to rebuild our understandings of race that do not destroy the cultural differences that in part underlie them, perhaps it will be possible to help families understand the importance of mattering to their children's healthy development.

Here is another real possibility: At the beginning of the chapter, I mentioned that it is highly unlikely that there is something inherent in race or ethnicity that would militate against a child's mattering to family. Perhaps the differences I found in my analysis are caused by the fact that what it means to matter to the family is specific to the understandings that have developed over time as a part of the racial distinctions made by society. Indeed, it may be the case that each race/ethnicity constructs for itself an understanding of what it means to matter to one's family. If so, the measure I have constructed can be more valid for some racial/ethnic groupings than for others. It is especially important to determine if this is so, in order that it be possible to facilitate mattering to family, in whatever form it may take.

Lower levels of mattering within the lowest socioeconomic status levels indicate that, as a society, we must deal with the problem of restricted codes of communication and other factors that might inhibit mattering to family. Our society is very leery of interfering with family processes, and rightly so. Yet, as Bernstein (Bernstein & Henderson, 1973) and Sennett and Cobb (1972) have demonstrated, status differences in cognitive operation and orientation to the social world serve mainly to reproduce the status hierarchy in the United States. And this book has revealed significantly lower perceived mattering to family in adolescents from the lowest status levels in the Youth at Risk data.

Is there a way that society can encourage the development of elaborated codes of communication and authoritative parenting without violating the sanctity of the family? The process must include *both* parents and child. If, for example, the child learns elaborated codes only through programs offered at school, there could be two problems that might dampen their salutary effects. First, parents may be quite suspicious of any programs that may threaten or devalue the work they do at home. If so, they will be unlikely to support the programs and may even intentionally work to defeat them.

Second, if parents are not included, they will watch their children grow beyond them. Their restricted codes of communication and rule-bound approach to behavior will become ineffectual, as their children learn to question things and consider options. In short, the programs may well estrange child from parent.

Single-parent families need support so that the lone parent has the opportunity to assure her (usually) children that they do matter. If the major problem for mattering in single-parent families is that neither time nor energy is available to take on this critical aspect of child socialization (which cannot be done by anyone but members of the family), then it is incumbent on us collectively to provide the resources necessary for success.

In sum, although mattering is a part of the individual self-concept, it is good to remember that societal factors can both facilitate and inhibit the growth of mattering in teenagers (and probably children of all ages). If we view the failure to matter simply as an individual problem and not as a challenge to society as a whole, it is very unlikely that we will ever resolve it for the betterment of either the individual or society.

Too Much Mattering?

When self-esteem emerged as a pre-eminent concern in both the academic study of the self (Rosenberg, 1979) and the public desire to make children's lives better, after the initial enthusiasm a backlash arose against the concept (Baumeister, Campbell, Krueger, & Vohs, 2003; Hewitt, 1998). One major criticism was that one could have too much self-esteem, that people can come to an understanding of a self without flaws. As a result of this self-perception, those with "too high" self-esteem see themselves as superior to others, become egocentric, and engage in alienating and anti-social behaviors, like aggression (Baumeister, Smart, & Bowden, 1996).

There is little doubt that egocentric people will have great difficulty in relating to others, but this is not a problem of "too high" self-esteem. Rosenberg (1989) emphasizes that a realistically positive appraisal of the self can never be based on an understanding of the self as flawless. When he discusses high levels of self-esteem, he is careful to focus on what he calls *realistic* high self-esteem, the feeling that one is "good enough."

With realistically high self-esteem, individuals recognize their imperfections but believe that these imperfections do not overwhelm the positive aspects of themselves. In the final summation, the positive aspects, more seriously considered because they are more central to the self-concept, sufficiently outweigh the negatives. As Rosenberg (1989, p. 31; italics in the original) has written:

> The individual simply feels that he [*sic*] is a person of worth; he respects himself for what he is, but he does not stand in awe of himself nor does he expect others to stand in awe of him. He does *not* necessarily consider himself superior to others. . . . he does not feel that he is the ultimate in perfection but, on the contrary, recognizes his limitations and expects to grow and improve.

In fact, "too high" self-esteem can mean the opposite problem: Those who have unrealistically high self-esteem may not have high self-esteem at all. People with unrealistically high self-esteem recognize few, if any, faults in themselves, preferring selectively to perceive only the socially valuable components. ("Last year I was conceited, but now I'm perfect.") Indeed, the blanket denial of imperfections more likely signals a low level of realistic self-esteem. Such fantastic self-evaluations may be no more than an attempt to defend against a perception of the self that is problematic. As a result, true self-improvement is obviated, because one cannot change aspects of the self that one does not acknowledge.

And so it is with mattering. Inducing mattering in a child does not mean flooding him or her with a myriad of words and gestures. Being at the child's beck and call for continuous attention, investing in the child whenever it is demanded, and expecting too much from the child in the process of being a family will not induce mattering.

The sociologist Annette Lareau (2003) describes the process of "concerted cultivation," in which parents make sure that their children take advantage of every opportunity for social experience that comes their way. Of course, many advantages accrue to a child who engages in a wide variety of activities.

However, as she points out, there are also some notable disadvantages. Most relevant to the issue of mattering, children can develop a sense of entitlement, in which they come to expect that their parents (and other authority figures) will focus on their own needs and wants, irrespective of the needs and wants of others. It is important for parent and child to have a common understanding of the appropriate amount of inconvenience that the parent will endure for the sake of supporting the child. Some disappointment can be borne, if it is balanced by circumstances when the child comes first.

Academic deans at many colleges today lament the presence of what they call "helicopter" parents, who are in continual contact with them about the welfare of their children. From the most serious incidents (grave student misconduct) to the most trivial (their child has a cold), they hover above their children, just out of reach, but close enough to be involved in almost every aspect of the student's college life. Some may call this an expression of how much their children matter to them, but I do not.

Such behavior suggests a fusion between parent and child that does not connote mattering. In this kind of relationship, the child is then merely an "ego extension" (Rosenberg, 1979) of the parent. If children "matter" only to the extent that they follow the parents' directives or live up to the parents' standards of the parent, there will be no real mattering. Instead, it is likely to create the egocentrism and resultant anti-social behavior Baumeister and his colleagues found in "high self-esteem' participants in their studies. (And, as I have shown, much of adolescent self-esteem is highly related to the young person's sense of mattering to the family.) Ultimately, the most serious consequence could be a delay in full maturation. The great task of mattering is to encourage children to do their best. Then, congratulate them when they succeed and comfort them when they fail.

In sum, true mattering calls for a relationship that balances connection with autonomy. Young people must know that their parents are interested in them in times of serenity and are there for them in times of need. At the same time, they must know that their parents give them the chance to make their own lives, in age- and stage-appropriate ways. Mattering gives children the confidence as they mature to explore new things while relying on old ones. It is a relationship that assures that children will keep the family within their hearts, even as they create a self that will be truly their own.

The Future of Mattering

> *Gay and Fred Eisenhauer, whose son, Wyatt, an Army Ranger, was killed last May in Iraq by an improvised bomb, are still hoping to receive their son's watch, eyeglasses and cellphone. The phone is precious because it holds a recording of their son's voice. A combat patch they were promised has never arrived.*
>
> *"I know these are little things," Mrs. Eisenhauer said. "What makes it important to me is that my son was good enough to go over there [Iraq] to fight, but he is not important enough to get his stuff back to his family."*
>
> Lizette Alvarez, *New York Times*

Mattering is an exciting new concept in social psychology. Thanks to the pioneering efforts of Morris Rosenberg, we now have in clear, conceptual form an understanding of what I believe is the most fundamental motivator of human behavior. The results in this book have demonstrated the power of mattering. Whether directly or indirectly, through self-esteem and other mediators, mattering to one's family serves a strong, protective role against many of the anti-social and self-destructive behaviors to which adolescents may fall prey. It is good to know that something so simple, on the one hand, and so difficult, on the other, can work such wonders. Simple, because it really does not take much (besides time and energy) to provide and its consequences are immediate. Difficult, because it often requires conscious insight and discipline on the part of the parent. Like most aspects of parenting, inculcating mattering in children is not a "natural" or "instinctive" process. Ultimately, it is worth the effort, because the protective nature of mattering continues throughout the life course.

So, what next? The possibilities are almost endless. Because mattering is such a central aspect of the self, it is almost certainly the primary motivation for a wide range of human behavior. I have examined an important subset: anti-social behaviors (perhaps unrealistically) intended to establish or restore mattering to those who are without it and, for the truly desperate, self-destructive behaviors that will provide an escape from the agony of not mattering.

But there are many other areas where mattering plays a strong role. Just a few examples come to mind quickly. Surely, mattering has something to do with the building and maintaining of social relationships, from friendship to romantic involvement. Does mattering have any role in the prevention of mental illness, or the success of its treatment? Perhaps mattering is involved in the journey through the life course, including educational or occupational aspiration.

I have investigated a teenager's mattering to family, and this is clearly important, but there are many other sources of mattering in adolescence and throughout the life course. Considering individual sources of mattering, perhaps many students' progress in life is intimately tied to whether they mattered to a teacher whom they admired. Coaches can play this role for their athletic charges. And mattering to a loved one must be a sine qua non for a successful romantic relationship.

Beyond specific individuals, mattering to other social institutions beside the family can be important. This is surely the case with mattering to school. I wonder how many students whom I teach and advise believe that they matter to the "elite" institution of higher learning at which they have matriculated. Can a person matter to the military, whose ultimate goal is to break down the person's self in order to teach him or her to kill without compunction?

Other subpopulations in our society need to be studied. If one thinks about who is likely to matter, certain groups stand out as at risk. The elderly may very well believe that they are surplus members of our society. A glance at the structural and individual problems of health care and end-of-life treatment does nothing to contradict the hypothesis. The scandalous stories surfacing occasionally in the mass media chronicle the often inhumane conditions in which the elderly are forced to live out their last days.

The disabled among us may wonder if they matter much, given the stigma that many of them face. The simple problem of inaccessibility to building entrances signals that those with disability do not matter to our society. People may proclaim otherwise, but Goffman (1963) reminds us that if people can be defined as meaningfully different from the norm, the difference can quickly become a hierarchy. Those lower in the hierarchy become somehow inferior, and they do not "deserve" to matter as much. The disabled, often with obvious signs of their plight, are targets for such a redefinition.

The unemployed are equally likely to feel they do not matter, at least to the businesses that formerly employed them and perhaps to all of society as well. They may understand themselves only as fodder for the economic system, to be used as necessary and then left to their own devices. Indeed, when Marx and Engels (1848/2002) speak of the *lumpenproletariat*, the lowest among the working class, whom today we would call "the underclass" (Auletta, 1999), they are surely referring to those who do not matter to society.

So far, research on mattering (including my own) has been confined to the population of the United States. It is imperative to understand if mattering is a universal motivation, shared by people from all societies. Is mattering a meaningful concept in cultures that are fundamentally different from our own? If it is true that people all over the world feel the motivation to matter, it may be that the exact nature of mattering is culturally specific. For example, the symbolic universe of many Asian societies is very different from that of the United States. If Chinese children need to matter as much as our children do, is it induced and maintained in ways quite different from ours?

Finally, I am excited about the myriad possibilities of learning more about this complex entity/process called the self that have opened with the conceptualization and operationalization of mattering. Human beings are complex creatures, and the "common sense" approach to making sense of people is often misleading and ineffectual. In Chapter 1, I delineate some of the important research on mattering already available, but I look forward to much more. I believe that mattering will reveal many rewarding insights into behaviors and issues that are currently confusing or troubling. This is the purpose of scientific investigation, and the avenue opened by the discovery of mattering promises to be especially rich and fundamentally fruitful.

Appendix
Researching Mattering: A Scientific View

The Sample and the Procedure

Schulman, Ronca, and Bucubalas, Inc., conducted the cross-sectional survey by telephone for the Center for the Study of Youth Policy at the University of Pennsylvania. The survey comprised telephone interviews with 2,004 children between the ages of 11 and 18 residing at home. The sampling was stratified by telephone exchange and county; the data are self-weighted.

Telephone interviews were conducted during two time periods. The initial data collection period was between May and June 2000; the second data collection period occurred between October and November 2000. Approximately half the sample was surveyed in the initial period, while the remaining sample was interviewed during the fall. Interviews lasted, on average, 20 to 25 minutes. Refusals occurred for 19.3% of the total contacts; the completion rate of non-refusals was 80.6%.

Households that were contacted were initially screened for an eligible adolescent in the home. When more than one such child resided in the home, the interviewer selected the one who had the most recent birthday. Screening interviews were conducted with the parent (or parent figure) to obtain demographic information about the child and the family, including socioeconomic status (in the form of the adult respondent's level of educational attainment), number of children in the family, and family structure. The adult portion of the interview also included informed consent questions that asked permission to interview the youth.

The adolescent interview began with an informed consent question, in which the respondents acknowledged an understanding of the nature of the interview they were about to undergo. The first questions gathered demographic data on the child, such as age, sex, and race/ethnicity. In addition, respondents were asked how important religion is in their lives today.

Then followed the indices measuring mattering to family, and self-esteem. Each index was randomly ordered for each respondent, and the order of items within each index was also randomized.

In addition, adolescent respondents were asked the extent to which they engage in a wide range of behaviors, some anti-social (truancy, vandalism, dealing in contraband, theft from the family, violent behavior against people outside the family) and others self-destructive (illicit drug use, binge drinking, and planning and attempting suicide).

The items used to measure youth behavior were drawn from ongoing studies of the issue. This was done for the purpose of being able to compare this national survey of risk behavior to other efforts. The items covering delinquency, violence, binge drinking, and suicide were drawn from the Centers for Disease Control and Prevention's Youth Risk Behavior Survey.[1] Additional undesirable behavior items were selected from the University of Colorado's National Youth Survey (D. Elliott, Huizinga, & Menard, 1989), and the Monitoring the Future Survey (Johnston, O'Malley, & Bachman, 2003).

Characteristics of the Sample

The sample of adolescents was divided almost equally by gender. Non-Hispanic whites made up the large majority of respondents, followed by non-Hispanic blacks, Hispanics, Asian/Pacific Islanders, Native Americans, and others. The age distribution was fairly uniform. Table A.1 presents the demographic breakdown for the respondents.

With regard to the family's socioeconomic status, the educational attainment for the adult respondent spanned a wide range, from grammar school to post-college study. However, the lowest levels of status are underrepresented, a consequence of conducting the interviews

[1] The CDC YRBS is a national survey of youth risk behavior. The survey samples approximately 12,000 students from 200 schools, in 25 states. The survey is a questionnaire, with 95 questions, which is completed by the students in class.

Table A.1 Demographic Characteristics of the Sample

Characteristic	*Frequency*	*Percent*	*Valid Percent*
Sex: Male	996	49.7	49.7
Female	1008	50.3	50.3
Race: Non-Hispanic White	1442	71.0	71.6
Non-Hispanic Black	270	13.5	13.6
Hispanic/Latino	205	10.2	10.3
Asian/Pacific Islander	49	2.4	2.5
Native American	26	1.3	1.3
Other	14	0.7	0.7
Missing	18	0.9	–
Age: 11 Years Old	221	11.0	11.1
12 Years Old	238	11.9	11.9
13 Years Old	233	11.6	11.7
14 Years Old	258	12.9	12.9
15 Years Old	293	14.6	14.7
16 Years Old	303	15.1	15.2
17 Years Old	243	12.1	12.2
18 Years Old	211	10.5	10.6
Missing	4	0.2	–
Respondent Adult Education			
Grammar School	58	2.9	2.9
Less than High School	149	7.4	7.5
High School Diploma/GED	695	31.3	31.3
Some College/Vo-Tech	597	29.7	30.0
College Diploma	357	17.8	17.9
Postgraduate Study	208	10.4	10.4
Missing	11	0.5	–
Adult Marital Status			
Married/Living as Married	1388	69.3	70.3
Previously Married	419	20.8	21.2
Never Married	109	5.4	5.5
Missing	30	1.5	–
Importance of Religion			
Not Important	321	16.0	16.3
Fairly Important	652	32.5	33.2
Very Important	625	31.2	31.8
Extremely Important	367	18.3	18.7
Missing	39	0.2	–

by telephone. Most of the adult respondents were married or living as married.

Measuring Mattering

Respondents' perceptions of the degree to which they matter to family were measured using an index, constructed from items selected from an index I have developed with two research assistants (Elliott, Kao, & Grant, 2004). Because of the length of the interview, I had to trim the number of items from 24 to 15. I chose items based on their performance on the original analysis, with an eye to retaining as much content validity as possible.

The original items were designed to measure a general feeling of mattering, with the source of mattering being "others." The survey substituted "my family" in the items. Some items reflected the awareness facet of mattering (e.g., "For better or worse, my family generally knows when I am around"); others tapped their sense of importance to their families (e.g., "My successes are a source of great pride to my family"); and others reflected a sense of their families' reliance on them (e.g., "People in my family count on me to be there in times of need").

Responses were in Likert format, with five options ranging from "Strongly Disagree" to "Strongly Agree." These responses were then coded such that a score of 5 represents the response that indicates the *highest* level of mattering, and a score of 1 indicates the *lowest* level of mattering.

I constructed an index for mattering to family by summing the scores on the items. The resultant index consisted of 15 items, with possible scores for each index ranged from a low of 15 to a high of 75. The sample mean for mattering to family was 66.69 and the standard deviation was 7.71. The complete list of items, along with evidence of reliability in the form of Cronbach's alpha and corrected item-total correlations (cf. Nunnally & Bernstein, 1994) can be found in Table A.2.

Measuring Self-Esteem

The survey employed nine items from Rosenberg's (1979) Self-Esteem Index. Responses were in the same Likert format as for mattering; the responses were coded such that a score of 5 indicates

Table A.2 Reliability Analyses for the Indices Measuring Mattering, Self-Esteem, and Attitudes toward Violence

Item	*Item-Total Correlation*
Mattering to Family	
Awareness	
In my family's social gatherings, no one recognizes me.[a]	.398
My family does not seem to notice when I come or go.[a]	.458
My family is usually aware of my presence.	.373
Whatever else happens, my family does not ignore me.	.313
For whatever reason, it is hard to get my family's attention.[a]	.465
Importance	
My successes are a great source of pride to my family.	.397
There is no one in my family who really takes pride in my accomplishments.[a]	.404
I have noticed that my family will sometimes inconvenience themselves to help me.	.325
If the truth be known, no one in my family really needs me.[a]	.423
For better or worse, my family generally knows when I am around.	.421
When I have a problem, my family usually doesn't want to hear about it.[a]	.470
My family does not care what happens to me.[a]	.375
Reliance	
When people in my family need help, they come to me.	.398
People in my family count on me to be there in times of need.	.415
Quite a few people in my family look to me for advice on issues of importance.	.379
Cronbach's alpha	**.795**
Self-Esteem	
I feel that I do not have much to be proud of.[a]	.506
I feel that I have a number of good qualities.	.442
All in all, I am inclined to feel that I am a failure.[a]	.454
I feel able to do things as well as most people.	.358
I wish I could have more respect for myself.[a]	.403
On the whole, I am satisfied with myself.	.444
I certainly feel useless at times.[a]	.420

Table A.2 (*cont'd*)

Item	*Item-Total Correlation*
I take a positive attitude about myself.	.521
At times, I think I am no good at all.[a]	.526
Cronbach's alpha	**.771**
Attitude toward Violence	
I could see myself committing a violent crime in 5 years.	.406
I could see myself joining a gang.	.383
It is OK to use violence to get what you want.	.465
I try to stay away from places where violence is likely.[a]	.264
People who use violence get respect.	.371
Lots of people are out to get you.	.313
Carrying a gun or knife would make me feel safer.	.448
If a person hits you, you should hit them back.	.533
It is OK to beat up a person who is badmouthing me or my family.	.567
It is OK to carry a gun or knife if you live in a rough neighborhood.	.510
It is OK to do whatever it takes to protect yourself.	.375
It is good to have a gun.	.428
Parents should tell their children to use violence if necessary.	.436
If someone tries to start a fight with you, you should walk away.[a]	.437
Cronbach's alpha	**.804**

[a]Reverse coded

the *highest* level of self-esteem, and a score of 1 indicates the *lowest* level. In a potential range of 9 to 45, the mean level of self-esteem was 39.03, and the standard deviation was 5.70. As with the Mattering Index, the reliability information is available in Table A.2.

Measuring the Control Variables

Of course, other factors in a youth's life, beyond mattering and self-esteem, can contribute to the likelihood of engaging in anti-social and self-destructive behaviors. Research and theories of adolescence have suggested a number of personal and social factors that are meaningful precursors to such behavior. (See e.g. the University of Colorado's National Youth Survey, conducted by D. Elliott, Huizinga, & Menard, 1989, for a careful and thorough study of anti-social behavior, and the review of the causes of risky behavior presented by DiClemente, Hansen, & Ponton, 1996.) The Youth at Risk data provided information on many of these factors.

The control variables can be divided into two categories: those measured at the categorical or ordinal level of measurement and those measured at the interval or ratio level of measurement. I will discuss each group in turn.

Categorical and Ordinal Variables

Variables at these levels of measurement include sex, race/ethnicity, socioeconomic status, family structure, and religiosity. Although age is technically a ratio level variable, given the literature on self-concept disturbance in the early adolescent years, I was concerned that the effect of age on the dependent variables of interest would be non-linear. Accordingly, I treated the age levels as separate categories for the analyses I conducted.

I used the "effect" coding scheme to make contrasts for the categories of these variables (Pedhazur & Pedhazur, 1997). In the Logistic Regression analyses used for the behavioral outcome variables, the consequence for this coding pattern is to contrast the odds for the behavior for each category with the overall odds of engaging in the behavior. In the Ordinary Least Squares Regression analyses used for self-esteem and attitude toward violence as intervening variables, the consequence of effect coding is to contrast the mean value of the dependent variable for each category with the overall mean of the dependent variable.

Age. The respondents in the Youth at Risk survey ranged from age 11 to 18. Because the 11-year-olds had very low levels of reported dysfunctional behaviors, I always combined them with the 12-year-olds. Certain anti-social or self-destructive behaviors are even rarer among young people. In that case, I truncate age until the remaining categories are sufficient to obtain reliable estimates.

Sex. I utilized the question "Are you male or female?" to separate respondents by sex.

Race/Ethnicity. Race/ethnicity was measured by the item "Which of the following race or ethnic categories best describes you?" The response options were White/Caucasian, African-American, Hispanic or Latino, Asian or Pacific Islander, and Something Else. In order to distinguish multi-racial adolescents, respondents were allowed to place themselves in more than one group.

I classified respondents according to four categories: Non-Hispanic White, Non-Hispanic Black, Hispanic, and Other. The scarcity of respondents in the categories of Asian, Native American, multi-racial respondents, and those who listed themselves as "Something Else" made reliable discriminations among these groups impossible. Therefore, I combined these into a category labeled "Other." As a consequence, contrasts involving this residual category will not be meaningful; the category was retained in the analyses so that data from these respondents would not be lost for the other variables.

Socioeconomic Status. I used the educational attainment level of the parent (figure) who responded to the following item in the parent's screening interview: "What is the highest grade or year in school you have completed?" Response options were None or Grade 1–8; High School Incomplete (Grades 9–11); High School Graduate (Grade 12 or GED certificate); Business, Technical, or Vocational AFTER High School; Some College, No Four Year Degree; College Graduate (BA, BS, or Other Four Year Degree); Post-Graduate Training or Professional Schooling after College. The categories I created were less than high school, high school diploma (or GED), some college (including vocational training), college degree, and post-graduate education.[2]

[2] Recognizing that parents' education may not be the best measure of socioeconomic status (especially when one considers that the item did not ascertain the educational attainment of the principal wage earner in the household), I carried out an analysis using another indicator of status: total family income. From the report of income, I calculated the family's position with respect to the poverty line for the respondent's family size. The four categories created were below poverty, between poverty and the median income for the sample, between the median income and $75,000, and above $75,000.

The results for the two analyses were highly similar for virtually all of the dependent variables, both in the effects of the two status variables and in the effects of the other variables in the model as well. However, the data on the poverty variable were missing for 206 respondents. Because of the similarity of results and in order to preserve a greater level of power for statistical tests, I report the analysis using educational attainment as the measure of socioeconomic status.

Family Structure. Parent respondents were asked, "Are you married, living as married, widowed, divorced, separated, or have you never been married?" I constructed a trichotomous family structure variable by first distinguishing those who claimed to be married or living as married from all others. Unfortunately, the question wording did not allow me to distinguish between traditional intact families and stepfamilies. The second category includes single parents who had previously been married (widowed, divorced, or separated). The third category consisted of single parents who had never been married.

Religiosity. Adolescent respondents were asked: "How important is religion in your life today?" Response options included "Extremely Important" (18.7% of respondents), "Very Important" (31.8%), "Fairly Important" (33.2%), "Not Very Important" (12.6%), and "Not Important at All" (3.8%). Once again, because I was sensitive to issues of non-linearity in effects, I constructed three groups of respondents, combining "Not Very Important" and "Not Important at All" because of the small frequency in the latter category.

Ratio Variable

Number of Children in the Household. I used two items in the survey to construct a variable counting the number of children in the household. The adult respondent was asked, "How many teens age 11–18 currently live in this household?" Later, they were asked, "NOT counting yourself, how many people currently live in this household?" The age of each person identified in this manner was ascertained. For a given household and for each person identified, if the age was 10 years or below, that person was included as an additional child in the household. The sum of children identified by these two questions yields the number of children in the household.

Limitations of the Data Set

The 2000 National Youth at Risk Survey has several benefits as a data set. It is a nationally representative sample of all 11- to 18-year-olds and provides a broad and detailed set of data on a variety of topics associated with risky and anti-social behavior. Yet, there are certain limitations found within these data.

Although the data do include mattering for family and friends, they do not include an index for mattering at school (discarded because the questionnaire was too long). It would have been preferable to have all three targets for mattering (the central spheres of an adolescent's life) to gain a more complete understanding of the importance of mattering for an adolescent.

A variable that proved difficult to operationalize in the manner hoped for was family structure. Because of the question wording, I could not distinguish between households that comprised two biological parents and those with stepfamilies.

In addition, the survey simply does not include certain control variables that one would be interested in examining, because of prior research asserting its import. For example, catastrophic events (such as a major accident or the death of a parent or other friend) could lead to adolescent anti-social and self-destructive behavior. An especially vexing omission is the lack of data on peer behavior for the activities that are the focus of the analysis.

Plan of the Analysis

Phase 1: The (Total) Effect of Mattering on Behavior

For the variables measuring anti-social (Chapter 4) and self-destructive (Chapter 5) behaviors, each analysis consists of three phases. The aim of the first phase is to determine the effects of mattering on the various anti-social and self-destructive behaviors for the adolescents participating in the study. To accomplish this purpose, I constructed statistical models in which the main independent variables were the mattering index and the dependent variable was the particular behavior in question.

The analysis also included the control variables, to determine if mattering's effect is robust in the presence of other theoretically meaningful predictors of the behavior. If mattering remains a powerful influence on behavior with the control variables in the analysis, one has persuasive evidence that its effect is not due to its relationship with any of the other predictors in the model.

Each of the outcome variables was highly skewed, with most respondents not engaging in the behavior in question. Therefore, I dichotomized each variable to reflect those respondents who did not do the behavior from those who did to any degree. To analyze the dichotomous dependent variable, I conducted Logistic Regressions using the SAS software package to provide estimates of the predictive coefficient for each independent variable and determine its level of statistical significance.

Phases 2 and 3: Elaborating the Effect of Mattering

The second and third phases together establish the strength of self-esteem as a mediator between mattering and adolescent behavior. The analytical treatment follows the pattern discussed in Kenny, Kashy, and Bolger (1998). (See Figure A.1 for a pictorial representation of the elaborated model.)

The objective of the second phase is twofold: (1) to determine the effect of self-esteem on adolescent behavior and (2) to examine the resultant coefficients for mattering when self-esteem is included in the analysis. Regarding the first objective, a significant effect for self-esteem would mean that it is also an important predictor of the behavior, thereby establishing part of the link in the chain model of mattering to self-esteem to behavior depicted in Figure A.1.

Second, if there is no meaningful change in the coefficients for mattering to family in the elaborated model, one can conclude that self-esteem does not channel the effect of mattering on behavior. In contrast, a drop in the coefficients for mattering when self-esteem is

Figure A.1 Mattering, Self-Esteem, and Adolescent Behavior

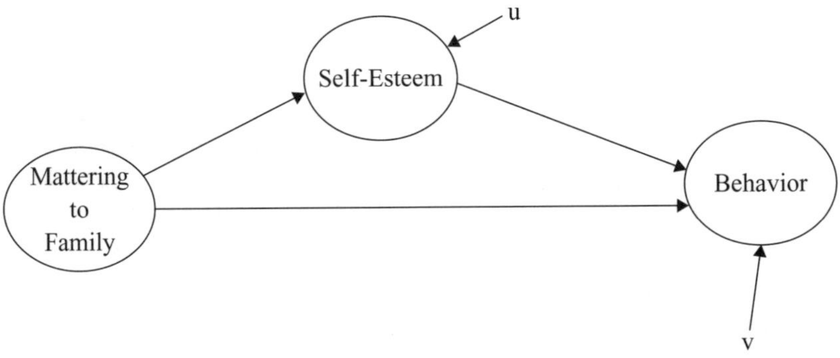

Note: Arrows from sources labeled with a lower case letter represent the contributions from factors not contained in the data (including randomness).

also in the model will suggest that the effects of mattering found in the first phase may be, at least in part, mediated by self-esteem. Indeed, if the effect of mattering fails to achieve significance, it is then reasonable to conclude that the entire effect of mattering on behavior is due to the mediating role played by self-esteem: Mattering predicts self-esteem, which, in turn, predicts adolescent behavior.

The third phase of analysis completes the investigation of the intervening properties of self-esteem. Even if self-esteem has a strong influence on adolescent behavior, if mattering to family does not relate to self-esteem, then mattering cannot be mediated by self-esteem; rather, mattering and self-esteem are independent influences on behavior. In order to substantiate self-esteem as a mediator of the relationship between mattering and behaviors, it is necessary to establish the first link in the chain depicted in Figure A.1.

To this end, I analyzed self-esteem as a function of mattering and the control variables. Because the dependent variable is measured (by design) at the interval level of measurement, I used Ordinary Least Squares Regression (again, with SAS) to estimate the contribution of each of the independent variables. A significant relationship between mattering on self-esteem, combined with a significant relationship between self-esteem and behavior from the second phase, would reveal self-esteem as a meaningful mediator of the relationship between mattering and behavior. Because the self-esteem variable consists of a range of responses along a continuum, Ordinary Least Squares Regressions of self-esteem on mattering to family and the control variables tests the hypothesis that mattering to family is a strong predictor of self-esteem.

Finally, for Chapter 6, I examine the control variables as predictors of levels of mattering to family. I use Ordinary Least Squares Regression analysis to estimate the contribution of each control variable and determine its statistical significance. For further explication of this relationship, I analyze the likelihood that a predictor variable will place a respondent at certain places in the distribution of mattering scores: below the mean, and below one, two, and three standard deviations under the mean. Because this categorization makes use of dichotomous dependent variables, I utilize Logistic Regression procedures for these analyses.

Reporting the Results of the Analyses

In reporting the results of the analyses in the first phase, I will present the probability that a respondent would engage in the targeted behavior as a function of varying levels of mattering to family. Because of its negatively skewed distribution, I will focus on the contrast across four levels of mattering: the mean, and one, two, and three standard deviations below the mean. In other words, the results I present will show how a diminution in mattering leads to an increased likelihood of the undesirable behavior in question.

Next, in the second phase, as self-esteem is added to the model, I will describe its independent contribution to these probabilities, using the same four-category discriminations that I use for mattering. In addition, I will present the changes in the contributions of mattering to the probabilities of behavior, due to the addition of self-esteem. Finally, I will show the part played by the control variables on the probability of the adolescent behavior.

Analyses not presented in this book demonstrate that no statistical interactions between the theoretical variables and any other variable emerged in the analysis (i.e., the effects of mattering and self-esteem were the same across levels of all other variables). Therefore, the pattern of variation in probabilities of the targeted behavior across levels of mattering and self-esteem will be the same for *any* combination of the other variables. The only change will be in the *absolute* probability of the behavior found across given levels of mattering. It is the *changes* in probabilities across the selected levels of mattering that are informative.

In Tables A.3 through A.17 (below) are the results of each of the Logistical Regressions and Ordinary Least Squares Regressions, in the order in which they are found in the chapters. The tables present the coefficient estimates, standard errors of the estimates, and the odds ratios (Logistic Regressions) or standardized coefficients (Ordinary Least Squares Regressions).

Table A.3 Ordinary Least Squares Regression of Self-Esteem on Mattering to Family and the Control Variables

Variable	*Coefficient*	*Standard Error*	*Standardized Coefficient*
Intercept	14.317***	1.090	–
Mattering to Family	0.371***	.016	.486
Eleven & Twelve	−0.659**	.244	−.064
Thirteen	−0.230	.307	−.019
Fourteen	−0.283	.285	−.025
Fifteen	−0.447+	.270	−.040
Sixteen	0.388	.263	.036
Seventeen	0.596*	.297	.051
Eighteen	0.635+	.328	.062
Male	0.619***	.114	.111
Female	−0.619***	.114	−.111
Non-Hispanic White	0.020	.204	.002
Non-Hispanic Black	1.103***	.289	.085
Hispanic	−0.571+	.316	−.040
Other	−0.551	.378	−.058
Less Than High School	−1.142***	.328	−.091
High School	0.199	.204	.022
Some College	0.102	.206	.011
College	0.234	.243	.022
Postgraduate	0.607*	.306	.048
Never Married	0.281	.357	.028
Previously Married	−0.180	.240	−.027
Married	−0.101	.215	−.010
Religion Not Important	−0.015	.237	−.002
Religion Fairly Important	−0.050	.185	−.006
Religion Very Important	−0.016	.188	−.002
Religion Extremely Important	0.081	.227	.008
Number of Children	0.008	.096	.002

+p < .10; *p < .05; **p < .01; ***p < .001
N = 1792

Table A.4 Logistic Regression of Truancy on Mattering to Family, Self-Esteem, and the Control Variables

	Mattering Only			*Mattering and Self-Esteem*		
Variable	*Coefficient*	*Standard Error*	*Odds Ratio*	*Coefficient*	*Standard Error*	*Odds Ratio*
Intercept	0.325	.5734	1.384	1.252*	.608	3.498
Mattering to Family	−0.025**	.008	0.975	−0.003	.010	0.997
Self-Esteem	–	–	–	−0.062***	.013	0.940
Eleven & Twelve	−1.276***	.193	0.279	−1.338***	.196	0.262
Thirteen	−0.716***	.203	0.489	−0.746***	.205	0.474
Fourteen	−0.310⁺	.166	0.733	−0.333*	.168	0.716
Fifteen	0.308*	.139	1.361	0.276*	.140	1.317
Sixteen	0.498***	.131	1.646	0.534***	.133	1.705
Seventeen	0.988***	.142	2.685	1.043***	.144	2.839
Eighteen	0.509**	.167	1.663	0.564***	.169	1.759
Male	0.641	.063	1.066	0.117⁺	.064	0.895
Female	0.641	.063	0.938	−0.117⁺	.064	1.117
Non-Hispanic White	−0.373***	.107	0.689	−0.384***	.108	0.681
Non-Hispanic Black	−0.622***	.166	0.537	−0.544***	.168	0.580
Hispanic	0.441**	.159	1.554	0.413**	.160	1.511
Other	0.554*	.181	1.740	0.515**	.183	1.674
Less Than High School	−0.104	.181	0.902	−0.181	.184	0.835
High School	0.030	.114	1.030	0.037	.115	1.038
Some College	0.229*	.112	1.257	0.238*	.229	1.499
College	0.111	.134	1.117	0.121	.136	1.129
Postgraduate	−0.266	.180	0.766	−0.216	.181	0.806
Never Married	−0.295	.215	0.744	−0.263	.215	0.769
Previously Married	0.221	.138	1.247	0.203	.138	1.225
Married	0.074	.125	1.077	0.061	.126	1.062
Relig. Not Important	0.417***	.119	1.518	0.419***	.121	1.520
Fairly Important	−0.043	.101	0.958	−0.051	.102	0.951
Very Important	−0.106	.105	0.899	−0.101	.106	0.904
Extremely Important	−0.268*	.131	0.765	−0.268*	.132	0.765
Number of Children	0.026	.055	1.027	0.031	.055	1.032

⁺p < .10; *p < .05; **p < .01; ***p < .001
N = 1758

Table A.5 Logistic Regression of Vandalism on Mattering to Family, Self-Esteem, and the Control Variables

	Mattering Only			*Mattering and Self-Esteem*		
Variable	*Coefficient*	*Standard Error*	*Odds Ratio*	*Coefficient*	*Standard Error*	*Odds Ratio*
Intercept	0.446	.585	1.562	0.995	.619	2.705
Mattering to Family	−0.037***	.009	0.964	−0.022	.010	0.978
Self-Esteem	–	–	–	−0.040**	.014	0.961
Eleven & Twelve	−0.288⁺	.160	0.750	−0.319*	.161	0.727
Thirteen	0.104	.182	1.109	0.084	.212	1.088
Fourteen	0.456**	.155	1.577	0.445**	.156	1.560
Fifteen	0.362*	.152	1.437	0.346*	.152	1.413
Sixteen	−0.244	.173	0.784	−0.224	.174	0.800
Seventeen	−0.110	.190	0.896	−0.084	.191	0.919
Eighteen	−0.280	.225	0.756	−0.248	.226	0.781
Male	0.373***	.072	1.451	0.401***	.073	1.495
Female	−0.373***	.072	0.689	−0.401***	.073	0.669
Non-Hispanic White	−0.219⁺	.118	0.803	−0.221	.119	0.681
Non-Hispanic Black	0.216	.164	1.240	0.265	.165	1.304
Hispanic	−0.178	.190	0.837	−0.206	.191	0.814
Other	0.181	.202	1.199	0.162	.203	1.176
Less Than High School	−0.135	.205	0.874	−0.192	.207	0.825
High School	−0.147	.128	0.863	−0.141	.129	0.868
Some College	0.196	.122	1.216	0.203⁺	.223	1.225
College	−0.066	.152	0.936	−0.050	.153	0.951
Postgraduate	0.152	.181	1.164	0.180	.182	1.198
Never Married	−0.255	.232	0.775	−0.250	.233	0.779
Previously Married	0.139	.150	1.149	0.135	.151	1.145
Married	0.116	.137	1.123	0.114	.137	1.121
Relig. Not Important	0.118	.140	1.125	0.116	.140	1.123
Fairly Important	0.213⁺	.110	1.237	0.218*	.110	1.244
Very Important	−0.179	.148	0.836	−0.156	.120	0.856
Extremely Important	−0.268*	.131	0.765	−0.178	.148	0.837
Number of Children	0.066	.057	1.069	0.069	.057	1.072

⁺p < .10; *p < .05; **p < .01; ***p < .001
N = 1789

Table A.6 Logistic Regression of Dealing in Contraband on Mattering to Family, Self-Esteem, and the Control Variables

	Mattering Only			*Mattering and Self-Esteem*		
Variable	*Coefficient*	*Standard Error*	*Odds Ratio*	*Coefficient*	*Standard Error*	*Odds Ratio*
Intercept	0.318	.703	1.374	0.805	.751	2.237
Mattering to Family	−0.038***	.010	0.962	−0.027*	.012	0.974
Self-Esteem	–	–	–	−0.032+	.017	0.968
Eleven through Fourteen	−1.426***	.194	.240	−1.459***	.196	0.233
Fifteen	0.201	.175	1.223	0.184	.175	1.202
Sixteen	0.489**	.160	1.630	0.500**	.160	1.648
Seventeen	0.322+	.185	1.379	0.338+	.186	1.402
Eighteen	0.414*	.202	1.513	0.437*	.202	1.548
Male	0.269**	.091	1.309	0.296**	.092	2.114
Female	−0.269**	.091	0.764	−0.296**	.092	0.743
Non-Hispanic White	−0.243	.157	0.784	−0.244	.157	0.783
Non-Hispanic Black	−0.015	.237	0.985	0.030	.238	1.031
Hispanic	0.264	.230	1.302	0.234	.231	1.263
Other	−0.006	.284	0.995	−0.020	.284	0.981
Less Than High School	−0.213	.257	0.809	−0.251	.259	0.778
High School	−0.081	.158	0.922	−0.074	.159	0.928
Some College	−0.183	.167	0.833	−0.183	.167	0.833
College	0.185	.186	1.203	0.184	.187	1.202
Postgraduate	0.291	.217	1.338	0.325	.218	1.384
Never Married	−0.029	.286	0.971	−0.010	.285	0.990
Previously Married	−0.036	.191	0.965	−0.043	.191	0.957
Married	0.064	.170	1.067	0.054	.170	1.055
Relig. Not Important	0.720***	.162	2.054	0.727***	.162	2.068
Fairly Important	0.288*	.142	1.333	0.289*	.144	1.335
Very Important	−0.335+	.169	0.734	−0.316+	.170	0.729
Extremely Important	−0.699**	.233	0.497	−0.700**	.233	0.497
Number of Children	0.006	.078	1.006	0.008	.078	1.008

+p < .10; *p < .05; **p < .01; ***p < .001
N = 1791

Table A.7 Logistic Regression of Theft from the Family on Mattering to Family, Self-Esteem, and the Control Variables

	Mattering Only			*Mattering and Self-Esteem*		
Variable	*Coefficient*	*Standard Error*	*Odds Ratio*	*Coefficient*	*Standard Error*	*Odds Ratio*
Intercept	−0.079	.789	0.925	0.705	.826	2.024
Mattering to Family	−0.044***	.012	0.957	−0.020	.014	0.981
Self-Esteem	–	–	–	−0.064***	.019	0.938
Eleven & Twelve	−0.523+	.285	0.593	−0.568*	.286	0.567
Thirteen	0.126	.279	1.134	0.092	.282	1.096
Fourteen	0.182	.254	1.200	0.151	.256	1.163
Fifteen	0.451*	.219	1.571	0.429+	.220	1.536
Sixteen	−0.043	.253	0.958	−0.005	.254	0.995
Seventeen	0.010	.279	1.010	0.064	.280	1.066
Eighteen	−0.202	.335	0.817	−0.163	.338	0.850
Male	−0.024	.108	0.977	0.026	.109	1.026
Female	0.024	.108	1.024	−0.026	.109	0.975
Non-Hispanic White	0.004	.187	1.004	−0.003	.188	0.997
Non-Hispanic Black	−0.353	.309	0.703	0.251	.311	0.778
Hispanic	0.070	.290	1.073	0.011	.294	1.011
Other	0.278	.310	1.321	0.243	.312	1.275
Less Than High School	−0.178	.319	0.837	−0.263	.322	0.769
High School	−0.040	.194	0.961	−0.039	.194	0.962
Some College	0.094	.191	1.099	0.100	.192	1.105
College	−0.067	.237	0.935	−0.049	.237	0.952
Postgraduate	0.191	.271	1.210	0.251	.274	1.285
Never Married	−0.085	.368	0.918	−0.067	.371	0.935
Previously Married	0.034	.238	1.035	0.020	.239	1.020
Married	0.051	.214	1.052	0.047	.215	1.048
Relig. Not Important	0.221	.203	1.247	0.218	.204	1.243
Fairly Important	0.231	.165	1.259	0.228	.166	1.257
Very Important	−0.380+	.204	0.684	−0.380+	.204	0.684
Extremely Important	−0.071	.226	0.931	−0.066	.226	0.936
Number of Children	0.011	.091	1.011	0.022	.056	1.022

+p < .10; *p < .05; **p < .01; ***p < .001
N = 1779

Table A.8 Ordinary Least Squares Regression of Attitude toward Violence on Mattering to Family, Self-Esteem, and the Control Variables

	Mattering Only			*Mattering and Self-Esteem*		
Independent Variable	*Coefficient*	*Standard Error*	*Standardized Coefficient*	*Coefficient*	*Standard Error*	*Standardized Coefficient*
Intercept	48.189***	1.762	–	51.113***	1 831	–
Mattering to Family	−0.285***	.026	–.243	−0.208***	029	–.178
Self-Esteem	–	–	–	−0.205***	038	–.134
Eleven & Twelve	–3.347***	.397	–.213	–3.470***	.395	–.220
Thirteen	1.660***	.501	–.090	–1.695***	.497	–.092
Fourteen	0.111	.459	.006	0.049	.456	.003
Fifteen	1.111**	.436	.066	1.018*	.433	.060
Sixteen	0.682	.426	.041	0.755^{+}	.423	.045
Seventeen	1.579***	.480	.088	1.695***	.477	.094
Eighteen	1.524**	.528	.097	1.649**	.524	.105
Male	2.056***	.185	.240	2.181***	.185	.255
Female	–2.056***	.185	–.240	–2.181***	.185	–.255
Non-Hispanic White	–1.274***	.331	–.087	–1.269***	.328	–.086
Non-Hispanic Black	1.144*	.468	.057	1.361**	.467	.068
Hispanic	0.312	.517	.014	0.207	.513	.015
Other	–0.182	.615	–.018	−0.299	.611	–.020
Less Than High School	–0.094	.533	–.005	−0.319	.530	–.017

Table A.8 *(cont'd)*

	Mattering Only			*Mattering and Self-Esteem*		
Independent Variable	*Coefficient*	*Standard Error*	*Standardized Coefficient*	*Coefficient*	*Standard Error*	*Standardized Coefficient*
High School	0.995**	.330	.071	1.034**	.328	.074
Some College	0.162	.334	.012	0.183	.332	.013
College	−0.429	.394	−.027	−0.379	.391	−.024
Postgraduate	−0.633	.495	−.033	−0.518	.492	−.027
Never Married	−0.215	.581	−.014	−0.140	.577	−.009
Previously Married	0.674⁺	.389	.065	0.627	.386	.060
Married	−0.459	.349	−.030	−0.487	.347	−.032
Religion Not Important	1.051**	.384	.072	1.055**	.381	.073
Religion Fairly Important	−0.068	.298	−.029	−0.078	.296	−.006
Religion Very Important	−0.331	.368	−.045	−0.336	.301	−.027
Number of Children	−0.197	.161	−.027	−0.196	.160	−.027

⁺p < .10; *p < .05; **p < .01; ***p < .001
N = 1773

Table A.9 Logistic Regression of Carry a Weapon on Mattering to Family, Self-Esteem, Attitude toward Violence, and the Control Variables

	Mattering Only			*Add Self-Esteem*			*Add Violence Attitude*		
Independent Variable	*Coefficient*	*Standard Error*	*Odds Ratio*	*Coefficient*	*Standard Error*	*Odds Ratio*	*Coefficient*	*Standard Error*	*Odds Ratio*
Intercept	0.2539	.733	1.289	0.371	.777	1.449	−4.934***	1.051	0.007
Mattering to Family	−0.048***	.011	0.954	−0.044***	.013	0.957	−0.026⁺	.014	0.974
Self-Esteem	–	–	–	−0.009	.018	0.991	0.021	.020	1.021
Attitude toward Violence	–	–	–	–	–	–	0.093***	.011	1.098
Eleven & Twelve	−0.465*	.223	0.628	−0.471*	.224	0.625	−0.017	.236	0.984
Thirteen	−0.518⁺	.299	0.595	−0.527⁺	.299	0.591	−0.347	.309	0.707
Fourteen	0.183	.214	1.201	0.180	.214	1.197	0.194	.226	1.214
Fifteen	0.212	.208	1.236	0.209	.208	1.232	0.130	.216	1.138
Sixteen	0.431*	.189	1.539	0.436*	.189	1.546	0.338⁺	.201	1.403
Seventeen	0.103	.246	1.108	0.107	.246	1.113	−0.173	.263	0.853
Eighteen	0.054	.260	1.056	0.066	.262	1.068	−0.140	.277	0.869
Male	1.000***	.123	1.453	1.006***	.124	2.732	0.774***	.127	2.141
Female	−1.000***	.123	0.368	−1.006***	.124	0.366	−0.774***	.127	0.461
Non-Hispanic White	0.412*	.174	1.509	0.413*	.174	1.511	0.573**	.183	1.774
Non-Hispanic Black	−0.714*	.306	0.490	−0.704*	.307	0.495	−0.972**	.324	0.379
Hispanic	0.100	.254	1.105	0.094*	.254	1.099	−0.929**	.343	0.395
Other	0.202	.302	1.224	0.197	.302	1.218	0.115	.265	1.122

Table A.9 (*cont'd*)

	Mattering Only			*Add Self-Esteem*			*Add Violence Attitude*		
Independent Variable	*Coefficient*	*Standard Error*	*Odds Ratio*	*Coefficient*	*Standard Error*	*Odds Ratio*	*Coefficient*	*Standard Error*	*Odds Ratio*
Less Than High School	0.241	.249	1.272	0.228	.250	1.256	0.276	.266	1.318
High School	0.082	.156	1.086	0.086	.157	1.090	−0.045	.166	0.956
Some College	−0.124	.170	0.884	−0.124	.170	0.884	−0.089	.177	0.915
College	−0.121	.201	0.886	−0.117	.201	0.890	−0.145	.211	0.865
Postgraduate	−0.079	.240	0.925	−0.074	.240	0.929	0.002	.252	1.002
Never Married	−0.043	.187	0.958	−0.045	.187	0.956	−0.148	.197	0.863
Previously Married	−0.186	.167	0.831	−0.188	.167	0.828	−0.143	.176	0.867
Married	0.228	.275	1.257	0.234	.275	1.263	0.290	.289	1.336
Religion Not Important	−0.121	.184	0.886	−0.121	.184	0.886	−0.265	.197	0.767
Religion Fairly Important	0.084	.143	1.088	0.086	.143	1.090	0.127	.150	1.135
Religion Very Important	0.025^{+}	.156	1.026	0.023	.156	1.023	0.040	.163	1.041
Religion Extremely Important	0.012	.200	1.012	0.013	.200	1.013	0.098	.209	1.103
Number of Children	−0.029	.078	0.971	−0.028	.078	0.972	0.011	.082	1.011

$^{+}p < .10$; $^{*}p < .05$; $^{**}p < .01$; $^{***}p < .001$
N = 1772

Table A.10 Logistic Regression of Violence outside the Family on Mattering to Family, Self-Esteem, Attitude toward Violence, and the Control Variables

	Mattering Only			*Add Self-Esteem*			*Add Violence Attitude*		
Independent Variable	*Coefficient*	*Standard Error*	*Odds Ratio*	*Coefficient*	*Standard Error*	*Odds Ratio*	*Coefficient*	*Standard Error*	*Odds Ratio*
Intercept	1.470**	.505	4.347	1.821***	.534	6.177	−4.116***	.724	0.016
Mattering to Family	−0.038***	.007	0.963	−0.029***	.008	0.971	−0.008	.010	0.992
Self-Esteem	–	–	–	−0.024*	.114	0.977	−0.00[illegible]	.013	1.001
Attitude toward Violence	–	–	–	–	–	–	0.11[illegible]***	.009	1.126
Eleven & Twelve	−0.692***	.135	0.501	−0.710***	.136	0.492	−0.32[illegible]*	.144	0.725
Thirteen	−0.045	.150	0.956	−0.054	.150	0.948	0.133	.163	1.142
Fourteen	0.341**	.130	1.407	0.335**	.131	1.398	0.369**	.142	1.446
Fifteen	0.160	.127	1.174	0.149	.128	1.160	0.027	.138	1.027
Sixteen	0.074	.126	1.077	0.084	.126	1.088	−0.013	.140	0.987
Seventeen	0.119	.142	1.126	0.133	.143	1.142	−0.062	.156	0.940
Eighteen	0.042	.161	1.043	0.063	.161	1.065	−0.131	.177	0.877
Male	0.373***	.056	1.453	0.390***	.057	1.477	0.158*	.063	1.171
Female	−0.373***	.056	0.688	−0.390***	.057	0.677	−0.158*	.063	0.854
Non-Hispanic White	−0.213*	.098	0.808	−0.213*	.098	0.808	−0.064	.107	0.938
Non-Hispanic Black	0.458***	.134	1.581	0.485***	.135	1.624	0.402**	.148	1.495
Hispanic	−0.287⁺	.156	0.751	−0.302⁺	.157	0.739	−0.389*	.172	0.678
Other	−0.042	.176	1.043	0.030	.177	1.031	0.051	.191	1.052

Table A.10 (*cont'd*)

	Mattering Only			*Add Self-Esteem*			*Add Violence Attitude*		
Independent Variable	*Coefficient*	*Standard Error*	*Odds Ratio*	*Coefficient*	*Standard Error*	*Odds Ratio*	*Coefficient*	*Standard Error*	*Odds Ratio*
Less Than High School	−0.015	.160	0.985	−0.045	.161	0.956	0.001	.175	1.001
High School	0.048	.099	1.049	0.053	.099	1.054	−0.088	.109	0.916
Some College	−0.036	.101	0.965	−0.031	.101	0.969	−0.055	.109	0.946
College	−0.086	.122	0.918	−0.080	.122	0.923	−0.041	.132	1.052
Postgraduate	0.089	.148	1.093	0.103	.149	1.108	0.183	.161	1.200
Never Married	0.066	.114	1.068	0.064	.115	1.066	−0.018	.127	0.983
Previously Married	−0.006	.103	0.994	−0.010	.103	0.990	0.045	.114	1.046
Married	0.095	.349	1.099	−0.053	.171	0.948	−0.027	.190	0.973
Religion Not Important	0.070	.114	1.073	0.071	.114	1.074	−0.058	.126	0.944
Religion Fairly Important	0.214*	.089	1.239	0.214*	.089	1.239	0.268**	.097	1.038
Religion Very Important	−0.171⁺	.094	0.843	−0.173⁺	.095	0.841	−0.157	.102	0.855
Religion Extremely Important	−0.113	.114	0.893	−0.112	.114	0.894	−0.054	.124	0.948
Number of Children	0.070	.047	1.073	0.327***	.059	1.386	0.111*	.051	1.118

⁺p < .10; *p < .05; **p < .01; ***p < .001
N = 1759

Table A.11 Logistic Regression of Illicit Drug Use on Mattering to Family, Self-Esteem, and the Control Variables

	Mattering Only			*Mattering and Self-Esteem*		
Variable	*Coefficient*	*Standard Error*	*Odds Ratio*	*Coefficient*	*Standard Error*	*Odds Ratio*
Intercept	−0.466	.918	0.628	−0.648	.984	0.523
Mattering to Family	−0.046***	.013	0.956	−0.050**	.016	0.951
Self-Esteem	–	–	–	0.013	.024	1.013
Eleven & Twelve	−0.498	.335	0.608	−0.488	.336	0.614
Thirteen	−0.267	.380	0.766	−0.256	.380	0.774
Fourteen	−0.607	.409	0.545	−0.604	.409	0.547
Fifteen	−0.243	.320	0.784	−0.241	.321	0.786
Sixteen	0.066	.297	1.068	0.060	.297	1.062
Seventeen	0.748**	.259	2.113	0.736**	.261	2.088
Eighteen	0.801**	.287	2.227	0.793**	.287	2.221
Male	−0.079	.127	0.924	−0.087	.128	0.917
Female	0.079	.127	1.082	0.087	.128	1.091
Non-Hispanic White	−0.062	.235	0.940	−0.062	.235	0.940
Non-Hispanic Black	−0.971*	.467	0.379	−0.987*	.468	0.373
Hispanic	0.359	.331	1.431	0.369	.331	1.446
Other	0.675*	.337	1.963	0.681*	.338	1.976
Less Than High School	−0.849⁺	.496	0.428	−0.835⁺	.497	0.434
High School	0.290	.228	1.336	0.286	.229	1.331
Some College	−0.037	.251	0.964	−0.038	.251	0.963
College	0.156	.285	1.168	0.156	.284	1.169
Postgraduate	0.441	.304	1.554	0.431	.305	1.538
Never Married	0.117	.257	1.124	0.119	.257	1.127
Previously Married	−0.146	.234	0.864	−0.142	.235	0.868
Married	0.029	.393	1.030	0.023	.394	1.023
Relig. Not Important	0.191	.263	1.210	0.185	.264	1.203
Fairly Important	0.621**	.209	1.860	0.623**	.210	1.864
Very Important	0.057	.244	1.059	0.056	.244	1.058
Extremely Important	−0.868**	.396	0.420	−0.864*	.396	0.422
Number of Children	0.017	.114	0.983	−0.020	.114	0.981

⁺p < .10; *p < .05; **p < .01; ***p < .001
N = 1792

Table A.12 Logistic Regression of Binge Drinking on Mattering to Family, Self-Esteem, and the Control Variables

	Mattering Only			*Mattering and Self-Esteem*		
Variable	*Coefficient*	*Standard Error*	*Odds Ratio*	*Coefficient*	*Standard Error*	*Odds Ratio*
Intercept	0.839	.747	2.315	1.543⁺	.847	4.677
Mattering to Family	−0.044***	.011	0.957	−0.029*	.013	0.972
Self-Esteem	–	–	–	−0.044*	.017	0.957
Eleven through Fifteen	−1.342***	.160	0.261	−1.388***	.161	0.249
Sixteen	0.152	.161	1.164	0.155	.161	1.168
Seventeen	0.326⁺	.171	1.385	0.344*	.271	1.410
Eighteen	0.864***	.165	2.373	0.890**	.166	2.434
Male	0.045	.094	1.046	0.084	.096	1.088
Female	−0.045	.945	0.956	−0.084	.096	0.919
Non-Hispanic White	0.333⁺	.185	1.396	0.339⁺	.185	1.404
Non-Hispanic Black	−0.511	.313	0.600	−0.440	.315	0.643
Hispanic	−0.223	.311	0.800	−0.258	.312	0.772
Other	0.401	.309	1.493	0.360	.312	1.433
Less Than High School	−0.230	.294	0.795	−0.275	.295	0.759
High School	0.092	.168	1.097	0.112	.168	1.118
Some College	−0.003	.173	0.997	−0.001	.174	0.999
College	0.250	.197	1.284	0.245	.198	1.277
Postgraduate	−0.110	.250	0.896	−0.081	.251	0.923
Never Married	−0.152	.193	0.859	−0.166	.194	0.847
Previously Married	−0.110	.170	0.896	−0.127	.170	0.881
Married	0.262	.280	1.299	0.293	.281	1.340
Relig. Not Important	0.321⁺	.172	1.379	0.331⁺	.172	1.393
Fairly Important	0.300*	.148	1.349	0.291*	.148	1.338
Very Important	−0.184	.171	0.832	−0.193	.172	0.825
Extremely Important	−0.436*	.222	0.646	−0.430⁺	.222	0.651
Number of Children	−0.149⁺	.091	0.862	−0.145	.091	0.865

⁺p < .10; *p < .05; **p < .01; ***p < .001
N = 1786

Table A.13 Logistic Regression of Depression on Mattering to Family, Self-Esteem, and the Control Variables

	Mattering Only			*Mattering and Self-Esteem*		
Variable	*Coefficient*	*Standard Error*	*Odds Ratio*	*Coefficient*	*Standard Error*	*Odds Ratio*
Intercept	1.624**	.589	5.071	3.288***	.648	26.787
Mattering to Family	−0.053***	.009	0.949	−0.010	.010	0.991
Self-Esteem	–	–	–	−0.119***	.014	0.888
Eleven & Twelve	−0.751***	.193	0.472	−0.885***	.201	0.413
Thirteen	0.215	.180	1.239	0.204	.186	1.226
Fourteen	0.012	.176	1.012	−0.039	.183	0.962
Fifteen	0.104	.162	1.110	0.023	.169	1.023
Sixteen	−0.093	.168	0.911	−0.039	.173	0.961
Seventeen	0.215	.174	1.240	0.339⁺	.179	1.403
Eighteen	0.298	.189	1.347	0.398*	.198	1.488
Male	−0.366***	.075	0.693	−0.287***	.078	0.751
Female	0.366***	.075	1.442	0.287***	.078	1.332
Non-Hispanic White	−0.090	.124	0.914	−0.098	.129	0.906
Non-Hispanic Black	−0.115	.180	0.892	0.674	.185	1.070
Hispanic	−0.118	.200	0.888	−0.209	.209	0.811
Other	0.323	.211	1.381	0.240	.221	1.271
Less Than High School	0.082	.198	1.085	−0.055	.206	0.947
High School	0.109	.129	1.115	0.120	.133	1.127
Some College	0.075	.131	1.078	0.096	.135	1.101
College	0.038	.157	1.039	0.055	.162	1.057
Postgraduate	−0.304	.214	0.738	−0.216	.219	0.805
Never Married	0.316*	.145	1.372	0.311*	.150	1.365
Previously Married	−0.145	.136	0.865	−0.176	.141	0.839
Married	−0.171	.229	0.842	−0.135	.237	0.873
Relig. Not Important	0.268⁺	.137	1.307	0.266⁺	.143	1.304
Fairly Important	0.039	.116	1.039	0.016	.120	1.016
Very Important	−0.078	.122	0.925	−0.068	.126	0.934
Extremely Important	−0.228	.150	0.796	−0.214	.154	0.807
Number of Children	0.013	.062	1.013	0.022	.064	1.022

⁺p < .10; *p < .05; **p < .01; ***p < .001
N = 1785

Table A.14 Logistic Regression of Planned Suicide on Mattering to Family, Self-Esteem, Depression, and the Control Variables

	Mattering Only			*Add Self-Esteem*			*Add Depression*		
Independent Variable	*Coefficient*	*Standard Error*	*Odds Ratio*	*Coefficient*	*Standard Error*	*Odds Ratio*	*Coefficient*	*Standard Error*	*Odds Ratio*
Intercept	0.507	.897	1.660	1.833⁺	.953	6.254	0.630	1.060	1.878
Mattering to Family	−0.064***	.013	0.938	−0.025	.016	0.975	−0.017	.017	0.974
Self-Esteem	–	–	–	−0.103***	.022	0.902	−0.060**	.023	0.942
Depression: Yes	–	–	–	–	–	–	1.186***	.159	3.279
Depression: No	–	–	–	–	–	–	−1.186***	.159	0.305
Eleven through Thirteen	−0.675*	.303	0.509	−0.758*	.309	0.469	−0.569⁺	.321	0.566
Fourteen	0.113	.321	1.119	0.061	.325	1.062	0.164	.343	1.178
Fifteen	0.111	.291	1.118	0.028	.298	1.029	−0.051	.319	0.951
Sixteen	0.264	.281	1.302	0.317	.287	1.373	0.287	.309	1.332
Seventeen	−0.379	.377	0.685	−0.192	.377	0.825	−0.359	.395	0.698
Eighteen	0.565⁺	.321	1.760	0.544⁺	.344	0.752	0.528	.342	1.696
Male	−0.981***	.192	0.375	0.914***	.196	0.401	−0.808***	.196	0.446
Female	0.981***	.192	2.668	−0.914***	.196	2.495	0.808***	.196	2.242
Non-Hispanic White	−0.161	.236	0.852	−0.167	.241	0.845	−0.134	.254	0.875

Non-Hispanic Black	−0.432	.373	0.649	−0.206	.380	0.814	−0.353	.395	0.702
Hispanic	0.291	.358	1.338	0.226	.368	1.253	0.374	.380	1.453
Other	0.302	.394	1.352	0.149	.410	1.161	0.113	.434	1.120
Less Than High School	−0.441	.413	0.643	−0.543	.418	0.581	−0.611	.429	0.543
High School	−0.099	.261	0.906	−0.100	.266	0.905	−0.174	.276	0.840
Some College	0.197	.242	1.218	0.194	.245	1.214	0.203	.262	1.225
College	0.178	.293	1.195	0.127	.301	1.135	0.080	.319	1.084
Postgraduate	0.164	.379	1.179	0.323	.381	1.381	0.502	.404	1.625
Never Married	0.295	.357	1.343	0.304	.235	1.355	0.586	.376	1.796
Previously Married	0.046	.250	1.047	0.042	.256	1.043	−0.195	.268	0.823
Married	−0.341	.228	0.711	−0.346	.234	0.707	−0.391	.240	0.676
Religion Not Important	0.362	.246	1.437	0.380	.249	1.462	0.216	.266	1.241
Religion Fairly Important	−0.044	.226	0.957	−0.085	.230	0.919	−0.011	.243	0.989
Religion Very Important	−0.105	.240	0.901	−0.102	.245	0.903	0.072	.259	0.930
Religion Extremely Important	−0.213	.279	0.808	−0.193	.283	0.824	−0.132	.301	0.876
Number of Children	0.096	.115	1.100	0.092	.118	1.096	0.107	.124	1.113

$^+p < .10$; $^*p < .05$; $^{**}p < .01$; $^{***}p < .001$
N = 1784

Table A.15 Logistic Regression of Attempted Suicide on Mattering to Family, Self-Esteem, Depression, and the Control Variables

	Mattering Only			*Add Self-Esteem*			*Add Depression*		
Independent Variable	*Coefficient*	*Standard Error*	*Odds Ratio*	*Coefficient*	*Standard Error*	*Odds Ratio*	*Coefficient*	*Standard Error*	*Odds Ratio*
Intercept	0.871	.979	2.390	2.203*	1.035	9.055	1.292	1.114	3.641
Mattering to Family	−0.075***	.015	0.9287	−0.039*	.018	0.961	−0.040*	.018	0.961
Self-Esteem	–	–	–	−0.100***	.024	0.905	−0.064**	.024	0.938
Depression: Yes	–	–	–	–	–	–	0.901***	.172	2.463
Depression: No	–	–	–	–	–	–	−0.901***	.172	0.406
Eleven through Thirteen	−0.106	.297	0.900	−0.161	.303	1.340	0.002	.312	1.002
Fourteen	0.317	.348	1.373	0.292	.351	1.340	0.359	.361	1.432
Fifteen	−0.235	.369	0.790	−0.368	.376	0.692	−0.442	.391	0.642
Sixteen	0.045	.338	1.081	0.103	.351	1.108	0.070	.366	1.073
Seventeen	−0.044	.389	0.957	0.162	.391	1.175	0.025	.405	1.025
Eighteen	0.023	.427	1.023	−0.027	.441	0.973	−0.014	.440	0.986
Male	−0.964***	.216	0.382	−0.907***	.220	0.404	−0.822***	.219	0.440
Female	0.964***	.216	2.621	0.907***	.220	2.477	0.822***	.219	2.275
Non-Hispanic White	0.003	.276	1.003	0.005	.279	1.005	0.041	.284	1.042

Non-Hispanic Black	−0.305	.414	0.737	−0.059	.423	0.943	−0.2[illegible]2	.432	0.817
Hispanic	−0.385	.495	0.681	−0.444	.501	0.641	−0.342	.503	0.710
Other	0.687⁺	.413	1.987	0.499	.428	1.646	0.5[illegible]2	.434	1.653
Less Than High School	−0.320	.522	0.726	−0.409	.524	0.664	−0.4[illegible]4	.534	0.616
High School	0.442	.294	1.555	0.427	.299	1.532	0.411	.303	1.508
Some College	0.375	.298	1.455	0.390	.301	1.477	0.368	.309	1.445
College	0.143	.372	1.154	0.124	.378	1.132	0.100	.388	1.105
Postgraduate	−0.639	.604	0.528	−0.531	.605	0.588	−0.394	.612	0.674
Never Married	0.359	.399	1.432	0.355	.412	1.426	−0.411	.303	1.508
Previously Married	−0.087	.285	0.917	−0.109	.293	0.897	−0.270	.299	0.763
Married	−0.272	.256	0.762	−0.246	.263	0.782	−0.258	.263	0.773
Religion Not Important	0.193	.286	1.213	0.202	.287	1.224	0.053	.298	1.065
Religion Fairly Important	0.079	.251	1.083	0.040	.254	1.041	0.092	.262	1.096
Religion Very Important	−0.089	.277	0.915	−0.076	.282	0.927	−0.011	.290	0.989
Religion Extremely Important	−0.184	.311	0.832	−0.167	.314	0.846	−0.144	.325	0.866
Number of Children	−0.025	.137	0.975	−0.024	.139	0.976	−0.030	.144	0.971

⁺p < .10; *p < .05; **p < .01; ***p < .001
N = 1781

Table A.16 Ordinary Least Squares Regression of Mattering to Family on the Control Variables

Variable	*Coefficient*	*Standard Error*	*Standardized Coefficient*
Intercept	65.729***	.497	–
Eleven & Twelve	−0.566	.360	−.042
Thirteen	−0.225	.455	−.014
Fourteen	−0.097	.427	−.006
Fifteen	−0.430	.401	−.030
Sixteen	0.038	.394	.003
Seventeen	0.521	.444	.033
Eighteen	0.758	.488	.057
Male	−0.394*	.170	−.054
Female	0.394*	.170	.054
Non-Hispanic White	0.825**	.303	.066
Non-Hispanic Black	0.495	.428	.029
Hispanic	−0.324	.469	−.017
Other	−0.997^{+}	.563	−.080
Less Than High School	−1.074*	.481	−.066
High School	0.209	.302	.017
Some College	0.334	.307	.028
College	0.644^{+}	.361	.047
Postgraduate	−0.113	.454	−.007
Never Married	−0.981^{+}	.522	−.077
Previously Married	0.304	.354	.020
Married	0.685*	.316	.053
Religion Not Important	−2.239***	.348	−.181
Religion Fairly Important	0.027	.274	.003
Religion Very Important	1.163***	.277	.111
Religion Extremely Important	1.048**	.336	.085
Number of Siblings	−0.141	.147	−.023

$^{+}p < .10$; *p < .05; **p < .01; ***p < .001
N = 1821

Table A.17 Placement on the Mattering to Family Index Continuum as a function of the Control Variables

	One Standard Deviation Below the Mean			*Two Standard Deviations Below the Mean*		
Predictor	*Coefficient*	*Standard Error*	*Odds Ratio*	*Coefficient*	*Standard Error*	*Odds Ratio*
Intercept	−1.687***	.185	0.185	−2.837***	.308	0.059
11 & 12	0.032	.147	1.039	−0.339	.278	0.712
13	0.094	.180	1.099	0.006	.302	1.006
14	−0.088	.178	0.916	−0.130	.301	0.878
15	0.254	.155	1.289	−0.121	.288	0.886
16	−0.182	.168	0.833	0.113	.250	1.119
17	−0.214	.193	0.808	0.167	.282	1.181
18	0.098	.193	1.103	0.306	.289	1.358
Male	0.044	.069	1.045	0.001	.116	1.001
Female	−0.044	.069	0.957	−0.001	.116	0.999
Non-Hispanic White	−0.280*	.117	0.756	−0.204	.208	0.816
Non-Hispanic Black	−0.086	.168	0.918	−0.040	.289	0.961
Hispanic	0.120	.174	1.128	0.555*	.275	1.743
Other	0.246	.201	1.279	−0.312	.406	0.732
Less Than High School	0.128	.186	1.137	0.078	.303	1.082
High School	0.114	.120	1.121	0.075	.201	1.078
Some College	−0.060	.127	0.942	0.036	.208	1.036
College	−0.242	.158	0.785	−0.346	.284	0.708
Postgraduate Study	0.059	.185	1.061	0.157	.305	1.170
Never Married	0.145	.192	1.156	0.161	.291	1.175
Previously Married	−0.096	.137	0.909	0.159	.203	1.172
Married	−0.050	.120	0.952	−0.320⁺	.187	0.726
Religion Not Important	0.667***	.123	1.949	0.921***	.185	2.512
Fairly Important	−0.078	.111	0.925	−0.190	.196	0.827
Very Important	−0.389**	.121	0.678	−0.655**	.228	0.519
Extremely Important	−0.200	.141	0.818	−0.076	.234	0.927
Number of Children	0.051	.058	1.053	0.023	.098	1.023

⁺p < .10; *p < .05; **p < .01; ***p < .001
N = 1821

A Caveat

No data set is perfect. As careful and exacting as researchers are, deficiencies always come to light only after examining the data. However, once the problems are discovered, there may be ways of minimizing the damage that they do to the analysis.

And so it is with the Youth at Risk study. Planning the analysis, it became clear that there were problems, not fatal but unfortunate, that would complicate the understanding of adolescent dysfunctional behavior.

One concern is a function of the method used to conduct the survey. It is very convenient and less intrusive to use the telephone to gather data. The respondents are not face to face with the interviewer, producing a heightened sense of anonymity and therefore a greater willingness to be candid in replying to the questions. In addition, mailed questionnaires can simply be ignored, resulting in high refusal rates; although respondents can, of course, not answer the telephone or decline to continue, it requires more effort.

For all these advantages, there is a problem with the method. Some adolescents still live in homes without a telephone, and they are not randomly distributed across the United States population. Rather, they are much more likely to be located in very poor households, some even in homeless shelters. Inaccessible to the interviewer, these adolescents cannot have a voice in this investigation. The sociologist Delbert Elliott (Elliott, Huizinga, & Menard, 1989) has shown a strong relationship between socioeconomic status and problematic behavior in adolescence. Because socioeconomic status is related to mattering, the cost of efficiency and convenience in gathering data may very well be a less than perfect understanding of mattering and its relationship to behavior.

On the other hand, reaching a wider range of adolescents at the lowest levels is not likely to eliminate or reverse the results I report in this book. If anything, one might expect them to become even more pronounced. And so, the loss of generalizability for the results I obtain may be relatively small. In any case, further studies that use a research method better designed to reach the poorest of the poor will shed light on the issue. The problem becomes an opportunity for continued research to extend the validity of mattering as an important motivation for behavior to a part of the population that is often underrepresented in social and behavioral science research.

A second drawback in the data could also influence the validity of some of the results reported in the following chapters. Unfortunately, in the interview, there is nothing to indicate whether members of the respondent's family or friends engage in any of the behaviors under examination. This is most unfortunate but cannot be remedied. Delbert Elliott (Elliott, Huizinga, & Menard, 1989) has confirmed that adolescent delinquent behavior is highly associated with friends' delinquent behavior. In addition, parents' and siblings' behavior are sometimes linked to that of their children. For example, parental use of illicit substances plays a large role in whether or not teenagers themselves are abusers (Hoffman & Cerbone, 2002).

The critical issue here is the question of whether mattering to family and self-esteem are associated with the family's or friends' problematic behavior. It is almost certainly the case that this is so, at least with some of the behaviors in question (such as drug use or violence). In that case, failure to include these factors in the analysis will, to some degree, distort the results for the two motivations. To some extent, the contributions of the omitted variables will have been absorbed by mattering, self-esteem, or both.

Although this defect cannot be remedied in the Youth at Risk sample, future studies can be designed to include measures of friends' and family members' anti-social and self-destructive behaviors. Analysis of such data would have to be quite sophisticated. For example, it must take into account the significant likelihood that the relationships between friends' and the family's behavior, on the one hand, and the adolescent respondent's behavior, on the other, is bi-directional. That is, the probability of one person's engaging in the behavior is influenced by the probability that the other also enacts it.

This "chicken-and-egg" conundrum can be dissected. But it is not easy and can be done only under certain circumstances. As I discussed when examining the outcomes of carrying a weapon and engaging in physical violence in Chapter 4, a longitudinal study over at least two time periods will do the trick. However, success will be determined by the extent to which perceived mattering to family changes over the several periods.

Alternatively, if one could find variables, one related *exclusively* to family members' behavior, friends' behavior, and the respondents' behavior, one could perform an analysis on cross-sectional data (gathered at only one point in time) to tease out the bi-directionality of the relationship. As I said before, this is a tall order.

Nevertheless, it would be a singular advance in the study of family process in general and mattering in particular to determine the nature of the reciprocities involving an adolescent's behavior and that of friends or other family members. In general, the problem is a useful reminder that in the social and behavioral sciences, researchers are never at a point at which they can assert that all that needs to be known about an issue has been discovered. Rather than be discouraged, such awareness can be an impetus to continue the pursuit of knowledge. It is part of the simultaneously comforting and vexing realization that we social psychologists will never be out of a job.

References

Ackard, D. M., Neumark-Sztainer, D., Story, M., & Perry, C. (2006). Parent–child connectedness and behavioral and emotional health among adolescents. *American Journal of Preventative Medicine, 30,* 59–66.

Ainsworth, M., Blehar, M. E., Waters, E., & Wall, S. (1978). *Patterns of attachment: A psychological study of the strange situation.* Hillsdale, NJ: Erlbaum.

Ali, A., & Toner, B. B. (2001). Self-esteem as a predictor of attitudes toward wife abuse among Muslim women and men in Canada. *Journal of Social Psychology, 141,* 23–30.

Allport, G. H. (1953). *The individual and his religion.* New York: Macmillan.

Amundson, N. E. (1993). Mattering: A foundation for employment counseling and training. *Journal of Employment Counseling, 30,* 146–152.

Anderson, C. A., Benjamin, A. J., Jr., & Bartholow, B. D. (1998). Does the gun pull the trigger? Automatic priming effects of weapon pictures and weapon names. *Psychological Science, 9,* 308–314.

Andrews, P. W. (2006). Parent–offspring conflict and cost-benefit analysis in adolescent suicidal behavior. *Human Nature, 17,* 190–211.

Anthony, D. B., Wood, J. V., & Holmes, J. G. (2007). Testing sociometer theory: Self-esteem and the importance of acceptance for social decision-making. *Journal of Experimental Social Psychology, 43,* 425–432.

Arnett, J. J. (1999). Adolescent storm and stress, reconsidered. *American Psychologist, 54,* 317–326.

Aspy, C. B., Oman, R. F., Vesely, S. K., McLeroy, K., Rodine, S., & Marshall, L. (2004). Adolescent violence: The protective effects of youth assets. *Journal of Counseling and Development, 82,* 268–276.

Athens, L. (1992). *The creation of dangerous violent criminals.* Urbana: University of Illinois Press.

References

Auletta, K. (1999). *The underclass.* Woodstock, NY: Overlook.

Bahr, S. J., Hoffmann, J. P., & Yang, X. (2005). Parental and peer influences on the risk of adolescent drug use. *Journal of Primary Prevention, 26,* 529–551.

Barber, B. K., & Buehler, C. (1996). Family cohesion and enmeshment: Different constructs different effects. *Journal of Marriage and the Family, 58,* 433–441.

Barnes, G. M., Hoffman, J. H., Welte, J. W., Farrell, M. P., & Dintcheff, B. A. (2006). Effects of parental monitoring and peer deviance on substantive use and delinquency. *Journal of Marriage and the Family, 68,* 1084–1104.

Barnes, G. M., Reifman, A. S., Farrell, M. P., & Dintcheff, B. A. (2000). The effects of parenting on the development of adolescent alcohol misuse: A six-wave latent growth model. *Journal of Marriage and the Family, 62,* 175–186.

Baumeister, R. F. (1990). Suicide as escape from self. *Psychological Review, 97,* 90–113.

Baumeister, R. F. (1993). Understanding the inner nature of low self-esteem: Uncertain, fragile, protective, and conflicted. In R. F. Baumeister (Ed.), *Self-esteem: The puzzle of low self-regard* (pp. 201–218). New York: Plenum.

Baumeister, R. F. (1998). The self. In D. T. Gilbert, S. T. Fiske, & G. Lindzey (Eds.), *The handbook of social psychology* (4th ed., Vol. 1) (pp. 680–740). Boston: McGraw-Hill.

Baumeister, R. F., Campbell, J. D., Krueger, J. I., & Vohs, K. D. (2003). Does high self-esteem cause better performance, interpersonal success, happiness, or healthier lifestyles? *Psychological Science, 4,* 1–44.

Baumeister, R. F., & Leary, M. R. (1995). The need to belong: Desire for interpersonal attachments as a fundamental human motivation. *Psychological Bulletin, 117,* 497–529.

Baumeister, R. F., Smart, L., & Bowden, J. M. (1996). Relation of threatened egotism to violence and aggression. *Psychological Review, 103,* 5–33.

Baumeister, R. F., Twenge, J. M., & Nuss, C. K. (2002). Effects of social exclusion on cognitive processes: Anticipated aloneness reduces intelligent thought. *Journal of Personality and Social Psychology, 83,* 817–827.

Baumrind, D. (1966). Effects of authoritative parental control on child behavior. *Child Development, 37,* 887–907.

Baumrind, D. (1971). Current patterns of parental authority. *Developmental Psychology Monograph, 4,* 1–103.

Baumrind, D. (1991). The influence of parenting style on adolescent competence and substance use. *Journal of Early Adolescence, 11,* 56–95.

Beck, A. T., Ward, C. H., Mendelson, M., Mock, J., & Erbaugh, J. (1961). An inventory for measuring depression. *Archives of General Psychiatry, 5,* 462–467.

Bem, D. (1972). Self-perception theory. In L. Berkowitz (Ed.), *Advances in experimental social psychology* (Vol. 6, pp. 1–62). New York: Academic.

Berger, P. L. (1969). *The sacred canopy: Elements of a sociological theory of religion*. New York: Anchor.

Berger, P. L., & Luckmann, T. (1966). *The social construction of society: A treatise in the sociology of knowledge*. New York: Anchor.

Berkowitz, L. (1993). *Aggression: Its causes, consequences, and control*. Philadelphia, PA: Temple University Press.

Berkowitz, L., & LePage, A. (1967). Weapons as aggression-eliciting stimuli. *Journal of Personality and Social Psychology*, *7*, 202–207.

Bernstein, B. (1961). Social class and linguistic development: A theory of social learning. In A. H. Halsey, J. Floud, & C. A. Anderson (Eds.), *Education, economy, and society* (pp. 288–314). Glencoe, IL: Free.

Bernstein, B., & Henderson, D. (1973). Social class differences in the relevance of language to socialization. In B. Bernstein (Ed.), *Class, codes and control*. Vol. 2: *Applied studies towards a sociology of language* (pp. 24–47). Boston: Routledge & Kegan Paul.

Blaine, B., & Crocker, J. (1995). Religiousness, race and psychological well-being: Exploring social psychological mediators. *Personality and Social Psychology Bulletin*, *21*, 1031–1041.

Blaine, B. E., Trevedi, P., & Eshelman, A. (1998). Religious belief and the self-concept: Evaluating the implications for psychological adjustment. *Personality and Social Psychology Bulletin*, *24*, 1040–1052.

Blum, R. W., Beuhring, T., Shew, M. L., Bearinger, L. H., Sieving, R. E., & Resnick, M. D. (2000). The effects of race/ethnicity, income, and family structure on adolescent risk behaviors. *American Journal of Public Health*, *90*, 1879–1884.

Blumer, H. (1969). *Symbolic interactionism: Perspective and method*. Englewood Cliffs, NJ: Prentice-Hall.

Blumstein, P. (1975). Identity bargaining and self-conception. *Social Forces*, *53*, 476–485.

Bookwala, J., Frieze, I. H., & Smith, C. (1992). Predictors of dating violence: A multivariate analysis. *Violence and Victims*, *7*, 297–311.

Bowlby, J. (1969). *Attachment and loss*. Vol. 1: *Attachment*. New York: Basic.

Branje, S. J. T., van Lieshout, C. F. M., van Aken, M. A. G., & Haselager, G. J. T. (2004). Perceived support in sibling relationships and adolescent adjustment. *Journal of Child Psychology and Psychiatry*, *45*, 1385–1396.

Brehm, J. W. (1966). *A theory of psychological reactance*. New York: Academic.

Briere, J. (1987). Predicting self-reported likelihood of battering: Attitudes and childhood experiences. *Journal of Research in Personality*, *21*, 61–69.

Brim, O. G., Jr., & Wheeler, S. (1966). *Socialization after childhood: Two essays*. New York: Wiley.

British Broadcasting Corporation. (2007, April 19). Loner filled with anger and spite. Retrieved from http://www.BBCNews.com.

Brook, S. S., Brook, D. W., Gordon, A. S., Whiteman, M., & Cohen, P. (1990). The psychosocial etiology of adolescent drug use: A family interactional approach. *Genetic, social, and general psychology monographs, 116*, 111–267.

Bushman, B. J., & Baumeister, R. F. (1998). Threatened egotism, narcissism, self-esteem, and direct and displaced aggression: Does self-love or self-hate lead to violence? *Journal of Personality and Social Psychology, 75*, 219–229.

Cable News Network. (1995, November 19). The road to Oklahama. Retrieved from http://www.CNN.com.

Castrucci, B. C., & Gerlach, K. K. (2006). Understanding the association between authoritative parenting and adolescent smoking. *Maternal and Child Health Journal, 10*, 217–224.

Cohen, Y., Spirito, A., & Brown, L. K. (1996). Suicide and suicidal behavior. In R. J. DiClemente, W. B. Hansen, & L. E. Ponton (Eds.), *Handbook of adolescent health risk behavior* (pp. 193–224). New York: Plenum.

Cooley, C. H. (1922). *Human nature and the social order* (rev. ed.). New York: Scribner's & Sons.

Cotten, N. U., Resnick, J., Browne, D. C., Martin, S. L., McCarraher, D. R., & Woods, J. (1994). Aggression and fighting behavior among African-American adolescents: Individual and family factors. *American Journal of Public Health, 84*, 618–622.

Criss, M. M., & Shaw, D. S. (2005). Sibling relationships as contexts for delinquency training in low-income families. *Journal of Family Psychology, 19*, 592–600.

Crocker, J., & Luhtanen, R. K. (2003). Level of self-esteem and contingencies of self-worth: Unique effects on academic, social, and financial problems in college students. *Personality and Social Psychology Bulletin, 29*, 701–712.

Crowne, D. P., & Marlowe, D. (1960). A new scale of social desirability independent of psychopathology. *Journal of Consulting Psychology, 24*, 349–354.

Damon, W. (1995). *Greater expectations.* New York: Free.

Dai, Y., Nolan, R. F., & White, B. (2002). Response to moral choices as a function of self-esteem. *Psychological Reports, 90*, 907–912.

DeWall, C. N., & Baumeister, R. F. (2006). Alone but feeling no pain: Effects of social exclusion on physical pain tolerance and pain threshold, affective forecasting, and interpersonal empathy. *Journal of Personality and Social Psychology, 91*, 1–15.

DiClemente, R. J., Hansen, W. B., & Ponton, L. E. (Eds.). (1996). *Handbook of adolescent health risk behavior.* New York: Plenum.

Dinkmeyer, D., & McKay, G. (1973). *Raising a responsible child.* New York: Simon & Shuster.

Dollard, J., Doob, L. W., Miller, N. E., Mowrer, O. H., & Sears, R. R. (1939). *Frustration and aggression.* New Haven, CT: Yale University Press.

Dominguez, M. M., & Carton, J. S. (1997). The relationship between self-actualization and parenting style. *Journal of Social Behavior and Personality, 12,* 1093–1100.

Durkheim, E. (1933). *The division of labor in society.* New York: Free.

Durkheim, E. (1951). *Suicide.* New York: Free.

Eagly, A. H., & Chaiken, S. (1998). Attitude structure and function. In D. T. Gilbert, S. T. Fiske, & G. Lindzey (Eds.), *The handbook of social psychology* (4th ed., Vol. 1, pp. 269–322). Boston: McGraw-Hill.

Elkind, D. (2007). *The hurried child: Growing up too fast, too soon* (25th anniversary ed.). New York: Perseus.

Elliott, D. S., Huizinga, D., & Menard, S. (1989). *Multiple problem youth: Delinquency, substance abuse, and mental health problems.* New York: Springer-Verlag.

Elliott, D. S., Huizinga, D., & Morse, B. (1986). Self-reported violent offending: A descriptive analysis of juvenile violent offenders and their offending careers. *Journal of Interpersonal Violence, 1,* 472–514.

Elliott, G. C. (1979). Some effects of deception and level of self-monitoring on planning and reacting to a self-presentation. *Journal of Personality and Social Psychology, 37,* 1282–1292.

Elliott, G. C. (1982). Self-esteem and self-presentation among the young as a function of age and gender. *Journal of Youth and Adolescence, 11,* 135–153.

Elliott, G. C. (1989). Self-serving attributions in the face of reality: The effect of task outcome and potential cause on self–other attributions. *Human Relations, 11,* 1015–1032.

Elliott, G. C., Colangelo, M., & Gelles, R. J. (2005). Mattering and suicide ideation: Establishing and elaborating a relationship. *Social Psychology Quarterly, 68,* 223–238.

Elliott, G. C., Kao, S., & Grant, A.-M. (2004). Mattering: Conceptualization and validation of a social psychological concept. *Self and Identity, 3,* 330–354.

Elliott, G. C., & Rosenberg, M. (1989). Self-esteem and social integration. In M. Rosenberg, *Society and the adolescent self-image* (pp. 240–259). Wesleyan, CT: Wesleyan University Press.

Elliott, G. C., Ziegler, H. L., Altman, B. M., & Scott, D. R. (1982). Understanding stigma: Dimensions of deviance and coping. *Deviant Behavior: An Interdisciplinary Journal, 3,* 275–300.

Emler, N., & Reicher, S. (1995). *Adolescence and delinquency.* Cambridge, MA: Blackwell.

Erikson, E. (1950). *Child and society*. New York: W. W. Norton.

Eron, L. D., Gentry, J. H., & Schlegel, P. (Eds.). (1994). *Reason to hope: A psychosocial perspective on violence and youth*. Washington, D. C.: American Psychological Association.

Evans, E., Hawton, K., & Rodham, K. (2004). Factors associated with suicidal phenomena in adolescents: A systematic review of population-based studies. *Clinical Psychology Review*, *24*, 957–979.

Evening Star. (1967, July 27). Press conference at the Student Nonviolent Coordinating Committee headquarters, Washington, D. C., p. 1.

Fenigstein, A., Scheier, F., & Buss, A. H. (1975). Public and private self-consciousness: Assessment and theory. *Journal of Consulting and Clinical Psychology*, *43*, 522–527.

Festinger, L. (1957). A theory of social comparison processes. *Human Relations*, *7*, 117–140.

Field, T., Diego, M., & Sanders, C. (2001). Adolescent depression and risk factors. *Adolescence*, *36*, 491–498.

Firestone, I. J., Kaplan, K. J., & Russell, J. C. (1973). Anxiety, fear, and affiliation with similar-state versus dissimilar-state others: Misery sometimes loves nonmiserable company. *Journal of Personality and Social Psychology*, *26*, 409–414.

Flouri, E. (2004). Correlates of parents' involvement with their adolescent children in restructured and biological two-parent families: The role of child characteristics. *International Journal of Behavioral Development*, *28*, 148–156.

Franck, E., & De Raedt, R. (2007). Self-esteem reconsidered: Unstable self-esteem outperforms level of self-esteem as vulnerability marker for depression. *Behaviour research and therapy*, *45*, 1531–1534.

Franke, T. M. (2000). The role of attachment as a protective factor in adolescent violent behavior. *Adolescent and Family Health*, *1*, 40–57.

Frensch, K. M., Pratt, M. W., & Norris, J. E. (2007). Foundations of generativity: Personal and family correlates of emerging adults' generative life-story themes. *Journal of Research in Personality*, *41*, 45–62.

Garnefski, N., & Diekstra, R. F. W. (1997). Adolescents from one parent, stepparent and intact families: Emotional problems and suicide attempts. *Journal of Adolescence*, *20*, 201–208.

Geuzaine, C., Debry, M., & Liesens, V. (2000). Separation from parents in late adolescence: The same for boys and girls? *Journal of Youth and Adolescence*, *29*, 79–91.

Gilligan, J. (1996). *Violence: Reflections on a national epidemic*. New York: Vintage.

Ginott, H. G., Ginott, A., & Goddard, H. W. (2003). *Between parent and teenager: The bestselling classic that revolutionized parent–child communication* (rev. ed.). New York: Three Rivers.

Goff, B. G., & Goddard, H. W. (1999). Terminal core values associated with adolescent problem behaviors. *Adolescence, 34*, 47–60.

Goffman, E. (1959). *The presentation of self in everyday life.* New York: Anchor.

Goffman, E. (1963). *Stigma: Notes on the management of spoiled identity.* Englewood Cliffs, NJ: Prentice-Hall.

Goffman, E. (1967). The nature of deference and demeanor. In E. Goffman, *Interaction Ritual* (pp. 47–95). New York: Doubleday Anchor.

Goffman, E. (1971). *Relations in public.* New York: Harper Colophon.

Goldstein, S., & Brooks, R. (Eds.). (2004). *Handbook of resilience in children.* New York: Springer-Verlag.

Gordon, T. (1975). *Parent effectiveness training.* New York: New American Library.

Gottfredson, M. R., & Hirschi, T. (1990). *A general theory of crime.* Stanford, CA: Stanford University Press.

Guillermo-Ramos, V., Jaccard, J., Turrisi, R., & Johansson, M. (2005). Parental and school correlates of binge drinking among middle school students. *American Journal of Public Health, 95*, 894–899.

Hackney, C. H., & Sanders, G. S. (2003). Religiosity and mental health: A meta-analysis of recent studies. *Journal for the Scientific Study of Religion, 42*, 43–55.

Hall, P. A., Elias, L. J., & Crossley, M. (2006). Neurocognitive influences on health behavior in a community sample. *Health Psychology, 25*, 778–782.

Halpern, C. T., Campbell, B., Agnew, C. R., Thompson, V., & Udry, J. R. (2002). Associations between stress reactivity and sexual and nonsexual risk taking in young adult human males. *Hormones and Behavior, 42*, 387–398.

Handel, G., Cahill, S. E., & Elkin, F. (2007). *Children and society: The sociology of children and childhood socialization.* Los Angeles, CA: Roxbury.

Harrington, N. (2005). It's too difficult! Frustration intolerance beliefs and procrastination. *Personality and Individual Differences, 39*, 873–883.

Harris, K. M., Duncan, G. J., & Boisjoly, J. (2002). Evaluating the role of "nothing to lose" attitudes on risky behavior in adolescence. *Social Forces, 80*, 1005–1039.

Harter, S. (1999). *The construction of the self: Developmental perspectives.* New York: Guilford.

Haugen, R., & Lund, T. (2002). Self-concept, attributional style and depression. *Educational Psychology, 22*, 305–315.

Hawkins, J. D., Catalano, R. F., & Miller, J. Y. (1992). Risk and protective factors for alcohol and other drug problems in adolescence and early adulthood: Implications for substance abuse prevention. *Psychological Bulletin, 112*, 64–105.

Heath, D. B. (1983). Alcohol and aggression: A "missing link" in worldwide perspective. In E. Gottheil, K. A. Druley, T. E. Skoloda, & H. M. Waxman (Eds.), *Alcohol, drug abuse and aggression* (pp. 89–103). Springfield, IL: Charles C. Thomas.

Heide, K. H. (1995). *Why kids kill parents: Child abuse and adolescent homicide.* Thousand Oaks, CA: Sage.

Heimer, K. (1997). Socioeconomic status, subcultural definitions, & violent delinquency. *Social Forces, 75,* 799–833.

Heimpel, S. A., Elliot, A. J., and Wood, J. V. (2006). Basic personality dispositions, self-esteem, and personal goals: An approach-avoidance analysis. *Journal of Personality, 74,* 1293–1319.

Henderson, V. L., & Dweck, C. S. (1990). Motivation and achievement. In S. S. Feldman and G. R. Elliott (Eds.), *At the threshold: The developing adolescent* (pp. 308–329). Cambridge, MA; Harvard University Press.

Hess, R. D., & Shipman, V. (1965). Early experience and the socialization of cognitive modes in children. *Child Development, 36,* 869–886.

Hewitt, J. P. (1998). *The myth of self-esteem: Finding happiness and solving problems in America.* New York: St. Martin's.

Hinton, S. E. (1967). *The outsider.* New York: Viking.

Hirschi, T. (1969). *Causes of delinquency.* Berkeley, CA: University of California Press.

Hoffman, J. P., & Cerbone, F. G. (2002). Parental substance use disorder and the risk of adolescent drug abuse: An event history analysis. *Drug and Alcohol Dependency, 66,* 255–264.

Horesh, N., & Apter, A. (2006). Self-disclosure, depression, anxiety, and suicidal behavior in adolescent psychiatric inpatients. *Crisis, 27,* 66–71.

Hunter, E. (1954). *The blackboard jungle.* New York: Pocket.

Hutton, F. (2005). Risky business: Gender, drug dealing and risk. *Addiction Research & Theory, 13,* 545–554.

Isen, A. M., & Hastorf, A. H. (1982). Some perspectives on cognitive social psychology. In A. H. Hastorf and A. M. Isen (Eds.), *Cognitive social psychology* (pp. 1–26). New York: Elsevier/North Holland.

Jacobson, K. C., & Crockett, L. J. (2000). Parental monitoring and adolescent adjustment: An ecological perspective. *Journal of Research on Adolescence, 10,* 65–97.

James, W. (1902). *The varieties of religious experience.* New York: Random House.

Jessor, R. J. (Ed.). (1998). *New perspectives on adolescent risk behavior.* New York: Cambridge University Press.

Johnston, L. D., O'Malley, P. M., & Bachman, J. G. (2003). *Monitoring the future: National survey results on drug use, 1975–2002.* Vol. 1: *Secondary school students* (NIH Publication No. 03-5375). Bethesda, MD: National Institute on Drug Abuse.

Jones., E. E., & Berglas, S. (1978). Control of attributions about the self through self-handicapping strategies: The appeal of alcohol and the role of underachievement. *Personality and Social Psychology Bulletin*, *4*, 200–206.

Jones, S., & Israel, P. (2001). *Others unknown: Timothy McVeigh and the Oklahoma City bombing conspiracy.* New York: Public Affairs.

Jourard, S. M. (1971). *Self-disclosure.* New York: Wiley.

Kandel, D. B., Kessler, R. C., & Margulies, R. Z. (1978). Antecedents of adolescent initiation into stages of drug use: A developmental analysis. In D. B. Kandel (Ed.), *Longitudinal research on drug use: Empirical findings and methodological issues* (pp. 73–99). Washington, D. C.: Hemisphere.

Karavasilis, L., Doyle, A. B., & Markiewicz, D. (2003). Associations between parenting style and attachment to mother in middle childhood and adolescence. *International Journal of Behavioral Development*, *27*, 153–164.

Kaufmann, D., Gesten, E., Santa Lucia, R. C., Salcedo, O., Rendina-Gobioff, G., & Gadd, R. (2000). The relationship between parenting style and children's adjustment: The parents' perspective. *Journal of Child and Family Studies*, *9*, 231–245.

Kenny, D. A., Kashy, D. A., & Bolger, N. (1998). Data analysis in social psychology. In D. T. Gilbert, S. T. Fiske, & G. Lindzey (Eds.), *The handbook of social psychology* (4th ed., Vol. 1, pp. 233–265). New York: McGraw-Hill.

Kenny, M. E., & Sirin, S. R. (2006). Parental attachment, self-worth, and depressive symptoms among emerging adults. *Journal of Counseling and Development*, *84*, 61–71.

Kim, J.-Y., McHale, S. M., Crouter, A. C., & Osgood, D. W. (2007). Longitudinal linkages between sibling relationships and adjustment from middle childhood through adolescence. *Developmental Psychology*, *43*, 960–973.

Kimmel, M. S. (2007). *The gendered society* (3rd ed.). New York: Oxford University Press.

Kinnier, R. T., Metha, A. T., Okey, J. L., & Keim, J. (2001). Adolescent substance abuse and psychological health. *Journal of Alcohol and Drug Education*, *39*, 101–111.

Kuhns, J. B., III. (2005). The dynamic nature of the drug use/serious violence relationship: A multi-causal approach. *Violence and Victims*, *20*, 433–454.

Lamborn, S. D., Mounts, N. S., Steinberg, L., & Dornbusch, S. M. (1991). Patterns of competence and adjustment among adolescents from authoritative, authoritarian, indulgent, and neglectful families. *Child Development*, *62*, 1049–1065.

Landsheer, J. A., & Hart, H. (1999). Age and adolescent delinquency: The changing relationship among age, delinquent attitude, and delinquent activity. *Criminal Justice and Behavior, 26*, 373–388.

Lareau, A. (2003). *Unequal childhoods: Class, race, and family life*. Berkeley, CA: University of California Press.

Lecky, P. (1945). *Self-consistency: A theory of personality*. New York: Island.

Lewinsohn, P. M., Rohde, P., Seeley, J. R., & Baldwin, C. L. (2001). Gender differences in suicide attempts from adolescence to young adulthood. *Journal of the American Academy of Child and Adolescent Psychiatry, 40*, 427–434.

Lewis, H. B. (1971). *Shame and guilt in neurosis*. New York: International Universities Press.

Lopez, J. S., Martinez, J. M., Martin, A., Martin, J. M., Martin, M. J., & Scandroglio, B. (2001). An exploratory multivariate approach to drug consumption patterns in young people based on Primary Socialization Theory. *Substance Use and Misuse, 36*, 1611–1649.

Lowry, R., Powell, K. E., Kann, L., Collins, J. L., & Kolbe, L. J. (1998). Weapon-carrying, physical fighting, and fight-related injury among adolescents. *American Journal of Preventive Medicine, 14*, 122–129.

Luster, T., & Oh, S. M. (2001). Correlates of male adolescents carrying handguns among their peers. *Journal of Marriage and the Family, 63*, 714–726.

McCall, G. J., & Simmons, J. L. (1978). *Identities and interactions: An examination of human associations in everyday life*. New York: Free.

McClelland, D. C., Atkinson, J. W., & Clark, R. A. (1976). *The achievement motive*. Oxford, UK: Irvington.

McCourt, F. (2005). *Teacher man*. New York: Scribner.

McLanahan, S., & Sandefur, G. (1994). *Growing up with a single parent: What hurts, what helps*. Cambridge, MA: Harvard University Press.

Mak, L., & Marshall, S. K. (2004). Perceived mattering in young adults' romantic relationships. *Journal of Personal and Social Relationships, 21*, 469–486.

Malecki, C. K., & Demaray, M. K. (2003). Carrying a weapon to school and perceptions of social support in an urban middle school. *Journal of Emotional and Behavioral Disorders, 11*, 169–178.

Mare, R. D. (1991). Five decades of educational assortative mating. *American Sociological Review, 56*, 15–32.

Markowitz, F. E. (2001). Attitudes and family violence: Linking intergenerational and cultural theories. *Journal of Family Violence, 16*, 205–218.

Markus, H. (1977). Self-schemas and processing information about the self. *Journal of Personality and Social Psychology, 35*, 63–78.

Marlatt, G. A., Baer, J. S., Donovan, D. M., & Kivlahan, D. R. (1988). Addictive behaviors: Etiology and treatment. *Annual Review of Psychology, 39*, 223–252.

Marshall, S. K. (2001). Do I matter? Construct validation of adolescents' perceived mattering to parents and friends. *Journal of Adolescence, 24*, 473–490.

Marshall, S. K., & Lambert, J. D. (2006). Parental mattering: A qualitative inquiry into the tendency to evaluate the self as significant to one's children. *Journal of Family Issues, 27*, 1561–1582.

Martin, K. A., & Brawley, L. R. (2002). Self-handicapping in physical achievement settings: The contributions of self-esteem and self-efficacy. *Self and Identity, 1*, 337–351.

Marx, K. (1876/1992). *Capital: A critique of political economy.* New York: Penguin Classics.

Marx, K., & Engels, F. (1848/2002). *The communist manifesto.* New York: Penguin Classics.

Maslow, A. (1970). *Motivation and personality* (2nd ed.). New York: Harper & Row.

Masterson, S. S., & Stamper, C. L. (2003). Perceived organizational membership: An aggregate framework representing the employee–organization relationship. *Journal of Organizational Behavior, 24*, 473–490.

Matsueda, R., & Heimer, K. (1997). A symbolic interactionist theory of role-transitions, role-commitments, and delinquency. In T. P. Thornberry (Ed.), *Developmental theories of crime and delinquency* (pp. 163–213). New Brunswick, NJ: Transaction.

Mead, G. H. (1934). *Mind, self and society.* Chicago: University of Chicago Press.

Menninger, K. A. (1968). *The crime of punishment.* New York: Viking.

Merton, R. K. (1938). Social structure and anomie. *American Sociological Review, 3*, 672–682.

Merwin, R. M., & Ellis, J. B. (2004). Children's reasons for living, self-esteem, and violence. *Archives of Suicide Research, 8*, 251–261.

Michel, L., & Herbeck, D. (2002). *American terrorist: Timothy McVeigh and the tragedy at Oklahoma City.* New York: Avon.

Miller-Perrin, C. L., & Perrin, R. D. (2007). *Child maltreatment: An introduction.* Thousand Oaks, CA: Sage.

Mills, C. W. (1959). *The sociological imagination.* New York: Oxford University Press.

MSNBC. (2007, April 30). Special report: Tragedy at Virginia Tech. Retrieved from http://www.MSNBC.com.

Myers, J. E., & Bechtel, A. (2004). Stress, wellness, and mattering among cadets at West Point: Factors affecting a fit and healthy force. *Military Medicine, 169*, 475–482.

National Institute of Mental Health. (n.d.). Depression. Retrieved from http://www.nimh.nih.gov/health/publications/depression/complete-publication.shtml.

New York Times. (2007a, April 22). Massacre in Virginia: The gunman. Retrieved from http://www.NYTimes.com.

New York Times. (2007b, April 20). Experts shy from instant diagnoses of gunman's mental illness, but hints abound. Retrieved from http://www.NYTimes.com.

New York Times. (2007c, December 6). Gunman at an Omaha Mall Kills 8 and Himself. Retrieved from http://www.NYTimes.com.

Nock, M. K., & Kessler, R. C. (2006). Prevalence of and risk factors for suicide attempts versus suicide gestures: Analysis of the National Comorbidity Survey. *Journal of Abnormal Psychology, 115*, 616–623.

Nunnally, J. C., & Bernstein, I. H. (1994). *Psychometric theory* (3rd ed.). New York: McGraw Hill.

Oates, R. K., and Forrest, D. (1985). Self-esteem and early background of abusive mothers. *Child Abuse & Neglect, 9*, 89–93.

O'Donnell, L., O'Donnell, C., Wardlaw, D. M., & Steuve, A. (2004). Risk and resiliency factors influencing suicidality among urban African American and Latino youth. *American Journal of Community Psychology, 33*, 37–49.

O'Keefe, M. (1998). Factors mediating the link between witnessing interparental violence and dating violence. *Journal of Family Violence, 13*, 39–57.

Omi, M., & Winant, H. (1994). *Racial formation in the United States* (2nd ed.). New York: Routledge.

Orpinas, P., Murray, N., & Kelder, S. (2007). Parental influences on students' aggressive behaviors and weapon carrying. *Health Education and Behavior, 26*, 774–787.

Overholser, J. C., Adams, D. M., Lehnert, K. L., & Brinkman, D. C. (1995). Self-esteem deficits and suicidal tendencies among adolescents. *Journal of the American Academy of Child and Adolescent Psychiatry, 34*, 919–928.

Paetsch, J. J., & Bertrand, L. D. (1999). Victimization and delinquency among Canadian youth. *Adolescence, 34*, 351–367.

Pearlin, L. I., & LeBlanc, A. J. (2001). Bereavement and the loss of mattering. In T. J. Owens, S. Stryker, & N. Goodman (Eds.), *Extending self-esteem theory and research* (pp. 285–300). New York: Cambridge University Press.

Pedhazur, E. J., & Pedhazur, J. (1997). *Multiple-regression in behavioral research: Explanation and prediction.* New York: Wadsworth.

Perl, R. F. (1992). United States. In S. B. MacDonald and B. Zagaris (Eds.), *International handbook on drug control* (pp. 67–88). Westport, CT: Greenwood.

Phinney, J. S., Kim-Jo, T., Osorio, S., & Vilhjalmsdottir, P. (2005). Autonomy and relatedness in adolescent–parent disagreements: Ethnic and developmental factors. *Journal of Adolescent Research, 20*, 8–39.

Pilowsky, D. J., Wickramaratne, P., Nomura, Y., & Weissman, M. M. (2006). Family discord, parental depression, psychopathology in offspring: 20-year follow-up. *Journal of the American Academy of Child and Adolescent Psychiatry, 45*, 452–460.

Ponzetti, J. J., Jr., & James, C. M. (1997). Loneliness and sibling relationships. *Journal of Social Behavior and Personality, 12*, 103–112.

Popkin, M. (1983). *Active parenting*. Atlanta: Active Parenting.

Popkin, R. H. (Ed.). (1998). *Dialogues concerning natural religion: Of the immortality of the soul and of suicide of miracles, by David Hume*. Indianapolis, IN: Hackett.

Powers, A. S., Myers, J. E., Tingle, L. R., & Powers, J. C. (2004). Wellness perceived stress, mattering, and marital satisfaction among medical residents and their spouses: Implications for education and counseling. *Family Journal: Counseling and Therapy for Couples and Families, 12*, 26–36.

Pysczynski, T., & Greenberg, J. (1987). Toward an integration of cognitive and motivational perspectives on social inference: A biased hypothesis-testing model. In L. Berkowitz (Ed.), *Advances in Experimental Social Psychology* (Vol. 20, pp. 297–340). San Diego, CA: Academic.

Rayle, A. D. (2005). Adolescent gender differences in mattering and wellness. *Journal of Adolescence, 28*, 753–763.

Rayle, A. D. (2006a). Mattering to others: Implications for the counseling relationship. *Journal of Counseling and Development, 84*, 483–487.

Rayle, A. D. (2006b). Do school counselors matter? Mattering as a moderator between job stress and job satisfaction. *Professional School Counseling, 9*, 206–215.

Rayle, A. D., & Myers, J. E. (2004). Counseling adolescents toward wellness: The roles of ethnic identity, acculturation, and mattering. *Professional school counseling, 8*, 81–90.

Reich, R. (1992). *Work of nations: Preparing ourselves for 21st century capitalism*. New York: Vintage.

Reifman, A., & Watson, W. K. (2003). Binge drinking during the first semester of college: Continuation and desistance from high school patterns. *Journal of American College Health, 52*, 73–81.

Richards, M. H., Miller, B. V., O'Donnell, P. C., Wasserman, M. S., & Colder, C. (2004). Parental monitoring mediates the effects of age and sex on problem behaviors among African American urban young adolescents. *Journal of Youth and Adolescence, 33*, 221–233.

Roberts, J. E., Shapiro, A. M., & Gamble, S. A. (1999). Level and perceived stability of self-esteem prospectively predict depressive symptoms during psychoeducational group treatment. *British Journal of Clinical Psychology, 38*, 425–429.

Rosenberg, M. (1973). Which significant others? *American Behavioral Scientist, 16*, 829–860.

Rosenberg, M. (1979). *Conceiving the self.* New York: Basic.

Rosenberg, M. (1989). *Society and the adolescent self-image* (rev. ed.). Middletown, CT: Wesleyan University Press.

Rosenberg, M., & McCullough, B. C. (1981). Mattering: Inferred significance and mental health. *Research in Community and Mental Health, 2,* 163–182.

Rosenberg, M., & Pearlin, L. I. (1978). Social class and self-esteem among children and adults. *American Journal of Sociology, 84,* 53–77.

Rosenberg, M., & Simmons, R. G. (1972). *Black and white self-esteem: The urban school child.* Washington, D. C.: American Sociological Association.

Rubin, L. (1996). *The transcendent child: Tales of triumph over the past.* New York: HarperPerennial.

SAS Institute. (1999). *SAS/STAT user's guide, Version 8.* Cary, NC: SAS Institute.

Schachter, S. (1959). *The psychology of affiliation: Experimental studies of the sources of gregariousness.* Oxford: Stanford University Press.

Schachter, S. (1964). The interaction of cognitive and physiological determinants of emotional state. In L. Berkowitz (Ed.), *Advances in experimental social psychology* (Vol. 1, pp. 49–80). New York: Academic.

Scheiman, S., & Taylor, J. (2001). Statuses, roles, and the sense of mattering. *Sociological Perspectives, 44,* 469–484.

Scherzer, T., & Pinderhughes, H. L. (2002). Violence and gender: Reports from an urban high school. *Violence and Victims, 17,* 57–72.

Seaman, M. (1959). On the meaning of alienation. *American Sociological Review, 24,* 183–791.

Sedikides, C., & Strube, M. J. (1995). The multiply motivated self. *Personality and Social Psychology Bulletin, 21,* 1330–1335.

Segraves, M. (2004). Midlife women's narratives of living alone. *Health Care for Women International, 25,* 916–932.

Sennett, R. (1980). *Authority.* New York: Vintage.

Sennett, R. (2003). *Respect in a world of inequality.* New York: W. W. Norton.

Sennett, R., & Cobb, J. (1972). *The hidden injuries of class.* New York: Vintage.

Serrano, R. A. (1998). *One of ours: Timothy McVeigh and the Oklahoma City bombing.* New York: W. W. Norton.

Sewell, W. H., Haller, A. O., & Portes, A. (1994). The educational and early occupational attainment process. In D. B. Grusky (Ed.), *Social stratification in sociological perspective* (2nd ed., pp. 410–421). Boulder, CO: Westview.

Sharff, J. W. (1998). *King Kong on 4th street: Families and the violence of poverty on the Lower East Side.* Boulder, CO: Westview.

Shea, M. E., & Pritchard, M. E. (2006). Is self-esteem the primary predictor of disordered eating? *Personality and Individual Differences, 42,* 1527–1537.

Simmons, R., Rosenberg, F., & Rosenberg, M. (1973). Disturbance in the self-image at adolescence. *American Sociological Review*, *38*, 553–568.

Simons, R. L., Simons, L. G., Burt, C. H., Brody, G. H., & Cutrona, C. (2005). Collective efficacy, authoritative parenting and delinquency: A longitudinal test of a model integrating community- and family-level processes. *Criminology*, *43*, 989–1029.

Smith, H. M., & Betz, N. E. (2002). An examination of efficacy and esteem pathways to depression in young adulthood. *Journal of Counseling Psychology*, *49*, 438–448.

Snyder, M. (1974). The self-monitoring of expressive behavior. *Journal of Personality and Social Psychology*, *30*, 526–537.

Snyder, M. (1987). *Public appearances / private realities.* New York: W. H. Freeman.

Southall, D., & Roberts, J. E. (2002). Attributional style and self-esteem in vulnerability to adolescent depressive symptoms following life stress: A 14-week prospective study. *Cognitive Therapy and Research*, *26*, 563–579.

Spicer, R. S., & Miller, T. R. (2000). Suicide acts in 8 states: Incidence and case fatality rates by demographics and method. *American Journal of Public Health*, *90*, 1885–1891.

Stahl, A. L. (2003). Delinquency cases in juvenile courts, 1999. *OJJDP Fact Sheet*, *#2*, p. 1.

Steger, M. F., & Frazier, P. (2005). Meaning in life: One link in the chain from religiousness to well-being. *Journal of Counseling Psychology*, *52*, 574–582.

Steinberg, L. (1990). Autonomy, conflict, and harmony in the family relationship. In S. S. Feldman & G. R. Elliott (Eds.), *At the threshold: The developing adolescent* (pp. 255–276). Cambridge, MA; Harvard University Press.

Steinberg, L. (2001). We know some things: Parent–adolescent relationships in retrospect and prospect. *Journal of Research on Adolescence*, *11*, 1–9.

Steinberg, L., & Silverberg, S. (1986). The vicissitudes of autonomy in early adolescence. *Child Development*, *57*, 841–851.

Straus, M. A., & Gelles, R. J. (1995). *Physical violence in American families: Risk factors and adaptations to violence in 8,145 families.* New Brunswick, NJ: Transaction.

Stryker, S., & Burke, P. J. (2000). The past, present, and future of an identity theory. *Social Psychology Quarterly*, *63*, 284–297.

Sugarman, D. B., & Frankel, S. L. (1996). Patriarchal ideology and wife-assault: A meta-analytic review. *Journal of Family Violence*, *11*, 13–40.

Sullivan, H. S. (1947). *Conceptions of modern psychiatry: The first William Alanson White memorial lectures.* Washington, D. C.: William Alanson White Psychiatric Foundation.

Swaim, R. C., Henry, K. L., & Kelly, K. (2006). Predictors of aggressive behaviors among rural middle school youth. *Journal of Primary Prevention, 27*, 229–243.

Swann, Jr., W. B., & Ely, R. J. (1984). A battle of wills: Self-verification versus behavioral confirmation. *Journal of Personality and Social Psychology, 46*, 1287–1302.

Swann Jr., W. B., Stein-Seroussi, A., & Giesler, R. B. (1992). Why people self-verify. *Journal of Personality and Social Psychology, 62*, 392–401.

Tangney, J. P. (1990). Assessing individual differences in proneness to shame and guilt: Development of the Self-Conscious Affect and Attribution Inventory. *Journal of Personality and Social Psychology, 59*, 102–111.

Taylor, J., & Turner, R. J. (2001). A longitudinal study of the role and significance of mattering to others for depressive symptoms. *Journal of Health and Social Behavior, 42*, 310–325.

Thomas, W. I., & Thomas, D. S. (1928). *The child in America: Behavior, problems and programs.* New York: Knopf.

Thornton, B., Audesse, R. J., Ryckman, R. M., & Burckle, M. J. (2006). Playing dumb and knowing it all: Two sides of an impression management coin. *Individual Differences Research, 4*, 37–45.

Twenge, J. M., Baumeister, R. F., Tice, D. M., & Stucke, T. S. (2001). If you can't join them, beat them: Effects of social exclusion on aggressive behavior. *Journal of Personality and Social Psychology, 81*, 1058–1069.

Udry, J. R., & Campbell, R. C. (1994). Getting started on sexual behavior. In A. S. Rossi (Ed.), *Sexuality across the Life Course* (pp. 187–208). Chicago: University of Chicago Press.

United States Department of Health and Human Services, Substance Abuse and Mental Health Services Administration, Office of Applied Studies. (2004). *National Household Survey on Drug Abuse, 2001*, 2nd ICPSR version. Research Triangle Park, NC: Research Triangle Institute [producer], 2002, Ann Arbor, MI: Inter-University Consortium for Political and Social research [distributor].

United States Department of Health and Human Services, Substance Abuse and Mental Health Services Administration, Office of Applied Studies. (2006). *National Survey on Drug Use and Health, 2005*, [Computer file]. ICPSR04596-v1. Research Triangle Park, NC: Research Triangle Institute [producer], 2006. Ann Arbor, MI: Inter-university Consortium for Political and Social Research [distributor].

Updegraff, K. A., Thayer, S. M., Whiteman, S. D., Denning, D. J., & McHale, S. M. (2005). Relational aggression in adolescents' sibling relationships: Links to sibling and parent–adolescent relationship quality. *Family Relations, 54*, 373–385.

Waite, L. J., & Gallagher, M. (2000). *The case for marriage: Why married people are happier, healthier, and better off financially.* New York: Doubleday.

Wallerstein, J. S., Lewis, J. M., & Blakeslee, S. (2000). *The unexpected legacy of divorce.* New York: Hyperion.

Washington Post. (2007, June 19). Va. Tech shooter seen as "Collector of Injustice." Retrieved from http://www.WashingtonPost.com.

Watson, D., Suls, J., & Haig, J. (2002). Global self-esteem in relation to structural models of personality and affectivity. *Journal of Personality and Social Psychology, 83*, 185–197.

Watson, J. B. (1939). *Behaviorism.* Chicago: University of Chicago Press.

Webster, D. W., Gainer, P. S., & Champion, H. R. (1993). Weapon carrying among inner-city junior high school students: Defensive behavior vs aggressive delinquency. *American Journal of Public Health, 83*, 1604–1607.

Weiner, B., Frieze, I., Kukla, A., Reed, L., Rest, S., & Rosenbaum, R. M. (1972). Perceiving the causes of success and failure. In E. E. Jones, D. E. Kanouse, H. H. Kelley, R. E. Nisbett, & S. Valins, *Attribution: Perceiving the causes of behavior* (pp. 95–120). Hillsdale, NJ: Lawrence Erlbaum Associates.

White, H. R., McMorris, B. J., Catalano, R. F., Fleming, C. B., Haggerty, K. P., & Abbott, R. D. (2006). Increases in alcohol and marijuana use during the transition out of high school into emerging adulthood: The effects of leaving home, going to college, and high school protective factors. *Journal of Studies on Alcohol, 67*, 810–822.

Wild, L. G., Flisher, A. J., & Lombard, C. (2004). Suicidal ideation and attempts in adolescents: Associations with depression and six domains of self-esteem. *Journal of Adolescence, 27*, 611–624.

Williams, K. D. (2001). *Ostracism: The power of silence.* New York: Guilford.

Yeh, H.-C., & Lempers, J. D. (2004). Perceived sibling relationships and adolescent development. *Journal of Youth and Adolescence, 33*, 133–147.

Yoder, K. A. (1999). Comparing suicide attempts, suicide ideators, and non-suicidal homeless and runaway adolescents. *Suicide and life-threatening behavior, 29*, 25–36.

Ziyadeh, N. J., Prokop, L. A., Fisher, L. B., Rosario, M., Field, A. E., Camargo, C. A., Jr., et al. (2007). Sexual orientation, gender, and alcohol use in a cohort study of U. S. adolescent girls and boys. *Drug and Alcohol Dependence, 87*, 119–130.

Zuckerman, M. (1994). *Behavioral expressions and biosocial bases of sensation seeking.* New York: Cambridge University Press.

Index

Note: page numbers in *italics* denote figures or tables

Index